Essential Computer Applications

◪ Information and Communication Systems, Databases, Spreadsheets, Word Processing and the Internet

Fourth Edition

◪ Séamus O'Neill and Gerard Morgan

Updated by Séamus O'Neill

Gill & Macmillan

Gill & Macmillan Ltd
Hume Avenue
Park West
Dublin 12
with associated companies throughout the world
www.gillmacmillan.ie

© Séamus O'Neill and Gerard Morgan 2000, 2007
978 07171 4264 4
Print origination in Ireland by TypeIT, Dublin

The paper used in this book is made from the wood pulp of managed forests. For every tree felled, at least one tree is planted, thereby renewing natural resources.

Contents

Chapter 1: Information and Communication Systems

An introduction to information   **1**
Data and information   1
Types of information   3
Attributes of good information   4
    Relevant   4
    Concise   4
    Accurate   4
    Complete   5
    Timing   5
    Clarity   5
    Cost effective   5
    Feedback loop in an information system   6
    Exception reporting   6
Types of information systems   7
    Personal system (PS)   7
    Transaction processing system (TPS)   7
    Management information system (MIS)   7
    Decision support systems (DSS)   8
    Expert systems (ES)   8
    Qualitative information (soft)   9
    Quantative information (hard)   9

Hardware   **9**
Types of computer systems   10
    Supercomputers   10
    Mainframe computers   10
    Minicomputer   10
    Microcomputer   10
Types of microcomputers (PCs)   11
    Desktops   11
    Notebooks (or laptops)   11
    Palmtops   11

Parts of a typical microcomputer system 12
The four-stage model of a computer 12
Input hardware 12
    Keyboard 12
    Mouse 13
    Scanner 13
    Magnetic card reader 13
    Smart card reader 13
    Voice data entry (VDE) 14
    Optical character recognition (OCR) 14
    Magnetic-ink character recognition (MICR) 14
    Optical mark recognition (OMR) 15
    Touch-sensitive screen 15
Processing hardware 17
    The central processing unit (CPU) 17
    Computer memory 17
    The representation of data 18
    Memory size 18
Output hardware 19
    Monitor 19
    Graphics card 20
    Sound card 20
    Speakers 20
    Printers 20
    Buying a printer 21
    Plotters 22
    Wide-format printers 22
    Computer output on microfiche/film 23
    Bluetooth 23
Auxiliary storage 24
    Diskettes or 'floppy disks' 24
    Fixed disks or 'hard disks' 24
    Zip disks 25
    Formatting a disk 25
    Care of disks 26
    Compact discs 26
    DVDs 26
    Storing and accessing data on CDs and DVDs 27
    USB flash drive 27
    Other storage media 27
    Ports 28
    PS/2 port 28
    USB port 29
    Parallel port 29
    Ethernet or network port 29
    Video port or monitor port 29

IEEE 1394 or firewire port   29
Serial port   30
Sound ports   30
USB to serial port adapter   30
Power port   30
Hardware specification example   30

Software   **32**
Types of software   32
The operating system   32
Application programs   33
Device drivers   33
Software licensing   33
Freeware and shareware   33
Easy-to-use (user-friendly) programs   34

Networks   **34**
Network categories   34
Network architectures   35
Wireless networking   36

Other information and technology (ICT) equipment   **38**
Telephone   38
Mobile telephone   38
Blackberry   38
Facsimile transmission (fax)   38
Photocopier   38
All-in-one printer   38

Data-processing concepts   **39**
Elements of a computer file   39
Key field   39
Types of record   39
Fixed length records   39
Variable lengths records   39
Types of file   40
Transaction file   40
Reference file   40
Master file   40
File organisation   40
Serial   40
Sequential   40
Index sequential   40
Random or direct access   40
Updating disk files   40
Stages of data collection   41

1. Data collection	41
2. Data transmission	41
3. Data preparation	41
4. Input	41
Methods of data processing	42
Batch processing	42
On-line transaction processing	42
Real-time processing	42
The information and communication technology environment	**44**
Definitions	44
Risks to computer systems	44
Methods of minimising the risks to the information technology environment	45
Physical methods	45
Logical methods	45
Procedural methods	46
The Data Protection Act 1988	47
The Freedom of Information Act 1997 and Freedom of Information (Amendments) Act 2003	47
Improving the information and communication technology environment for users – ergonomics	47
1. Analysis of workstations	48
2. Requirements for workstations	48
3. Daily routine for users	48
4. Eyes and eyesight	48
5. Provision of training	48
6. Provision of information	48
Questions	**50**
Multi-choice questions	50
Short-answer questions	53
Structured questions	53
Sample structured questions (FETAC)	54
Sample assignments (FETAC)	54
Sample short answer questions (FETAC)	55
Glossary of computer terms	**56**

Chapter 2: Introduction to Databases

Introduction	**62**
What is a database?	62
What is a file?	62
What is a record?	63

What is a field?	63
Why is information now stored in computer databases?	63
Holding a database on computer	**63**
1. Defining the data entry form	64
2. Entering data into the file	65
3. Editing the file	65
Adding and deleting records	65
Changing the contents of records	66
4. Searching the file	66
Searching for records by their position in the file	66
Searching for records using one condition	67
Searching for records using more than one condition	67
Searching for records using variable symbols	67
5. Displaying selected fields	68
6. Sorting the file	69
Alphabetical sorting	69
Numeric sorting	70
Reverse sorting	70
Multi-level sorting	70
Group sorting	71
7. Indexing the file	71
8. Changing the record structure	73
Changing the field width	73
Deleting a field from the record structure	73
Adding a new field to the record structure	74
Changing a field name	74
Changing the order of fields	74
Careful planning	75
9. Performing mathematical operations	75
Performing mathematical operations on data items	75
The summation function	76
10. Creating reports	76
Summary	**77**
Glossary of database terms	**77**

Chapter 3: Practical Database Assignments

Guidelines for students	**79**
1. The data entry screen	79
2. Entering data	79
3. Creating reports	80
4. Using Microsoft Access	80

Functions and commands required   80
Assignment 1   82
Assignment 2   83
Assignment 3   84
Assignment 4   85
Assignment 5   86
Assignment 6   87
Assignment 7   88
Assignment 8   89
Assignment 9   91
Assignment 10   92
Assignment 11   94
Assignment 12   96
Assignment 13   98
Assignment 14   100
Assignment 15   102
Assignment 16   105
Assignment 17   107
Assignment 18   109
Assignment 19 FETAC Database Methods Sample Paper 1   111
Assignment 20 FETAC Database Methods Sample Paper 2   114

Chapter 4: Introduction to Spreadsheets

Introduction   118
What is a spreadsheet?   118
What does a spreadsheet look like?   118
What can be put into a spreadsheet?   119

Example 1   **120**
1. Setting up the spreadsheet   121
2. Entering formulae   122
3. The summation function   123
4. Improving the appearance of the spreadsheet   123
        Changing the format of numbers   123
        Aligning the labels   123
5. Replication   124
        Straight copying   125
        Range copying   125
        Formula copying   125
        The importance of replication   125
6. Editing the spreadsheet   126
        Simple editing   126
        Inserting rows or columns   127

7.	Considering 'what if?' situations	129
8.	The 'logical if' function	130
	'What if?' again	131
9.	Other facilities	132
	Quick cursor movement	132
	Non-scrolling titles	133
	Printing part or all of the spreadsheet	133
	Turning off automatic recalculation	134
	Using the 'look-up' function	134
	Summary of the standard facilities of a spreadsheet program	134
	Creating a spreadsheet	134

Example 2	**135**
Questions	135
Solution	136

Graphing the data	**138**

Example 3	**139**
The bar graph	139
The pie graph	140

Financial matters	**140**
Depreciation	140

Example 4	**141**
Loan repayments	141

Example 5	**142**
Investment venture	143

Example 6	**143**

Using macros	**144**
Macro basics	144
Creating a macro	144
Building a macro manually	145

Example 7	**145**
Planning	146
Entering	146
Documenting	146
Naming	146
Executing	147
Saving	147
Recording a macro	147

Interactive macros   148
Example 8   **148**

Conclusion   **149**

Glossary of spreadsheet terms   **149**

Chapter 5: Practical Spreadsheet Assignments

Assignment 1   154
Assignment 2   155
Assignment 3   155
Assignment 4   157
Assignment 5   158
Assignment 6   159
Assignment 7   161
Assignment 8   162
Assignment 9   163
Assignment 10   165
Assignment 11   167
Assignment 12   169
Assignment 13   171
Assignment 14   172
Assignment 15   174
Assignment 16   176
Assignment 17   178
Assignment 18   179
Assignment 19   181
Assignment 20   184
Assignment 21 FETAC Spreadsheet Methods Sample Paper 1   185
Assignment 22 FETAC Spreadsheet Methods Sample Paper 2   189

Chapter 6: Computer Applications Projects

Introduction   **195**

A project idea   **195**

Producing a database project   **196**
Design phase   196
Implementation phase   196
Conclusion phase   197

Common questions   197

Producing a spreadsheet project   **197**
Design phase   197
Implementation phase   198
Conclusion phase   198
Common questions   198

Chapter 7: Introduction to Word Processing

Facilities of a word processor   **199**
1. Elementary editing: deleting and inserting   199
2. More advanced editing: moving text   201
3. Enhancing the appearance of a document   203
        Changing the font and font size   204
        Centring and underlining   204
        Altering the line spacing   205
        Setting new margins   205
4. The 'find and replace' facility   206
5. Setting tabs   207
6. Stored paragraphs   208
        Letter 1: Comprising stored paragraphs 1, 2 and 4   209
        Letter 2: Comprising stored paragraphs 1, 3 and 4   210
7. Merge printing   210
        Letter 1: South-west region   212
        Letter 2: South-east region   213
        Letter 3: Central region   214
8. Other facilities   214

Applications of word processing   **216**
Standard letters   216
Contracts and agreements   216
Reports   216
Mailshots   216
Regularly updated lists   216

Advantages of word processor use   **216**
Storage of text   216
Time savings   217
Quality   217
Security   217
Ease of use   217

Disadvantages of word processor use   **217**

Cost   217
Staff training   217
Poor checking   217
Health   217

Conclusion   **218**

Questions   **218**
Multi-choice questions   218
Short-answer questions   219

Glossary of word processing terms   **219**

Chapter 8: Practical Word Processing Assignments

Assignment 1   223
Assignment 2   224
Assignment 3   225
Assignment 4   226
Assignment 5   227
Assignment 6   228
Assignment 7   229
Assignment 8   229
Assignment 9   231
Assignment 10   232
Assignment 11   233
Assignment 12   234
Assignment 13   235
Assignment 14   238
Assignment 15   239
Assignment 16   239
Assignment 17   241
Assignment 18   242
Assignment 19   243
Assignment 20 FETAC sample exam   245

Chapter 9: The Internet and the World Wide Web

History and structure of the Internet   **254**
What is the Internet?   254
How does the Internet work?   254

What is the World Wide Web?   **256**

How did the Internet develop? 256
Who owns and pays for the Internet? 257
Internet connection requirements 258
    Connecting to the Internet 258
    Connection methods 258
    Dial-up access 258
    Broadband 258
Hardware required 260
Software required 261
Internet service provider 261
    Evaluating an ISP 261
IP addresses and domain names 262
Intranet 263

The World Wide Web and other Internet facilities **263**
The basics 263
    Uniform resource locator (URL) 263
    Hyperlinks 264
    The browser 264
    Plug-ins 265
Conducting a search 266
    Search tools 266
    Directories 266
    Search engines 267
    Multi-engine search tools 268
    Portal sites 268
    Advice on how to search the World Wide Web 269
Other Internet facilities 270
    File transfer protocol 270
    Downloading software 271
    Voice over IP 271
    Internet relay chat 271
    Instant messaging 272
    Blogs 272
    Multimedia conferencing 273
    Radio and television on the Web 273
    Podcasts 273
    On-line games 274
    Electronic business (e-business) 274
Security and confidentiality 275
    Virus protection 276
    Filtering software 276
    Firewalls 277
    Encryption 278
    Digital signatures 278
    Cookies 278

Spyware   279
Phishing   279

Chapter 10: Electronic Mail and Web Publishing

Electronic mail   **281**
How does e-mail work?   281
What is an e-mail address?   281
Characteristics of an e-mail program   281
Component parts of an e-mail message   283
    Managing mailboxes   284
    Emoticons and acronyms   284
    Good e-mail etiquette   285
    Web-based e-mail accounts   285
    Mailing lists   286
Usenet newsgroups   286
    Spam   288

Web publishing   **288**
Website evaluation   288

Creating a web page   **290**
Web editor program   291
Text editor and HyperText Mark-up Language (HTML)   291
Sample travel agent website   292
How the HTML tags work   294
    Inserting a graphic   295
    Changing colours   295
    Using backgrounds   296
    File formats   296

Questions   **298**

Glossary of Internet terms   **298**

Chapter 11: Practical Internet Assignments

E-mail Assignments   **301**
Assignment 1   301
Assignment 2   301
Assignment 3   302
Assignment 4   302
Assignment 5   303

Searching the World Wide Web   **303**

Assignment 6   303
Assignment 7   303
Assignment 8   303
Assignment 9   303
Assignment 10   304
Assignment 11   304
Assignment 12   304
Assignment 13   304
Assignment 14   305
Assignment 15   305

Web publishing   **305**

Assignment 16   305
Assignment 17   306
Assignment 18   307
Assignment 19   308
Assignment 20   308

Dedicated to our parents

Acknowledgments

We would like to acknowledge all of the people who made this book possible, in particular: Jacqui O'Sullivan and Margaret Buckley, Principal and Deputy Principal, respectively, of Crumlin College of Further Education; the staff and students at Crumlin College for their co-operation, especially the CPC and CT1 classes for their tireless testing of assignments; Val Canavan, John Smyth, Aoife Fox, Eithne Frayne, Irene Murtagh, Michael Phillips and Brenda Quinn for their advice and encouragement; and Marion O'Brien, Emma Farrell and Hubert Mahony and all of the staff at Gill & Macmillan.

From Séamus O'Neill, special thanks to Margaret and Patrick Murtagh, my wife Caroline, and children, James and Richael, for their support and encouragement.

From Gerard Morgan, special thanks to my wife Mary, and sons, Darragh and Oisin, for their support and encouragement.

Additional resources for *Essential Computer Applications Fourth Edition:*

For Lecturers

Easy to use online support material for this book is available at

www.gillmacmillan.ie/lecturers.

To access lecturer support material on our secure website:

1. Go to www.gillmacmillan.ie/lecturers

2. Log on using your username and password. If you don't have a password, register online and we will e-mail your password to you.

For Students

Data files for assignments are available to students at

www.gillmacmillan.ie/students.

1. Go to www.gillmacmillan.ie/students

2. Click on 'Support Material' on top right of page

3. Click on title of book to access the data files.

Chapter 1
Information and
Communication Systems

Before deciding to explore the four application areas outlined in this book, we must have some basic background knowledge of computing. To use a comparison: before beginning to drive a car on the road, we need to have some idea of the working of gears and other equipment in the car. We also need to know the rules of the road. Similarly, before using computers we should know about the equipment and procedures we are likely to use.

This chapter will cover the following areas:
1. An introduction to information
2. Hardware
3. Software
4. Networks
5. Other information and communication technology (ICT) equipment
6. Data processing concepts
7. The ICT environment.

An introduction to information

Data and information

The distinction between data and information is important.

Data is the term used to describe basic raw facts about activities of a business. These facts are subsequently used to produce useful information. Examples of data would include the hours worked by an individual, the rate of pay and the quantity of goods ordered by a customer.

Information is obtained when data is assembled or processed in a meaningful and useful way. Examples of information would include the average overtime hours in a year, the total payroll expense for the year and a trading profit and loss account.

e.g. hours worked   e.g. payroll details

Data processing to produce information

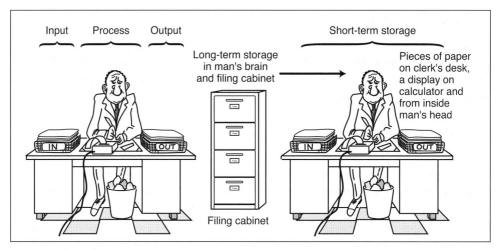

Manual data processing

Data processing on computer

Types of information

Information has no value in itself. Its value is derived from its ability to assist and improve decision making. Information is now considered so important that it is regarded as a factor of production in addition to land, labour, enterprise and capital. There are three main reasons why information is needed in organisations.

1. It is necessary to keep a record of events in the company in order to maintain its operational activities. Employees must be paid, invoices must be sent to customers and retained for billing, and statistical information must be kept for the government. This type of information is referred to as **transactional** or **operational information** (see information flows diagram on p. 4).

2. Those responsible for running the organisation need information about what is happening in order to plan and control activities. They need to know the cost of stock, the lead times, machine efficiency and level of sales in order to get an indication of current performance and improve in the future. This information is used by middle management. It is referred to as **tactical information**.

3. Historical information and business environmental information needs to be retained to plan for long-term development and forecasts and to maintain competitive advantage. Management need to know summary accounting data, information on competitors and market trends. Using this information, long-term decisions can be made, such as how the business should be financed, what business the organisation should be in and how to compete successfully in the market. This type of information is referred to as **strategic information**.

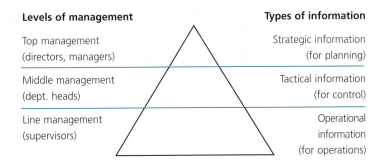

Levels of management	Types of information
Top management (directors, managers)	Strategic information (for planning)
Middle management (dept. heads)	Tactical information (for control)
Line management (supervisors)	Operational information (for operations)

The information pyramid

As you go down the pyramid:
1. More *structured* information is required
2. More *internal* information is required
3. More *detailed* information is required
4. More *historical* information is required
5. More *repetitive* information is required.

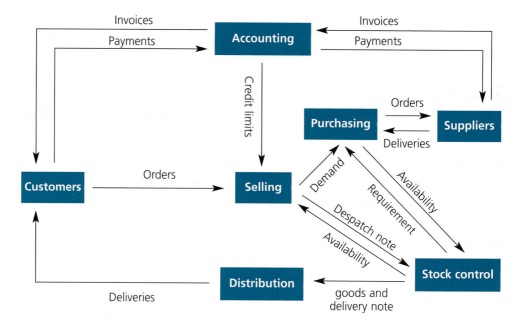

Information flows (simplified) in a non-manufacturing organisation

Attributes of good information

Good information is that which is used and which creates value. Good information should have the following characteristics.

◢ Relevant

The information must be relevant for the purpose. Often information given or produced is irrelevant. This can make understanding more difficult.

◢ Concise

The preference is for 'need to know' information rather than 'nice to know information'. The general rule is to give as little information as possible consistent with effective use. This is often called exception reporting, e.g. where only major or important differences between actual figures and budgets are reported.

◢ Accurate

The information must be sufficiently accurate for the purpose. The level of accuracy will depend on the decision level involved. Transactional information may need to be very accurate (down to the nearest penny or second). Strategic information does not need such accuracy.

Complete

The information must be complete. This requires close liaison with information providers and users.

Timing

Good information is that which is communicated in time to be used, otherwise the information will be useless.

Clarity

Clarity is improved by the use of different presentation techniques such as graphs, photographs, insert diagrams and three-dimensional models.

Cost effective

The value or benefit to the organisation of obtaining the information should exceed the cost of acquiring it, i.e. cost effective = benefits from information > cost of information.

For information to have value it must result in some benefit, e.g. reduced costs, gained competitive advantage, increased sales, prevented fraud. It is often difficult to directly compare costs and benefits as some of the benefits can be intangible (difficult to quantify). However, cost/benefit analysis can be carried out to calculate the net benefit of a new information system. This involves calculating all the costs of the new system and comparing it with the future benefits of the system. The process uses a variety of mathematical techniques such as net present value, payback period calculations, cash flow and internal rates of returns figures.

Examples of typical costs of a new information system may include:
- Equipment costs – hardware
- Software costs
- Installation costs – new buildings, wiring, special conditions
- Development costs – consultancy, systems analysis fees, testing, programmers' fees
- Personnel costs – training, new staff, redundancy, relocation
- Operating costs – consumables, maintenance, rent, power, back-up, data transmission.

Examples of possible benefits of a new system may include:

Tangible benefits:	Intangible benefits:
• saving in staff costs	• competitive advantage
• less wastage	• quicker response time to customers
• space saving	• greater customer satisfaction
• better control over stock.	• improved staff morale
	• better decision making.

◪Feedback loop in an information system

In any system it is very important to make certain that the system is regulated and controlled to ensure it is performing optimally. Standards or goals are often set as guidelines for acceptable performance or output. A control mechanism allows the output of the system to be compared to the standard. Any deviations from the standard are acted upon and fed back into the system. This is referred to as the feedback loop.

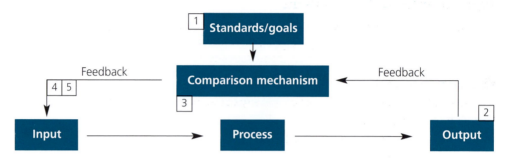

System with a feedback loop

Elements of the feedback loop:
1. A standard or goal is set for the system output
2. A measure of the actual output is made by a sensor
3. A comparison of the actual output with the standard set is made by the control mechanism
4. A report of the deviations from the standard is considered
5. An appropriate action is taken which is then fed back into the system.

◪Exception reporting

Exception reporting is where management only become involved in an activity when it falls outside the range of acceptable performance standards. In order to manage by exception, reporting upper and lower limits must be set. Output within the limits requires no action from management.

For example, a standard production rate of 2,000–2,200 shirts is set for daily production for a clothing manufacturer. A manager will only follow up on variations outside of this range, i.e. below 2,000 or above 2,200 units.

Advantages of exception reporting:
1. Managers do not waste time monitoring activity that is progressing normally
2. Fewer decisions need to be made
3. Attention can be given to both positive and negative deviations
4. Computer systems are especially suited to exception monitoring.

Disadvantages of exception reporting:
1. Not always easy to set workable standards
2. This method is not proactive, but reactive. Proactivity may be needed to anticipate problems before they happen.

Types of information systems

There are many different types of information systems and they can vary in complexity and scope. Here are some examples of such systems.

Personal system (PS)

A personal information system is necessary to carry out everyday activities in our daily lives. Such information may include:

- a diary of appointments and special dates
- names, addresses and phone numbers
- personal accounts
- travel timetables
- work schedules
- recipe book
- manuals
- contents of a filofax
- watch.

By using these sources of information, we can conduct our normal day-to-day activities. The information could be highly structured and stored on a PC or diary or it could all be in our memory.

Transaction processing system (TPS)

A TPS is necessary for the day-to-day running of a *business*. As transactions occur within the organisation, the data and information must be immediately recorded and maintained on file. Typically these include all forms of accounting ledger updates, invoicing, credit control and stock control.

Transaction processing systems process high volumes of routine structured data. The information generated from these systems provides information which is most useful for line managers or supervisors and it forms the basis for all other information systems.

Management information system (MIS)

MIS is a general term used to describe a computer system that converts data from external and internal sources into information which can be communicated to all levels of managers. This information enables managers to make timely and informed decisions.

Management information systems are the controlling mechanism for the entire organisation. A MIS includes all management information, including TPS, decision support systems and expert systems.

◼ Decision support systems (DSS)

The main aim of DSS is to *support* managers when making decisions. Most problems suited to DSS are in a non-structured form (not routinely produced by the system). In order to make decisions, managers must construct models or query databases to generate information to aid decision making. Using a variety of tools and procedures, the manager can generate this information. These tools include modelling software, spreadsheets, forecasting programs, large interactive database management systems and expert systems.

A simple example might include managers using spreadsheet software to develop 'what if' financial models, such as evaluating different investment options or calculating the cost benefit calculations for a number of different alternative computer systems.

Applications of DSS:
- Accounting models – estimating future results using accounting rules, e.g. budgeting
- Risk analysis
- Optimisation models – calculating optimal results under different constraints, e.g. production planning
- Ad hoc data analysis – unusual/extraordinary queries on a database.

◼ Expert systems (ES)

An expert system is a computer program which draws upon the knowledge of human experts captured in a knowledge base to solve problems that normally require human expertise. Unlike DSS, which *supports decisions*, the ES *makes decisions*.

Expert systems contain three elements.

Knowledge base
The base consists of facts, theories, relationships, rules (including subconscious rules), observations, definitions and other types of information gathered from experts, textbooks and manuals. Knowledge engineers gather this information onto common databases.

Inference engine
This is the computer program which provides the reasoning capability. These programs use artificial intelligence software systems to make decisions. It allows for searches and reasoning and allows conclusions or inferences to be made from the rules and knowledge base.

User interface/justifier
This allows the software to clarify information from the user.
Example: Eye Disease Diagnosis Expert System.
This is a medical diagnosis system for eye-related illness. The non-specialist user keys in

symptoms of the patient and the system will try to make a diagnosis. The system will use its knowledge base and inference engine and prompt the user for more information regarding symptoms to clarify its diagnosis. This system has been used in place of specialist medical staff in remote locations all around the world.

Applications of expert systems:
- Credit card issue systems
- Insurance claims
- Complex fault finding/diagnosis
- Farming advice
- Medical diagnosis.

Qualitative information (soft)

Qualitative information is information that is gathered from direct observation, opinions and case studies. The nature of the information may not always be factually true. The purpose of this type of information is to get an in-depth understanding of something and is exploratory in nature. The information is usually in the form of narrative. This form of information is very difficult to analyse or computerise. However, expert systems often use such information in their expert knowledge base.

Example:
In-depth interview details from shop floor workers on the problems associated with new work practices, or a list of rules (conscious or subconscious) that an expert uses to find a fault on a machine.

Quantitative information (hard)

This form of information is a collection of facts and records of actual happenings. The main purpose for gathering this information is to control activities and inform decisions. Most data capture techniques will record this type of information. In businesses this is the most common form of information.

Example:
Most business transactions generate this form of information.

Hardware

A computer is a programmable electronic device that can store and process data and display the results and/or information. The term 'hardware' is used to refer to any physical part of a computer system, such as the keyboard, monitor, printer or the disk drive.

Types of computer systems

Computer systems fall into one of four main categories according to their processing capabilities.

◩ Supercomputers

Supercomputers are very large, extremely fast and expensive computers capable of supporting hundreds, or even thousands, of users at the same time. They are used for specialised applications that require an immense amount of complex mathematical calculations, e.g. weather forecasting.

◩ Mainframe computers

Mainframe computers (or mainframes) are large, expensive computers capable of supporting hundreds, or even thousands, of users at the same time. They are used for very large processing tasks and perform many important business and government applications. Mainframes are more versatile than supercomputers in that they support more simultaneous programs, i.e. users can work on a greater number of different applications at the same time. A typical mainframe computer may have hundreds or thousands of dumb terminals attached.

A **dumb terminal** does not possess any processing power, rather, it allows the entry of data and the display of information. In contrast, an **intelligent terminal** has a built-in processing capability but no local disk or tape storage.

◩ Minicomputer

In cost, size and power, minicomputers lie between mainframes and microcomputers. They are capable of supporting from four to about 200 users at the same time. Minicomputers are usually found in medium-sized businesses or in divisions within a large organisation, e.g. in government departments.

Supercomputer, mainframe and minicomputer systems are classified as **multi-user systems** in that they can support two or more users simultaneously.

◩ Microcomputer

Microcomputers – also called personal computers (PCs) – are small, self-contained computers that fit on a desktop and are usually only used by one person. They are the least expensive type and are widely used in businesses for a variety of tasks, such as word processing, small database management, spreadsheets and e-mail. They are also used as home computers for a range of activities, e.g. family budgeting, accessing the Internet as well as for games. Microcomputers are classified as **single-user** systems.

For the purposes of this book, we will concentrate on microcomputers. However, much of the information here is also applicable to other computer systems. Also, as computers become more powerful and smaller, the division by size is becoming less useful. In particular, the distinction between mainframe computers and minicomputers is hard to draw, while a number of microcomputers joined together (networked) can perform many of the functions associated with minicomputers.

Types of microcomputers (PCs)

Microcomputers (PCs) fall into one of three categories.

Desktops

Desktop computers are designed to fit neatly on a desk in an office or at home. They are the most affordable and most common of all computers and are frequently used by businesses, schools and households.

Notebooks (or laptops)

Notebooks are small portable computers that run on either batteries or electricity. All of the components of a notebook computer – including the keyboard, mouse, speakers and screen – are built into a single unit. Notebook computers are ideal for people who work in a variety of locations, e.g. engineers and sales personnel.

Palmtops

Palmtops are small portable computers that literally fit in the palm of your hand. They are also known as handheld computers and personal digital assistants (PDAs). A major difference between notebook and palmtop computers is that palmtops are usually powered by off-the-shelf batteries, e.g. AA. Palmtops usually include a pen, called a stylus, that you use to select items on a small, touch-sensitive screen. Two examples of their uses are by doctors for patient tracking and by salespeople for managing data on sales and expenses.

Parts of a typical microcomputer system

The **keyboard** is used to get the information into the computer. The **CPU** is used to process this information, e.g. to do calculations. The **monitor** is used to display the result and the **printer** produces a copy of this display. The **disk drives** make it possible for the information (and programs) to be stored on disks for further use.

The four-stage model of a computer

In general, then, we can say that a computer has four main components:

- the hardware used to enter data, called **input devices**
- the hardware that produces results from entered data, called the **processor**
- the hardware that displays the results, called **output devices**
- the hardware used to store this information for later retrieval, called **auxiliary storage** or **backing storage**.

All the pieces of hardware outside the processor are called **peripherals**.

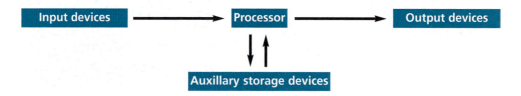

Input hardware

Keyboard

This is the most common means of entering data. It consists of an array of **keys** or switches, each one producing a particular character on the display when it is pressed. The character keys have a standard layout on all computer keyboards, called the 'QWERTY' layout after the first six letters on the top row; additional keys can include **cursor keys**, **function keys** and editing keys. The 'enter' key is used to implement a command or, in word processing, to mark the end of a paragraph. The 'escape' key is often used to cancel an operation.

◣Mouse

This is a small pointing device which may be connected by a wire to the computer (it vaguely resembles a real mouse!). It is moved about by hand on a flat surface, and the cursor on the screen follows its movements. Buttons on the top of the mouse can also be used to select options. Where used: various 'user-friendly' (easy-to-use) programs, especially graphics.

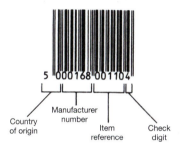

Country of origin | Manufacturer number | Item reference | Check digit

◣Scanner

Most consumer products now have bar codes on them. A scanner can read these codes by scanning the pattern of lines; this allows the product code to be entered without keyboarding. Scanners are also used for inputting whole pages of text and pictures into a computer. Where used: supermarkets; libraries.

◣Magnetic card reader

This is a machine that reads data from the magnetic strip on a plastic card. Where used: cash-dispensing machines (ATM); employee access to buildings.

◣Smart card reader

This is a device that can access and update data held on a smart card. This plastic card contains a computer chip that holds the data. It is more secure than a magnetic strip card, e.g. ATM card, as it can be programmed to self-destruct if the wrong password is entered more than the allotted number of times. Where used: to purchase goods and services or hold medical information.

Smart Card International

12345 54321 12345

◀ L. SMITH 12.08

Voice data entry (VDE)

Using a microphone connected to the computer, different commands or letters can be called out and then interpreted by special programs. Major advancements have been made in VDE technology for personal computers in recent times. It is now possible for a user to dictate whole documents and commands directly into the computer. Where used: word processing application (text entry); laboratories; computers for the physically disabled.

Optical character recognition (OCR)

This is an input method where a scanner is used to read the text of a document directly into the computer. Special typefaces that the machine recognises can be used, although modern systems can now read ordinary typefaces. Where used: processing of customer bills that have been received with payment; reading of authors' typescripts directly into typesetting systems.

Magnetic-ink character recognition (MICR)

Numerals of a special design can be printed with an ink that contains tiny pieces of magnetisable material, and these can then be read into the computer by a special scanner. The numbers along the bottom of a cheque are used by the computer to update a customer's bank account. They include code numbers representing the bank and branch, the customer account number, the number of the cheque (all of which are printed on each page of the cheque book before it is issued to the customer) and the amount (printed on the cheque after it has been presented to the bank). Where used: cheque books and other bank documents.

◪ Optical mark recognition (OMR)

With this system a reader connected to the computer can detect the presence or absence of a mark, with the position of the mark determining the value entered. Where used: National Lottery; electricity meter reading; multi-choice examination questions.

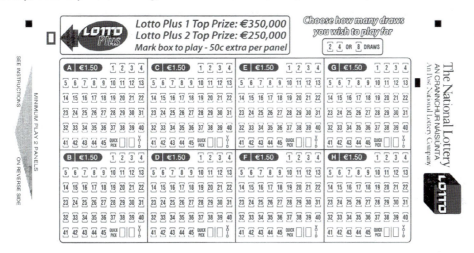

◪ Touch-sensitive screen

The screen displays choices and instructions, and the user simply touches the symbol representing the desired choice. Where used: information screens in banks, shopping centres and tourist offices.

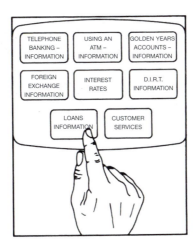

There are many other methods of entering data into a computer for processing. The choice of the most suitable input device depends on the nature of the data to be entered and the environment where the data is generated. A summary of the input devices described above is given on p.16.

	Speed	Volume of input	Advantages	Disadvantages	Where used
SUMMARY OF INPUT DEVICES					
keyboard	slow	medium	• standard QWERTY keyboard which people are familiar with	• slow • error prone	• text/data entry
OCR	fast	medium	• no keying required	• scanner and software are expensive • quality of document is important	• archiving • text entry • turnaround documents
OMR	fast	large	• no keying • less errors than keying • easy to complete	• special stationery required	• multi-choice examinations • meter reading • census recording • lotto
MICR	fast	large	• used as standard in worldwide banking • secure as writing over them does not affect the numbers read in	• need to post code cheques	• cheques • giros • travellers' cheques
bar codes	fast	small	• fast • fewer errors	• expensive hardware and software required	• retail stores • libraries
magnetic card	fast	small	• easy to use • portable • secure	• limited amount of data storage on the card	• ATM card • clock cards
smart card	fast	small	• easy to use • portable • secure	• easy to mislay	• financial transactions • medical records
mouse	fast	small	• easy to use	• limited – pointing device	• GUI-based software
touch-sensitive screens	fast	small	• very user friendly • no keying required	• limited – pointing device	• tourist information • banks
VDE	fast	large	• no keying • can move around while entering data	• expensive software • large memory requirements	• laboratories • word processing • handicapped
scanner for text/pictures	fast	large	• easy to use • no keying	• large memory requirements	• DTP • word processing • printing

Processing hardware

◤The central processing unit (CPU)

This is where all calculations and manipulations of the data are carried out: it could be considered the 'brain' of the computer. The CPU is contained on a tiny integrated circuit or 'microchip' that carries a large number of minute electronic circuits. The speed at which the CPU manipulates data is measured in gigahertz (GHz) or the number of billion cycles per second. For example, a 3.0 GHz computer has a clock which 'ticks' and 'tocks' 3 billion times each second. Each tick-tock is called a cycle. These cycles co-ordinate the movement of data inside the CPU.

There are three main areas in the CPU: the control unit, the arithmetic logic unit (ALU) and L1 cache memory.

The **control unit** takes instructions in a given sequence (rather like a set of traffic lights at a crossroads) and controls the movement of data inside the computer.

The **arithmetic logic unit (ALU)** performs mathematical functions and logical decisions, such as deciding whether one number is greater than another.

The **L1 cache memory** is a small high-speed memory. It is the first place that the CPU looks for its data.

The CPU is frequently referred to as the **microprocessor**.

◤Computer memory

The main memory or storage allows data to be stored for processing purposes and holds results. It also stores programs or sets of instructions. It is similar to our own memory. If you were asked to add three numbers without using a pen and paper, you would first have to put the numbers into your memory and then add them. The same is true with computers. In order to perform any calculations or processes, the computer must first have the data that is required in its memory.

There are two types of main storage: **read-only memory (ROM)** and **random-access memory (RAM)**.

The read-only memory (ROM) may not be written to by the computer system. The contents of ROM are entered at the time of manufacture and cannot be changed by the user. When the computer is turned off, this information is not lost; this form of storage is referred to as **'non-volatile memory'**. The information normally only takes up a small amount of the total memory of the computer. There are, however, some variations of ROM chips, namely PROM and EPROM chips. PROM (programmable ROM) is a chip which can be written to once by the user after its manufacture but is fixed once it has been written to. EPROM (erasable PROM) is a special type of PROM which can be erased using ultraviolet light.

The random-access memory (RAM) is memory that may be read from and written to by the programmer or user. It contains information currently being worked on. In our example above, the three numbers to be added would be contained in RAM while the calculation is being performed. Once the calculation has been completed, new data can be entered into RAM. RAM could be compared to an erasable notepad: the user can read the information from this memory and (unlike ROM) can change its contents. When the computer is switched off, however, this memory is completely cleared; this form of storage is known as **'volatile memory'**. Before you turn off your computer, always make sure to save your data if you want it for another day!

The representation of data

How is the data inside the computer represented? Computers can only understand the numerals 1 and 0 symbolising the presence (1) or absence (0) of an electrical pulse inside the computer. How, then, can computers deal with other numbers, letters and words?

Each character (numeral, letter or symbol) on the keyboard has its own unique code number. For example, the capital letter A has a character number 65. (The character numbers are allocated by an international agreement, which was based on an earlier one called the American Standard Code for Information Interchange (ASCII), and they are often still referred to as ASCII code – pronounced 'askey'.) The character numbers do not have to be known by the user: the computer automatically reads them when each key is pressed. The computer converts each character code into this 1 and 0 form, known as a binary number. For the letter A (character 65) this is 01000001. All the data inside the computer is made up of thousands of these pulses or no-pulses of electricity moving in and out of the memory very rapidly.

Each character is thus represented by a binary number, made up of a series of 1s and 0s. Each single 1 or 0 is called a bit, which is the smallest possible element in computer memory. A group of bits of the size that a particular computer handles – usually eight – is called a byte.

Memory size

Memory size is expressed in terms of the maximum number of bytes or characters the computer can hold in RAM at any time. The size is measured in megabytes (MB) or gigabytes (GB). Thus a computer that has a RAM with a capacity of 1 GB can keep a maximum of approximately 1 billion characters in its memory at any time.

Summary Chart of Memory Capacities

Term	Symbol	Value	Approx value
Bit	b	0 or 1	————————-
Byte	B	8 bits	————————-
Kilobyte	KB	1,024 bytes (2^{10})	One thousand bytes
Megabyte	MB	1,048,576 bytes	One million bytes
Gigabyte	GB	1,073,741,824 bytes	One billion bytes
Terabyte	TB	1,099,511,627,776 bytes	One thousand billion bytes

Having more RAM available in a computer means that it can manage more data and can also accommodate larger applications programs, thus making it more useful for processing purposes. When buying a computer you should be sure that is has adequate memory capacity for your requirements.

A hardware device is said to be on-line when it is connected to the CPU of the computer and under its control. A device is off-line if it is not under the control of the CPU.

Output hardware

When information has been entered and processed by the computer, we obviously need to see the result. Output devices allow this data to be viewed.

◥Monitor

The monitor, also called a **visual display unit (VDU)** or screen, is the most common means of displaying computer information. Monitors can be divided into two types: **cathode ray tube (CRT)** and **liquid crystal display (LCD)** monitors.

CRT monitors use the same technology as older television sets. They are cheaper and display brighter images than LCD monitors but are more expensive to run and emit small amounts of electromagnetic radiation. LCD monitors, in contrast, use an active-matrix technology to produce colour images (an explanation of this technology is beyond the scope of this book), emit less electromagnetic radiation but are more expensive and are difficult to view from an angle.

When purchasing a monitor, some of the factors that you must take into account are **size**, **resolution** and **dot pitch**. A monitor's size is measured in inches diagonally across the screen and ranges in size between 14 and 30 inches, but is normally between 17 and 19 inches. The monitor's resolution signifies the number or dots (or pixels) on the entire screen. For example, a 1,280 x 1,024 screen is capable of displaying 1,280 distinct dots on each of 1,024 lines, or about 1.3 million dots. The dot pitch is the distance between the dots and ranges from 0.15 to 0.30 millimetres – the closer the dots, the sharper the image.

◣Graphics card

A graphics card (also know as a graphic adapter, video card or video adapter) communicates directly with the main memory of the computer and is responsible for displaying images on the monitor. It contains memory and usually a co-processor for performing graphics calculations. For a graphics card, 128 MB of memory is recommended.

The two leading graphics cards are:

1. Accelerated graphics port (AGP) graphics card
2. Personal component interconnect express (PCIe) graphics card.

◣Sound card

A sound card (also know as an audio adapter or sound board) allows computers to record and play back sound. It supports both digital audio and MIDI formats and provides an input port for a microphone or other sound source and an output port to speakers and amplifiers.

Most computers come with a basic sound capability built in, but you can add a high-quality sound card to greatly improve the sound generated.

◣Speakers

Speakers allow you to hear sound from your computer, e.g. music. Typically, a pair of speakers is plugged into the computer's sound card and their cases are shielded so that they can be placed near monitors without causing magnetic interference. Many speaker systems now include a special speaker called a **subwoofer** to produce low sounds.

Speakers are often classified as active or passive. Active speakers have a built-in amplifier to boost the volume, whereas passive speakers do not possess a built-in amplifier and require an external amplifier.

The maximum volume of a set of speakers is determined by its total power output and this is given in watts (W).

◣Printers

The problem with a display is that it is only temporary: when the computer is switched off, the display is lost! Printers allow the information to be put onto paper, creating a permanent and portable display. The output from a printer on paper is called a print-out or sometimes **'hard copy'**.

Printers are divided into two main types – ink-jet and laser.

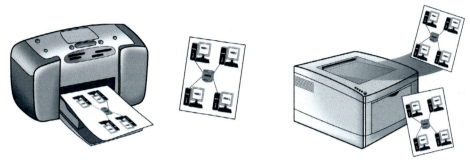

Ink-jet printer   *Laser printer*

Ink-jet printers are popular and work by sending a finely controlled jet of ink from an ink cartridge onto the paper to produce the required characters.

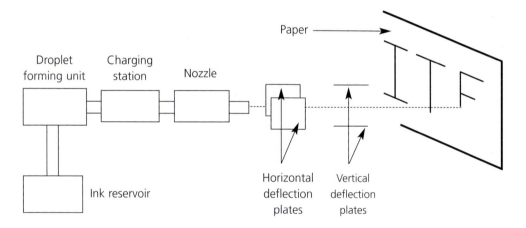

Ink-jet printer

The mode of operation of **laser** (**l**ight **a**mplification by **s**timulated **e**mission of **r**adiation) printers is similar to that of photocopiers and produces print using a fine, powdered ink called toner.

◤Buying a printer

Some of the factors that should be considered when buying a printer are purpose, speed, resolution and colour.

Purpose: Where will the printer be used? Will it be used in a small home office where the main output will be a small volume of word-processed documents, or will it be used in a busy advertising company with a high volume of printing?

Laser printers are more expensive than ink-jet printers but the actual running cost of a laser printer tends to be considerably cheaper than that of an ink-jet printer for high volumes of print.

Speed: This is measured in pages per minute (ppm) printed. Ink-jet printers can print text at two to six pages per minute while printing one page of graphics can take several minutes. Colour laser printers, in contrast, can print at up to sixteen pages per minute.

Resolution: The resolution of a printer determines the quality of text and graphics that a printer can produce and is measured in dots per inch (dpi). For example, print from a printer with a resolution of 1,200 dpi will be much sharper and more detailed than that from a printer with a resolution of only 600 dpi.

Colour: To print in colour, an ink-jet or colour laser printer is required. The initial purchase cost of the latter is considerably more expensive than the former.

Plotters

These are output devices which allow lines to be drawn using different colour pens. There are two basic types: the **flatbed** type where the pen moves up, down, across or to the side along a flat surface and the **drum plotter** where the paper is wrapped around a drum.

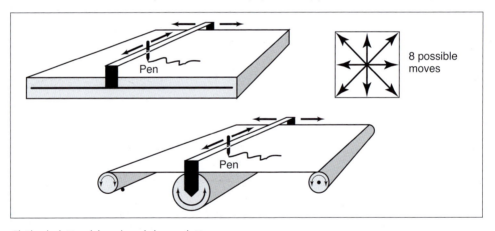

Flatbed plotter (above) and drum plotter

In general, plotters tend to be more expensive than printers. An example of the use of a plotter would be in producing hard-copy architectural plans of a house.

Wide-format printers

Wide-format printers are now gradually replacing plotters. These printers typically use ink-jet technology to print and can output drawings and images onto paper ranging from 0.5 to more than 4 metres in width.

Computer output on microfiche/film

This is where output is produced on film. This is done by means of a photographic technique where output is projected in a reduced form onto film. The film is not readable by the naked eye and requires a special magnifying reading device.

SUMMARY OF OUTPUT DEVICES					
Printer	**Relative**	**Volume speed***	**Advantages of output**	**Disadvantages**	**Where used**
ink-jet printer	slow	medium	• excellent quality • quiet	• running costs expensive • relatively slow	• low-volume/ high-quality output
laser printer	fast	large	• best quality • very fast • quiet	• running costs expensive	• high-volume/ high-quality output
plotters	slow	small	• attention to detail • different colours and pens	• slow • expensive software and hardware	• graphics • designs
monitor	fast	small	• no media expense	• temporary display • radiation omissions	• temporary output
speakers	–	–	• no media expense	• distracts others	• play sound
COM	fast	large	• large volume output on small media (space saving/ easier to distribute)	• need special viewing equipment • cannot be edited by hand	• libraries

Slow = 10 CPS to 300 LPM; fast = 300 LPM to 3,000 LPM.

Bluetooth

Bluetooth is a wireless technology that allows PCs and other devices to communicate with each other without cables. Bluetooth devices use radio signals to communicate and have a typical range of up to 10 metres. Some common Bluetooth devices are the mouse, keyboard and printer.

Auxiliary storage

All computer systems can store information for later retrieval. Magnetic disks of various types and sizes are the most common storage medium.

◣Diskettes or 'floppy disks'

Diskettes are small disks made of flexible plastic that are coated with a magnetisable material. These disks are removed from the disk drive when not in use and can be copied, filed, carried around or even sent through the post.

The first microcomputer disks had a diameter of 130 mm (5.25 inch) and were enclosed in a strong but flexible plastic envelope (hence the term 'floppy disk'). The latter was replaced by a disk with a diameter of 90 mm (3.5 inch) and is completely enclosed in a rigid plastic cartridge.

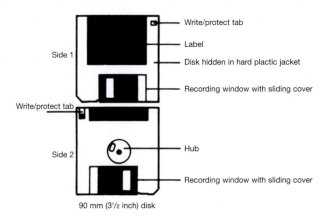

90 mm (3¹/₂ inch) disk

The information on the disk is stored in the form of spots of magnetisable material, each spot representing one bit (magnetised = 1, unmagnetised = 0). This information is stored on tracks or concentric rings or circles on the disk. A 90 mm (3.5 inch) disk can hold 1.44 MB of data. With the advent of newer portable storage media with larger capacities, this type of disk is falling into disuse.

◣Fixed disks or 'hard disks'

Fixed disks (usually called 'hard disks', in contrast to 'floppy disks') are permanently installed inside the case of the computer. They are made of a hard metal alloy with a magnetisable coating on both sides. These disks can store very large quantities of information of hundreds of gigabytes (1 gigabyte (GB) – 1000 million bytes). They can also access this information much faster than floppy disks.

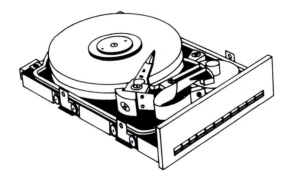

Hard disk

⬙ Zip disks

The zip disk can hold up to 750 MB of information, which is approximately 500 times the capacity of a floppy disk. These disks can be used in the same way as floppy disks and can be written to and changed. Zip disks are popular because of their portability and capacity. The disks have faster access speeds compared to floppy disks but are slower than hard disks. The main uses of zip disks include:

• storing large files, such as graphics, video clips and audio files
• exchanging large files
• archiving files
• backing up a hard disk.

⬙ Formatting a disk

A disk is formatted only once – before using it for the first time – and this simply divides the disk into sectors or slices. The procedure is similar to dividing a city into postal districts: the sectors allow data to be stored on specific areas on the disk for easy retrieval. Note: Some floppy discs are pre-formatted when purchased.

Here is an example to illustrate the retrieval method (simplified). When a file or document is stored on the disk it will have to be given a file name. Along with this name the computer will keep a record of where it recorded that file on the disk. For example, the file might be named 'CAR.doc'. When this file is saved the file name will be recorded on the outer track ('file allocation table', FAT) of the disk as CAR.doc 712. The number 712 is used to tell the computer where it has stored the file on the disk: 7 means the seventh sector and 12 means the twelfth track. When the computer needs to retrieve this data it will immediately position the read-write head at the twelfth track in the seventh sector.

This method of positioning the read-write head exactly on the spot where the data is stored is called **direct access system (DAS)**. This allows information to be retrieved from disks very rapidly.

◣ Care of disks

Magnetic disks must be treated with great care. For this reason, and because of possible loss of data from wear and tear on disks or power failure or hardware problems, you should keep contingency or 'back-up' copies of all data and program files. Back-up disks (which are exact copies of original disks) should be regularly updated, and used only in an emergency.

◣ Compact discs

Compact discs (CDs) are optical digital disks that can hold up to 700 MB of data. CDs can be classified into three different groups:
1. CD-ROMs (compact disc read-only memory) are recorded at the time of manufacture and cannot be erased. CD-ROMs are frequently used for the distribution of installation software and reference materials, e.g. technical manuals.
2. CD-Rs (compact disc-recordable) can be used to record data but are not erasable, i.e. they can be used only once to record data.
3. CD-RWs (compact disc-rewritable) can be used to erase and re-record data up to 1,000 times.

A CD-RW drive is used to record (or burn) data onto CD-Rs and CD-RWs. It can also perform all the normal functions of a CD-ROM drive, e.g. installing software or playing music. A CD-RW drive normally has three numbers associated with it, e.g. 52x32x52. The first number tells how fast the drive can read data, the second number tells how fast the drive can record data onto a CD-RW disc and the third number tells how fast a drive can record data onto a CD-R disc.

◣ DVDs

DVDs (digital video discs or digital versatile discs) are optical digital discs used for storing movies or data. DVDs look like CDs but have much greater capacities, ranging from 4.7 GB to 17 GB. Like CDs, they also can be classified into three different groups:
1. DVD-ROMs (digital versatile disc read-only memory) are impressed with data by the manufacturer and once written cannot be erased and rewritten with new data.
2. DVD-R and DVD+R are competing write-once formats for movies or users' data.
3. DVD-RW and DVD+RW are competing, rewritable (re-recordable) formats that can be rewritten up to 1,000 times. Companies like Dell, Hewlett-Packard and Sony support the DVD+RW format while Hitachi, Pioneer and Toshiba support the DVD-RW format.

A DVD +/- RW drive can record (or burn) DVDs in both formats. This drive typically has three numbers associated with it, e.g. 16x4x12. The first number tells how fast the drive can record data onto a DVD+R or DVD-R disk. The second number tells how fast the drive can record data onto a DVD+RW or a DVD-RW disk. The third number tells how fast the drive can read data from a DVD-ROM disk.

Another type of drive used with optical discs is the **combo drive.** It can read both CDs and DVDs. It can also write to CDs but not to DVDs.

Storing and accessing data on CDs and DVDs

In a CD or DVD burner, a production laser burns **pits** into the smooth surface of the disc, leaving flat surfaces (or **lands**) in between. The patterns of pits and lands represent data.

When data is being read, light from the laser is bounced off the pits and the lands. The transition from either land to pit or pit to land represents a 1, while the absence of a transition represents a 0. Together these 1s and 0s make up the binary language understood by computers.

Two reasons for the higher storage capacity of DVDs compared to CDs are:
1. Higher-density data storage: smaller pits placed closer together are used on DVDs.
2. Multi-layer storage: a DVD can have up to four layers, two on each side. The laser that reads the DVD can focus on the second layer through the first layer.

USB flash drive

USB flash drives (also called pen drives, key drives, memory sticks and thumb drives) are small, portable storage devices. They plug into a computer's USB port and come in a range of capacities, from 256 MB up to 16 GB. USB flash drives contain a special memory card called 'flash' memory, which is similar to that in digital cameras. This type of memory does not require a power source to retain the stored information.

Accessing and storing data on a USB flash drive is much faster than other types of removable storage, e.g. floppy disks or CDs. A USB flash drive is more durable than a portable hard disk in that it does not have any moving parts.

Other storage media

Magnetic tape, similar to that used in tape recorders, can also be used to store computer information. For business use, reel-to-reel tapes and tape streamers are used.

The main disadvantage of tapes is that only serial access is available, compared with the direct access possible with disks. This means that the tape must be wound forward until it reaches the spot where the information is stored, which can take several minutes in certain circumstances.

Magnetic tape is not used very often with business microcomputers, except occasionally for contingency or 'back-up' purposes.

SUMMARY OF BACKING STORAGE DEVICES							
	Floppy disk	**Hard disk**	**Magnetic tape**	**CD -ROM**	**Zip Disk**	**DVD-ROM**	**USB flash drive**
Access speed	slow	fast	varies	fast	fast (slower than hard disk)	fast	fast
Approx. capacity	1.44 MB, 2 MB	up to 1 TB*	up to 300 GB	up to 700 MB	up to 750 MB	4.7 GB to 17 GB	236 MB to 16 GB
Method of operation	DAS (direct access system)	DAS	SAS (serial access) system	DAS	DAS	DAS	
Where used	microcomputer systems, also to back up	micro, miniframe	mainframe, tape-streamers for back up on micros	micro, mini	micro back up large files	micro, mini	micro

*1TB (1 terabyte = 1,000 GB)

◼Ports

At the back of most computers are a number of connectors called **ports**. These allow the computer to be connected to the keyboard, printer and to other external (or **peripheral**) devices.

Most modern computers have the following ports.

◼PS/2 port

- A PS/2 port is also called a keyboard or mouse port.
- Most computers come with two PS/2 ports – one for the keyboard and the other for the mouse.
- They are usually coloured purple for the keyboard and green for the mouse.

USB port
- A USB port is used to connect different types of external devices, e.g. external hard drives, printers, mice, scanners.
- Most computers nowadays have at least two USB ports.

Parallel port
- A parallel port is used to connect external devices such as printers, scanners and zip drives.
- The 25-pin port is sometimes called a printer port.

Ethernet or network port
- For faster Internet connections and for networking, an ethernet or network port is used.
- This looks like an oversized telephone jack.

ETHERNET

Video port or monitor port
- This port is used to attach a computer display monitor to a computer's video card.
- The connector has fifteen holes. It looks like a serial port connector, but this port has holes, not pins.

IEEE 1394 or firewire port
- This port is used to transfer large amounts of data very quickly.
- Camcorders and other video equipment usually use this port to get data onto a computer.

Serial port

- A serial port is used to connect external modems or an older computer mouse to the computer.
- It comes in two versions:
  - a 9-pin version (on the left) or
  - a 25-pin model. The 9-pin version is found on most computers.

Sound ports

Three sound ports permit the connection of speakers, microphone and a stereo music system

USB to serial port adaptor

- You can also use your serial port device on your USB port with this adapter.

Power port

- The power port connects to the computer's power cable that plugs into a wall socket.

Hardware specification example

Advertisements often display detailed specifications of computers for sale. When considering the choice between one computer and another it is important to understand what the different specifications mean. Here is an example of one such specification and a brief explanation of each item.

> ## PC Specification
>
> Intel Pentium 4 3.0 Ghz processor
> 1024 MB DDR2 RAM
> 17" LCD monitor
> 250 GB hard disk
> 2 MB cache memory
> AGP 4/8X
> 16X DVD-ROM drive
> Integrated 10/100 LAN
> Windows XP Media Centre preloaded

Intel Pentium 4 3.0 Ghz processor
This is the type of Intel CPU chip in the PC. Its clock speed is 3 billion cycles per second. The higher the clock speed of the CPU, the quicker the computer can perform tasks.

1024 MB DDR2 RAM
1.024 billion bytes of information can be contained in the main memory (RAM). DDR2 is high-performance main memory and transfers sixty-four bits of data twice every clock cycle.

17" LCD monitor
This monitor uses less electricity and emits less electromagnetic radiation than CRT monitors.

250 GB hard disk
The maximum capacity is 250 billion bytes.

2 MB cache memory
Cache memory remembers instructions and data that the processor has executed or accessed previously and is faster than main memory (RAM). This computer has 2 MB capacity of this fast memory.

AGP 8X
An accelerated graphics port video card is installed. This enables 3-D images to access the computer's RAM faster when this is installed. The speed at which this card operates is eight times faster than the original AGP card developed by Intel.

16X DVD-ROM drive
A DVD-ROM drive is installed with a read speed sixteen times the original specification of the first-issue DVD-ROM drive.

Integrated 10/100 LAN
Each computer on a network must have a network interface card (**NIC**). Most modern network interface cards are 10/100 NICs and can operate at either 10 Mbps or 100 Mbps.

Windows XP Media Centre preloaded
Microsoft's graphical user interface operating system is pre-installed.

▦ Software

So far we have discussed the machinery or equipment that makes up a computer system: the 'hardware'. The problem is that if we had all this equipment available to us, the computer would still be useless. So what is missing? The answer is programs or 'software'.

The software is the set of instructions that enables the computer to perform its function. A car is useless without instructions to go fast or slow, stop or start. So, too, a computer is useless without the instructions for performing a particular task. For example, if we want to extract a trial balance from a computer, we must first have the accounting program (instructions) in the computer's memory.

Types of software

There are two types of software that need to be in place before we can use the computer: the **operating system** and **application programs**.

◆ The operating system

This is the set of instructions that looks after the internal running of the computer. Its functions include the following:

- providing a user interface to allow the person to give the computer instructions
- managing the memory of the computer as efficiently as possible
- error reporting and error handling
- handling the operation of input, output and backing storage devices
- running application software
- running utilities programs for displaying information on the screen, reading from disks, listing the contents of a disk, formatting disks, copying disks or files and so on.

The market-leading operating system used on most microcomputers is Microsoft Windows. It has a graphical user interface with icons (graphic symbols) and pull-down menus to select commands. Over the years, Windows has undergone many changes – Microsoft tends to introduce a new version of Windows to the market every three or four years. The three most recent versions of Windows in chronological order are Windows 2000, Windows XP and Windows Vista.

Two other popular operating systems are Linux for the PC and Mac OS X for Apple Macintosh computers.

The operating system instructions must be in the computer's memory before any other software can function. Programs work by communicating requests to the operating system, which acts as a kind of secretary to the application software.

Application programs

Application programs are computer programs that are written to make the computer perform specific tasks, such as:

- word processing
- spreadsheets
- graphics
- database management
- financial accounting
- website production.

Programs that perform specific functions such as these are often called applications (to distinguish them from programs that make the computer itself work more effectively, called the operating system as outlined above). Application programs are written in computer programming languages by large specialist companies, such as Microsoft, Adobe and Sage, and these programs can then be bought 'off the shelf' from computer suppliers. Alternatively, computer programs can be specially written (or customised) for a particular company's needs: this kind of program can be very expensive.

Device drivers

A **device driver** (or **driver**) is a computer program that enables the operating system to interact with a hardware device, e.g. a printer. Every device attached to a computer must have a driver. Some drivers come with the operating system, e.g. a keyboard driver. For other devices, you may need to install a new driver when you connect the device to the computer, e.g. a scanner driver.

Software licensing

A software licence allows an individual or group to use a piece of software. There are three distinct types of software licence:

1. A **single user** licence permits the software to be installed onto one computer only.
2. A **multiple user** licence allows software to be installed on a large number of computers, but only a set number of people can use the software at any one time.
3. A **site licence** allows unlimited use of a software program throughout the company or organisation.

Freeware and shareware

Freeware is copyrighted software given away for free by its author. The author allows people to use the software but not sell it. An example of freeware is Adobe Acrobat Reader, used for viewing documents in portable document format (**pdf**).

Shareware is copyrighted software that is distributed on the basis of an honour system and is generally free for a certain period of time, after which you have to pay a small fee to use it. An example of shareware is WinZip, used for compressing and decompressing files.

◤Easy-to-use (user-friendly) programs

Greater emphasis is placed nowadays on programs that are easy to learn and to use, or 'user-friendly' programs. Some or all of the following features may be found with such programs.

Sound: Sound may be used to signal to the user that a mistake has been made. Sound may also indicate that a task is complete or that the computer is awaiting more data.

Colour or contrast: Colour can highlight displays and improve the presentation of information.

Help facility: The user can give a special command to request help if needed. With some programs, if an error occurs the computer will automatically give the required explanation and offer ways to remedy the mistake. This is called 'on-line help'.

Icons: These are small symbols displayed on the screen to represent commands or options, and are usually selected by using a mouse. This means that complex commands do not have to be remembered.

Menus: The use of menus means that the user is guided through the application.

Program prompts: At no stage during the operation of a program should the user be left not knowing what to do next or in what form the information should be entered. Program prompts are messages telling the user the next action to take or offering choices, such as 'Press any key to continue', 'Do you want to exit the system (Y/N)?' or 'Do you want to save before exiting?'

On the other hand, poor choice of sound, graphics or colour may not enhance the ease of use of a particular program. Frequent beeps may be a source of irritation to the user, and may distract others working in the same room. The graphics and colour chosen may only serve to cause eye discomfort.

▦ Networks

A network can be defined as two or more computers linked together that allow users to share information and equipment.

Network categories

There are three main categories of network:

A **local area network (LAN)** is a small network of computers and ancillary equipment located close to each other, usually within the same building.

A **metropolitan area network (MAN)** is a number of local area networks linked together in the same geographical area, e.g. a university may decide to link all of its local area networks located on different campuses throughout a city into one metropolitan area network.

A **wide area network (WAN)** connects a number of local and/or metropolitan area networks together over a wide geographical area. The networks that make up the wide area network may be located throughout the world. The Internet is often described as the world's largest wide area network.

Network architectures

Networks can be classified into one of two main network architectures – **peer-to-peer** or **client/server**.

Peer-to-peer networks allow users to share their data and resources, e.g. printers, scanners and Internet access. They are decentralised in that each computer in a peer-to-peer network stores its own information and resources. There are no central computers that control the network. Peer-to-peer networks are suitable for a maximum of ten users.

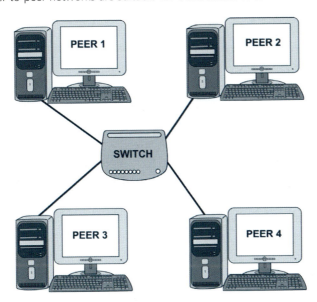

A **switch** is a device that can be used to connect the cables on a network. It can also direct information to a specific computer on a network. Typically, a cable runs from the network port on each computer to a port on the switch, thus linking the network interface card (NIC) in the computer to the switch. Switches with different numbers of ports can be purchased, e.g. 8-port and 24-port switches are commonplace.

Advantages:
1. Easy to configure
2. Does not require additional software
3. Does not require a network administrator
4. Reduced total cost.

Disadvantages:

1. Supports a small number of users
2. Does not provide a central location for saving files
3. Users are responsible for managing resources
4. Security is poor.

Client/server networks typically consist of a central computer (called a **server**) that provides information and resources to other computers (called **clients**) in the network.

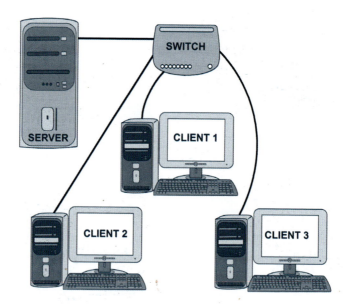

Advantages:

1. Can support a large number of users
2. Data is stored centrally and can be easily backed up
3. Management of resources is centralised
4. Provides a high level of security.

Disadvantages:

1. Planning, design and implementation can be complex
2. A network administrator must be employed
3. Server hardware and software is expensive.

Wireless networking

A wireless network (also know as a **wi-fi** network) uses wireless signals instead of cables to carry data. These signals can be produced using either infrared or radio waves. The latter is more popular, as it does not require a direct line of sight between sender and receiver.

A wireless network usually refers to a wireless local area network (**WLAN**). A WLAN can be installed as the sole network in a building or it can be used to extend an existing cabled network where cabling would be too difficult to implement.

Two devices are required to implement a WLAN: a wireless network interface card (NIC) installed in each PC and an **access point** installed in a prominent location in the room. The access point takes the place of the switch found in cabled networks in that it transmits and receives signals to and from the surrounding computers via their wireless NICs.

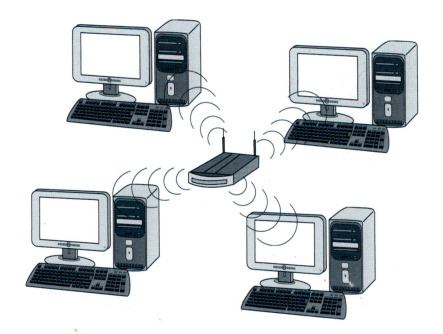

A **hotspot** is the area covered by an access point and provides public wireless broadband services to laptop users through a WLAN. Hotspots are found in public places, e.g. airports, colleges, hotels, libraries and train stations.

Advantages:
1. Elimination of unsightly and expensive cables
2. Offers mobility – a laptop with a wireless NIC can be configured to access the network
3. Radio frequencies used by wireless networks are unlicensed.

Disadvantages:
1. Potential for radio interference due to weather, other wireless devices or obstructions such as walls
2. Wireless NICs are more expensive than standard NICs
3. Network security can be expensive to implement.

Other information and communication technology (ICT) equipment

Telephone

Despite the increasing popularity of e-mail, the telephone remains the most popular and important method of communications in the office. Telephone technology is also advancing rapidly with such developments as digital and mobile phones.

Mobile telephone

The mobile phone is a portable wireless phone that allows communication from almost any location. This communication can take the form of a text message, a voice or video call. Newer models come with some or all of the following capabilities: digital camera, video capture, MP3 player, Blackberry, Bluetooth, a personal organiser or even mobile television. Most mobile phones also offer facilities for Internet access.

Blackberry

A Blackberry is a handheld wireless device that allows you to exchange e-mail messages. The demarcation line between the mobile phone and Blackberry has become blurred as most Blackberries now offer facilities for voice calls, Internet access and a built-in personal organiser.

Facsimile transmission (fax)

This is a popular and effective means of communication. Most businesses today have fax machines. These allow pictures, diagrams and text to be transmitted from place to place via the telephone lines. Fax operates in a similar way to a photocopier and is often described as a long-distance photocopier.

Photocopier

The photocopier can be described as a device for photographically reproducing written, printed or graphic material. Photocopiers are widely used in business, education and government.

All-in-one printer

This device has the facilities to copy, fax, print and scan documents. In effect, it takes the place of four separate devices – a photocopier, a fax, a printer and a scanner. Dell and Hewlett-Packard have a range of these devices on the market.

Data-processing concepts

Elements of a computer file

A **file** is a collection of records.

A **record** is made up of a collection of related fields.

A **field** consists of a number of characters.

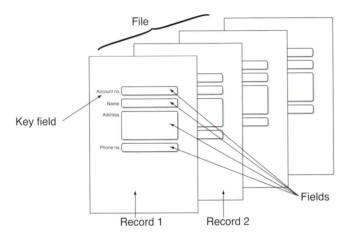

The elements of a file

◤ Key field

The key field is a field within a record that uniquely identifies the record, e.g. a bank account number.

Types of record

◤ Fixed length records

Every record of this type in the file will have the same fixed number of fields and characters. The maximum size of the fields is always specified. The main advantage of this type of record is that it is easier for programmers to use. The main disadvantage is that some space allocation may be wasted.

◤ Variable length records

With this type of record, not all records in the file are the same size. The number of fields may vary or the amount of characters in a particular field may vary. The main advantage of this type of record is that it is a better use of space. The main disadvantage is that programming can be difficult.

Types of file

Transaction file

This consists of records that relate to individual transactions that occur from day to day, e.g. sales invoices, orders.

Reference file

This contains reference data that is normally altered or updated infrequently, e.g. price lists, company regulations. It does not contain any transaction data.

Master file

This consists of reference data and transaction data that is built up over time, e.g. the payroll master file would contain reference data such as PRSI numbers and cumulative totals of pay and tax to date.

File organisation

File organisation refers to the way records are held on file. Usually a key field, e.g. student number or account code, is used to identify each record. The various types of file organisation are outlined below.

Serial

The key fields are stored one after the other but not in any logical order. This method is usually used for recording transaction data initially.

Sequential

Records are ordered by the the key field. Often transaction files are ordered sequentially before master files are updated.

Index sequential

Records are held sequentially but are accessed by means of an index.

Random or direct access

Records are not stored in any particular order. They are stored in addressable locations which are calculated based on the key field.

Updating disk files

Individual records on a disk are addressable directly (DAS). It is possible to write back to and update a record to the same place from which it was read. This involves overwriting the existing information with the new information. This is often referred to as **updating by overlay** or in **place**.

Updating consists of the following sequence:

- The transaction file data and master file data are read into main memory.
- The transaction data and master file data are matched and updated in the memory and transferred to the same place on the master disk.

Stages of data collection

◪1. Data collection
Data may be collected on manually prepared source documents, e.g. invoices, orders, etc., or the data could be captured in a machine sensible form at source, e.g. bar codes.

◪2. Data transmission
This involves sending source documents to a central location by post, telephone, electronic mail or fax for processing.

◪3. Data preparation
This can involve transcription of data from the source documents to a machine sensible form if there is no direct data capture and verification. **Data verification** is the process of checking that the original source information has been correctly transcribed. It is essentially a process of checking that the data input is identical to the source documents.

A common method of verification is to have the data rekeyed by another person and compared with the first entry. Misspelling and transposition errors can be detected. Tranposition errors are those where characters are mixed up, e.g. code 2343 is keyed in as 2334.

◪4. Input
The verified data is then subject to validation checks before processing. **Data validation** is a procedure which checks verified data before processing. Common validation checks are outlined below.

Range check: Checks whether the input data is within specific allowable ranges, e.g. accounts codes are only allowed between 0000 and 9999.

Limit check: Certain numbers are not allowed to be above or below a certain level, e.g. twenty-four hours in a day.

Existence check: Data is checked to ensure that all necessary fields are present.

Format check: Data is checked to ensure that it contains only characters of the correct type, e.g. there should only be numbers in numeric fields.

Reasonableness check: Checks that numbers are not unusually high or low. There have been cases of householders getting electricity bills for thousands of euro due to a meter reading error.

Check digits: These are used to check codes for validity. The computer calculates a check which is added to each code for validation purposes. For example: calculation of the check digit using 11 as the division factor. Original code: 9564

Multiply each digit by a weight starting one greater than the number of digits: 5432.

Product   9 * 5 = 45

           5 * 4 = 20

           6 * 3 = 18

           4 * 2 = 8

Sum the product = 91

Divide by 11 = 8 and remainder of 3

Subtract the remainder from 11 = 8 (11 − 3)

8 is the check digit

When the new code number is input to the computer, a weighting system is used. One is used for the right most digit and two for the next and so on. The product is calculated and summed. It is then divided by eleven and the remainder should be zero. If the remainder is not zero, the code is not valid.

New code: 95648

Product   9 * 5 = 45

           5 * 4 = 20

           6 * 3 = 18

           4 * 2 = 8

           8 * 1 = 8

Sum = 99

Divide by 11 = 9 and remainder 0

Thus this code would pass the validition test.

Note: An original code giving rise to check digit of '10' is normally discarded.

Methods of data processing

◪Batch processing

This involves individual source documents being grouped or batched manually or on computer and processed at a predetermined interval of time. For example, in an accounting system all the invoices for a week could be entered into the computer but not processed (updating the accounts) until the end of the week. At the end of the week all accounts relating to the batch would be processed in one run.

Advantages:

- Better control
- More efficient use of processing time

- Large tasks can be broken down into small batches
- Access to the computer not always required.

Disadvantages:

- Random enquiries not possible as files are not constantly up-to-date
- Causes peaks and lows in computer use
- Only applicable to certain applications.

Applications suited to batch processing:

- Payroll
- Accounting updates
- Sales statistics.

On-line transaction processing

This involves processing of transactions as they occur. An example would be an airline booking system. As bookings are received, they are immediately reserved on the system.

Advantages:

- Files always up-to-date
- No data preparation necessary
- Random enquiries possible.

Disadvantages:

- Computer power must always be available
- Back-up systems vital.

Applications suited to on-line processing:

- Airline booking system
- Electronic point-of-sale systems using bar code readers
- ATM.

Real-time processing

Real-time processing occurs where a computer must react immediately to new data received. It is usually found where computers are responsible for controlling systems.

Advantages:

1. Very fast response times
2. No data preparation necessary.

Disadvantages:

1. Very expensive systems are required
2. Specialised personnel usually required.

Applications suited to real-time processing:
1. Patient monitor in an intensive care unit
2. Process control at a chemical plant
3. Radar and aircraft collision avoidance.

▦ The information and communication technology environment

The aim of this section is to describe ways to minimise risks to the ICT environment.

Definitions

The **security** of computer systems 'is the establishment and application of safeguards to protect data, software and computer hardware from accidental or malicious modification, destruction or disclosure' (The British Computer Society).

The **privacy** of computer systems is part of overall security and involves methods of protection against unauthorised access or disclosure.

Data security is 'the means of ensuring that data is kept safe from corruption and that access to it is suitably controlled' (www.answers.com).

Data integrity refers to 'the accuracy of data and its conformity to its expected value, especially after being processed or transmitted' (Microsoft Computer Dictionary).

Risks to computer systems

1. INPUT FRAUD

This involves entering false or misleading information into a computer system. This is the most common method of fraud because the majority of users have input access.
Examples are:

- use of 'ghost' or fictitious employees on a payroll system
- creation of fictitious suppliers
- positive falsification, i.e. inserting additional data which is false
- negative falsification, i.e. where data is suppressed (not shown).

2. ALTERATION OF PROGRAMS

This is less common as very technical skills are required to alter commercial programs. The most common form of alteration is where a small slice or portion of an account is redirected into a secret account. This is called salami programming.

3. OUTPUT FRAUD

This is where computer output is suppressed, stolen or altered. Slow output devices mean that data is sometimes exposed to fraudulent attempts in a data queue.

4. UNAUTHORISED ACCESS

5. COMPUTER VIRUSES

These are computer programs designed as a prank or to damage data, which can copy themselves by attaching to other programs.

6. PHYSICAL DAMAGE FROM FIRE, FLOOD AND BREAK-INS

7. ENVIRONMENTAL FACTORS SUCH AS DUST, DAMPNESS AND HEAT

8. POWER SUPPLY CUT OFF AND PROXIMITY OF MAGNETIC FIELDS

9. LOSS OF DATA AND PROGRAMS

10. POOR PERSONNEL PROCEDURES

Methods of minimising the risks to the information technology environment

There are three main types of method:
- physical
- logical
- procedural.

Physical methods
- Air-conditioned rooms, especially for mainframe computers.
- Dust-free rooms.
- Controlled temperature systems.
- Back-up power supply (generator).
- Surge controller to control any variations in power going into computer systems.
- High-security locks on computer room doors.
- Limited access to keys.
- Locks on computer equipment.

Logical methods

These involve the use of computer programs to minimise risks.

- Use of non-display passwords for access to programs or data.
- The use of passwords to limit what the user can do on the system, e.g. the system manager's password will normally allow access to all areas whereas the computer operator may be restricted to data entry only.

- Built-in user monitor programs. These are programs which monitor the activities of every user of the system. Information such as log-on time, update activities, files read, menus visited, log-off time, etc. is stored for future reference. Printed summaries of this information are taken at regular intervals.
- Virus protection programs prevent viruses from infecting the computer. An alarm is usually sounded when a virus is present. These programs must be updated regularly to keep up with the many new viruses.
- Virus destruction software enables the user to delete or remove certain viruses if detected on a disk.
- Screen blank programs. These programs are time activated. After a set period of time of non-activity the screen will blank off. To reactivate the screen, the password must be given.

Procedural methods

Good personnel procedures are very important for minimising risks to computer systems.

- Back-up copies of data should be regularly made. These back-up copies (on disk or tape) should be stored in separate locations in fire-proof safes.
- Proper log-out procedure should be adhered to. The computer should not be switched off before logging out.
- Audit trials should be carried out randomly (once or twice yearly) and at regular intervals (twice a year). The audit trial will perform a full check on the working of the system and is particularly useful for detecting input fraud, program alterations and output fraud.
- Computer output should be shredded if not required or if confidential.
- Personnel should sign for important documentation.
- Proper care of hard disks:
    - regular checks for disk integrity
    - regular defragmentation of disks.
- Proper care of floppy and zip disks:
    - store away from electrical devices
    - store in disk boxes
    - never insert a disk in the disk drive before switching on the computer
    - always take the disk out before turning off the computer
    - never take a disk out when the drive is active
    - do not touch the surface of the disk
    - disks should be labelled clearly.
- Digruntled staff should be closely monitored.
- No employee should be put into a situation where there is a conflict of interest, e.g. a bank employee updating his/her own account.
- Personnel must follow legislation regarding data storage, e.g. the Data Protection Acts 1988 and 2003.

The Data Protection Act 1988

The eight principles of the Data Protection Act 1988 and Data Protection (Amendments) Act 2003 are as follows:

1. Personal data should be obtained and processed fairly and lawfully.
2. Personal data should only be kept for one or more specified, explicit and lawful purposes.
3. Personal data should be used and disclosed only in ways compatible with these purposes.
4. Personal data should be adequate, relevant and not excessive.
5. Personal data should be accurate and kept up-to-date.
6. Personal data should not be kept longer than deemed necessary.
7. An individual is entitled at reasonable intervals and without undue delay to find out
   — whether information is held about that individual
   — what the content of the information is
   and where appropriate, the individual can have the data edited or erased.
8. Appropriate measures should be used to limit access to personal data or for the destruction of personal data.

To ensure adherence to this Act, the following procedures should be adopted:
- Store only essential information.
- Improve the security of data using methods outlined above.
- Identify data elements which are sensitive, in particular personal details and monetary data.
- Adopt a policy of regularly updating information.
- Anticipate change – when designing or purchasing new software, ensure that it takes into account future anticipated changes or that it is flexible.

The Freedom of Information Act 1997 and Freedom of Information (Amendments) Act 2003

The Freedom of Information Acts established three new statutory rights. These are:
- A legal right for each person to access information held by public bodies.
- A legal right for each person to have official information relating to him/herself amended when it is incomplete or misleading.
- A legal right to obtain reasons for decisions affecting oneself.
- Obliges government departments and a range of statutory agencies to publish information on their activities and to make personal information available to citizens.

Improving the information and communication technology environment for users – ergonomics

Ergonomics is the study of work environments with a view to improving employee comfort and in turn employee productivity.

Ergonomic considerations were thought of as luxuries in the past. Today ergonomic considerations are now a management responsibility, enforceable by law. This is especially true with the passing of the EC Directive (90/270/EC) on Display Screen Equipment which came into force on 1 January 1993.

The regulations have six major requirements.

◤1. Analysis of workstations

Every employer must perform a suitable and sufficient analysis of user workstations to assess the risks which they may pose for the health and safety of users. Any risks identified must be reduced.

Common risks are:
- eyes (strain and glare)
- repetitive strain injuries (RSIs)
- musculo-skeletal (posture)
- mental stress
- space problems.

An ergonomics checklist can be very useful for analysing the workstations.

◤2. Requirements for workstations

These include:
- equipment should be adjustable
- glare-free working conditions
- software suitable for the task.

◤3. Daily routine for users

Where possible, users should have a mix of screen-based and non-screen-based work or, if this is not possible, the provision of breaks in work routine is essential.

◤4. Eyes and eyesight

Users have the right to request an eyesight test at their employer's expense. If it is found that corrective appliances are required for display screen work, then the employer is liable for the cost.

◤5. Provision of training

All users of workstations must be provided with adequate training in the areas of software use and health and safety issues.

◤6. Provision of information

All employers are required to ensure that all relevant information available is provided to users of workstations.

The diagram below shows a workstation that is ergonomically designed.

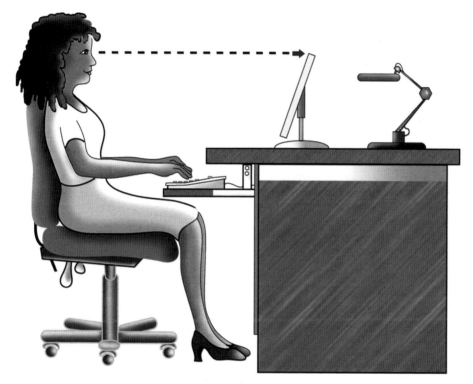

An ergonomically sound workstation

⠿ Questions

Multi-choice questions

1. Which of the following is the smallest computer system?
    (a) supercomputer
    (b) minicomputer
    (c) mainframe
    (d) microcomputer

2. A personal digital assistant (PDA) is:
    (a) a small hand-held computer
    (b) a battery pack for a notebook computer
    (c) a component within the CPU
    (d) a fast memory chip

3. A monitor is:
    (a) an output device
    (b) an input device
    (c) a peripheral device
    (d) an item of hardware
    (e) all of the above

4. ROM is:
    (a) non-volatile
    (b) storage
    (c) permanently required
    (d) all of the above

5. Typically, how many bits are there in one byte?
    (a) 4
    (b) 2
    (c) 65
    (d) 8

6. Which of the following disks holds the most information?
    (a) DVD-ROM
    (b) 90 mm (3.5 inch) disk
    (c) fixed (hard) disk
    (d) CD-ROM

7. Formatting a disk is usually done:
    (a) once before using a new disk
    (b) every time something is saved on the disk
    (c) every time the disk is full
    (d) to make a back-up copy of a file

8. The instructions that enable a computer to function are called:
    (a) hardware
    (b) applications
    (c) software
    (d) instructions

9. When purchasing a new printer, which of the following would you consider?
    (a) purpose
    (b) speed
    (c) resolution
    (d) all of the above

10. Which pair are the most commonly used input and output devices?
    (a) mouse, printer
    (b) keyboard, printer
    (c) VDE, monitor
    (d) keyboard, monitor

11. The information needed for long-term planning is called:
    (a) tactical
    (b) transactional
    (c) operational
    (d) strategic

12. To which of the following ports would you connect a printer?
    (a) serial
    (b) USB
    (c) firewire
    (d) network

13. Where records are stored in order of their key fields, the file organisation method is called:
    (a) index sequential
    (b) serial
    (c) sequential
    (d) random

14. Bluetooth:
    (a) is an accelerated graphics card
    (b) allows PCs and other devices to communicate without cables
    (c) is the latest high-capacity hard disk
    (d) all of the above

15. NIC is an acronym for:
    (a) network interrupt core
    (b) network instruction case
    (c) network interface card
    (d) network initialisation computer

16. Which of the following is not a computer network?
    (a) MAN
    (b) LAN
    (c) CAN
    (d) WAN

17. Which of the following operating systems is used on Apple Macintosh computers?
    (a) Linux
    (b) MAC OS X
    (c) Windows XP
    (d) Windows Vista

18. A device driver is a:
    (a) program that enables the operating system to interact with a hardware device
    (b) DIY computer assembly kit
    (c) tool used by PC technicians for replacing hard disks
    (d) very fast flash drive

19. The check digit for the code 4214 using division by 11 is:
    (a) 6
    (b) 5
    (c) 1
    (d) 39

20. Which of the following would not be used to combat input fraud?
    (a) passwords
    (b) monitoring disgruntled employees
    (c) virus protection
    (d) monitoring programs

Short-answer questions

1. Name four types of computer system and give an example of where each system is normally used.
2. What is an input device? Name six different input devices.
3. How is data inside the computer's memory represented?
4. What unit is computer capacity measured in?
5. What is a port?
6. What is a USB flash drive?
7. List conditions likely to damage disks.
8. What is the function of the operating system and how does it differ from application software?
9. What do the terms 'on-line' and 'off-line' mean? Give examples of on-line and off-line devices.
10. Explain the functions of ROM and RAM and how they differ.

Structured questions

1. Information in an organisation is often classified as strategic, tactical and operational.
   (a) Take an organisation with which you are familiar (e.g. a company or college) and explain the nature of the strategic, tactical and operational information, giving examples.
   (b) When communicating information to management, give five rules that should be observed so as to ensure that management will be satisfied with the information.
2. What method of data capture would you recommend as input to computer systems in each of the following situations:
   • time recording for employees in a company
   • multi-choice examination answers
   • sales orders in a mail order business.
   (a) Describe the main features of each method you would recommend for the applications given above.
   (b) Give possible advantages and disadvantages of each method described.
3. Describe the main features of any three output devices (other than printers) and indicate the most suitable application for each device.
4. (a) Explain what you understand by the term 'modern electronic office' and explain the principal hardware features of such an office.
   (b) List the possible benefits of the modern electronic office.
5. Owing to a combination of errors including an electrical fault and an error made by an inexperienced operator, the master file containing details of 10,000 insurance policy holders was destroyed.
   (a) Describe how this situation could be rectified if the master file was (i) on tape and (ii) on disk.

(b) Describe what precautions should have been taken so that the above situation could have been avoided.

6. 'Computer networks are widely used in business organisations today.'

   (a) List the main reasons why companies set up computer networks.

   (b) Using diagrams, describe two network architectures.

   (c) Discuss the relative advantages and disadvantages of each of the architectures.

Sample structured questions (FETAC)

1. (a) Distinguish clearly between data and information. (2 marks)

   (b) Describe the importance of the following in relation to information flows:

   comparison

   exception reporting

   feedback (3 marks)

   (c) Describe the following information systems and give an example of each.

   Transaction processing system (TPS)

   Decision support system (DSS) (5 marks)

2. The range of software available for computers is growing at a phenomenal rate.

   (a) Define the term 'software'. (1 mark)

   (b) Distinguish between 'systems software' and 'applications software' and give an example of each. (3 marks)

   (c) Describe the difference between 'off-the-shelf software' and 'custom software' and state the advantages of each type. (3 marks)

   (d) Describe three major functions performed by an operating system. (3 marks)

Sample assignments (FETAC)

Assignment 1 – Information Processing

Select an organisation of your choice and investigate the organisation under any five of the following headings:

1. Identify items of technology utilised in the organisation. Give their specification and outline their uses.

2. Identify examples of the following in the organisation:
   - operational information
   - tactical information
   - strategic information.

3. Describe the flow of information for one process or operation in the organisation and identify the data and information at each stage.

4. Describe one information process in the organisation in terms of efficiency and cost effectiveness.

vi. Describe the layout of technological equipment in ergonomic terms.

vii. Describe how the organisation deals with threats to data integrity and suggestions for improvements.

viii. List the applications software in use in the organisation and comment on their suitability.

ix. Another appropriate task.

Assignment 2 – Internet and E-mail (refer to Chapters 9 and 10)

(a) Select a specific topic in the module Information and Communication Systems and carry out the following tasks:

i. Use at least two search engines on the Internet to access information on the selected topic. Print one relevant search results page from each search engine.

ii. Select a page containing relevant information on the topic and print at least one page of relevant information.

iii. List the addresses of at least five sites visited in your search for information on the topic.

(b) Use e-mail to carry out the following tasks:

i. Compose an e-mail message and send it to multiple recipients, with an attachment.

ii. Create an e-mail address book for at least two individuals and two groups containing at least two addresses in each group.

Assignment 3 – Data Capture Form

You are employed in the marketing department of McNulty Shoes Ltd. You have been asked to create a data capture form to gather information on the firm's customers and their shopping habits. The form should contain the following:

i. have a minimum of ten fields

ii. have appropriate field names or questions

iii. have at least one text, numeric, logical, date and currency field

iv. field formats should be indicated or stated separately

v. field lengths should be indicated or stated separately

vi. fields should be grouped in an appropriate manner.

Sample short answer questions (FETAC)

1. List **four** attributes of information. (1 mark)

(i) _____   (ii) _____

(iii) _____   (iv) _____

2. List **four** advantages of using computers for information processing. (1 mark)

(i) _____   (ii) _____

(iii) _____   (iv) _____

3. State an appropriate input device for the following applications. (1 mark)

(i) Keying in text _____

(ii) Activating a card-phone _____

(iii) Selecting an item displayed on a computer screen _____

(iv) Producing a digital image from a photograph _____

4. List **two** types of error that could be caught by means of data verification. (1 mark)

(i) _____   (ii) _____

5. List **four** essential items required in order to connect to the Internet. (1 mark)

(i) _____   (ii) _____

(iii) _____   (iv) _____

▦ Glossary of computer terms

access point: a device found in wireless networks that transmits and receives signals to and from the surrounding computers.

access time: the amount of time to retrieve data from a storage device, measured from the instant of executing the command to retrieve data to the moment when the data is stored in a specified location.

ALU (arithmetic and logic unit): the part of the CPU that performs mathematical functions and logical decisions, such as deciding whether one number is greater than another.

application software: programs to perform specific tasks, such as word processing or database management, as distinct from system software (operating system), which maintains and organises the computer system.

ASCII (American Standard Code for Information Interchange): a term sometimes used to describe the system of allocating code numbers to different characters.

auxiliary ('backing') storage device: hardware used to store information for later retrieval.

bar code: a distinctive pattern of lines printed on a product or label, usually containing a code for the product number and capable of being entered into the computer by means of a suitable scanner.

binary number: a number system using only the digits 1 and 0, and therefore capable of being represented inside a computer by means of the presence (1) or absence (0) of an electrical current or magnetic charge.

bit: one digit in a binary number, either 1 or 0; the minimum unit of information in a computer system.

Blackberry: hand-held wireless device that allows the exchange of e-mail messages.

block: a group of records or words treated as a logical unit of data.

Bluetooth: a wireless technology that allows computers and other devices to communicate with each other without cables.

byte: a collection of bits, usually eight, to represent a single character.

cache memory: fast RAM memory which remembers instructions and information that the processor has executed or accessed *previously*.

catalogue: a listing of details of the files stored on a disk.

character: any of the signs used in creating text, whether a letter, a numeral or a symbol.

client/server network: a network in which some computers (servers) are dedicated to serving others (clients).

computer: a machine that processes data and supplies results.

contingency ('back-up') copy: a duplicate of data or program files kept in case of loss of this information; should be updated regularly and only used in an emergency.

control unit: the part of the CPU that takes instructions in a given sequence and controls the movement of data inside the computer.

corruption: the accidental alteration of data stored on any storage medium.

CPU (central processing unit): the part of the computer that decodes instructions and controls the hardware used to execute them; it consists of the control unit, arithmetic unit and cache memory.

cursor: a movable mark on the screen that shows where the next character will be displayed.

cursor keys: a group of keys that move the cursor left, right, up or down the display.

data: unprocessed source material.

data integrity: refers to the accuracy of data and its conformity to its expected value, especially after being processed or transmitted.

data security: the means of ensuring that data is kept safe from corruption and that access to it is suitably controlled.

default: an automatic option or value in a program that is used unless an alternative is specified (this term should not be confused with a fault of any kind).

device driver: a computer program that enables the operating system to interact with a hardware device.

direct access: a type of access used when reading information from a disk; the read–write head goes directly to the place on the disk where the data is stored.

directory: another term for 'catalogue'.

disk drive: an auxiliary storage device that enables data and programs to be stored and retrieved.

diskette/'floppy disk': a flexible plastic disk coated with a magnetisable material and enclosed in a plastic envelope or case.

dot-matrix printer: a printer that produces characters made up of patterns of dots.

dumb terminal: a VDU and keyboard link to a network. It has no local processing capability.

DVD: digital versatile disk or digital video disk. These optical disks (similar to CD-ROMs) can store large quantities of video, audio and computer data. Storage capacities for DVD are considerably higher than CD-ROMs.

editing keys: a group of keys that perform specialised functions, such as page up, page down, go to end of file, etc.

electronic mail (e-mail): facility to send messages directly from one computer to another or to a specific 'mail box'.

EPROM: erasable PROM (see below).

ergonomics: the study of the environment of work in order to improve efficiency.

file server: a computer which controls the sharing of resources in a network.

fixed (hard) disk: a rigid, non-removable disk coated in a magnetisable material.

flash drive: a fast, high-capacity storage medium that connects to a USB port on the computer.

formatting: the procedure used to prepare a blank disk before use for a particular computer; it divides the disk into sectors so that information can be stored and retrieved.

freeware: copyrighted software given away for free by its author.

function keys: a group of keys that can be programmed to execute commands or to choose options.

gigabyte: a unit of 1000 million bytes.

GUI: graphical user interface. Software where icons and graphics are used.

hardware: the physical components of a computer system.

hit rate: the percentage of master file records that are updated in an update run.

hotspot: the area covered by an access point and provides public wireless broadband services to laptop users through a WLAN.

information: processed data.

input device: any hardware device that enables data to be transmitted from the source into the computer.

intelligent terminal: a VDU, CPU, keyboard link to a network. It has local processing capability.

inter block gap: a blank space between blocks of information on a magnetic tape.

keyboard: an input device with a systematic arrangement of keys, used for entering instructions and data.

kilobyte (KB): a unit of 1,024 bytes (sometimes rounded to 1,000).

laptop: a small portable microcomputer (also called a notebook).

laser printer: a high-quality printer that uses a method of reproduction similar to a photocopier and prints whole pages at a time.

light pen: an input device used in conjunction with a screen to choose commands or data.

local area network (LAN): a network confined to one local site.

mainframe computer: a very large computer, capable of being used by many people at the same time.

megabyte (MB): a unit of 1,0048,576 bytes (sometimes rounded to 1 million).

menu: a list of the options available at any stage in the execution of a program.

metropolitan area network (MAN): a number of local area networks linked together in the same geographical area.

MICR (magnetic-ink character recognition): an input system that allows magnetic characters (usually found on cheques) to be read into a computer.

microcomputer: a self-contained desktop computer built around a microprocessor and that can be used by only one person at a time; sometimes called a 'personal computer' (PC).

microprocessor: an integrated circuit or 'microchip' that contains the ALU and control unit of a computer.

minicomputer: a medium-sized computer system, usually used by one department or a medium-sized company.

modem (modulator/demodulator): hardware required to convert a digital signal to a telephone signal and vice versa.

monitor: an output device like a television set that shows the stages in the operation of a program and displays the results; sometimes called a 'visual display unit' (VDU).

mouse: an input device housed in a palm-sized case used for pointing to commands or icons on the screen; the movement of the mouse on the desktop corresponds to the movement of the cursor on the display, and one or more buttons on the mouse can be used to select options or execute commands.

network: a group of computers linked together to communicate or share resources.

notebook: a small portable microcomputer (also called a laptop).

NLQ (near-letter-quality): a simulation of high-quality printing on a dot-matrix printer.

OCR (optical character recognition): an input system that reads printed or typewritten characters.

off-line: not under the direct control of the CPU.

OMR (optical mark recognition): an input device that can recognise the presence or absence of a mark.

on-line: under the control of the CPU.

operating system: all the software used to operate and maintain the computer system and utilities.

operational information: information required for day-to-day operations.

optical disk: a high-capacity storage medium from which data is read and to which data is saved using lasers.

output device: any hardware device that enables computer data to be displayed, transmitted or printed.

parallel port: a communications port that allows information to be received or transmitted in groups of bits.

palmtop: a small hand-held computer (also called a personal digital assistant or PDA).

parity bit: a bit appended to a byte. The state of the bit is such as to ensure that the parity is consistently either even or odd.

port/communications port: an external socket allowing peripheral devices to be connected to a computer.

peer-to-peer network: a network in which each computer has equivalent capabilities and responsibilities.

printer: an output device that produces printed text or graphics on paper.

PROM: programmable ROM (see below).

RAM (random-access memory): an area of electronic storage inside the computer used to hold current data and programs; information is constantly read from and written to this memory area.

ROM (read-only memory): an area of electronic storage used to hold instructions essential to the running of the computer; it is not possible to write to this area.

scanner: a device that can read images or text printed on paper and translate the information into a form the computer can use.

sector: a storage area on a disk.

seek time: the amount of time taken by a disk drive to move its head from one track to another.

serial port: a communications port that allows bits of data to be received or transmitted one after the other.

shareware: copyrighted software distributed on the basis of an honour system and is generally free for a certain period of time, after which a small fee must be paid to use it.

software: another name for programs.

software licence: allows an individual or group to use a piece of software.

strategic information: information required for long-term planning.

supercomputer: the largest and most powerful type of computer, capable of being used by many people at the same time.

tactical information: information required to plan for the medium term.

track: one of the concentric rings of data on a magnetic disk.

utility program: part of operating software which allows the user to carry out standard procedures such as formatting, copying files, etc.

validation: a procedure carried out by a computer to check if the data is complete and reasonable.

VDE (voice data entry): an input system that responds to the human voice.

VDU (visual display unit): another name for a monitor.

verification: a method of checking that the original data has been correctly entered. It often involves re-keying data.

viewdata: interactive information service via telephone connection.

wide area network (WAN): a network which spans over a wide area and is connected using telephone lines and other communication links.

WLAN: a wireless local area network.

WYSIWYG (what you see is what you get): this means that the image on the screen is very close to how it will appear when printed.

Chapter 2
Introduction to Databases

Introduction

When is the next available flight to New York? What is the current exchange rate for the Canadian dollar? Are there any rooms available at a certain hotel?

To answer these questions we may have to consult a travel agent, a bank clerk and the hotel receptionist, respectively. It is unlikely, however, that they will know these answers immediately. They may have to consult their respective databases.

What is a database?

A database is an organised collection of related information. It usually consists of one or more files that may be related to one another.

What is a file?

A file is a collection of similar records.

An employment agency, Bestmatch Recruitment, holds a personnel file on people looking for suitable employment. For simplicity, we will assume that there are only six people on the agency's file at present.

The information on each of the people seeking employment is arranged under these headings:

```
NAME         ADDRESS          PHONE_NO   SEX   JOB           YEARS

Murphy P     6 Greenore Pk    4449234    M     Secretary     2

Hopkirk L    16 Kilkenny Rd   8349042    F     Secretary     3

Maher K      56 Main St       8899593    M     Chef          0

Greene A     55 Wicklow Rd    5231772    F     Accountant    10

Burns J      57 Hazel Rd      7783924    M     Chef          2

Owens M      56 Ashe St       4931448    F     Pharmacist    4
```

- NAME: The person's name (surname and initial)
- ADDRESS: The person's home address
- PHONE_NO: The person's home telephone number
- SEX: The person's sex
- JOB: The job sought
- YEARS: The number of years' experience the person has of this work.

(Note that there is an underline character rather than a space in 'PHONE_NO': this is because some database programs need the parts of a heading to be joined together so that the computer can treat them as one word, and this character is the one usually used.)

What is a record?

A record is a complete unit of related data items organised in named fields. In our example, the information held on each person seeking a job is stored in a separate record. The third record in our file holds information on Kevin Maher.

What is a field?

A field is a space for a specified item of information in a record. In our example, 7783924 (a specific item of information) is held in the PHONE_NO field of the fifth record of the file. The content of a field is often referred to as a data item.

Why is information now stored in computer databases?

Information stored in a computer database can be:

(a) found extremely quickly, e.g. the number of three-bedroom houses in a certain area can be extracted from an estate agent's file;

(b) sorted and re-sorted quickly and efficiently, e.g. a personnel file can be sorted in chronological order of the date that each employee joined a company;

(c) kept up-to-date very easily, e.g. adding new member and erasing lapsed member details on a golf club membership file;

(d) used by other applications, e.g. the names and addresses of customers in a customer file can be extracted and used in producing mailshots by a word processor.

In summary, a database may consist of one or more files. Each file consists of a number of records, and each record comprises a number of fields.

Holding a database on computer

In order to hold a database on computer, we need a database program or **database management system (DBMS)**. On a microcomputer, this is a program that allows us to store information in a database, as well as to edit, organise or retrieve that information.

The database program is like our own private librarian, who looks after our database and carries out any editing, organising or retrieval requests from us.

We will now examine how to set up a database on a computer and how we can carry out various activities on the file, under the following headings:

1. Defining the data entry form
2. Entering data into the file
3. Editing the file
4. Searching the file

5. Displaying selected fields
6. Sorting the file
7. Indexing the file
8. Changing the record structure
9. Performing mathematical operations
10. Creating reports.

1. Defining the data entry form

Before we enter a new file into our computer database, we must define the data entry form.

A data entry form is a screen layout resembling a form that displays only one data record at a time, which makes it easier to enter and edit data.

We must decide the following:

(a) the heading of each field within the record structure, e.g. NAME, ADDRESS;

(b) the maximum width of each field. The longest address is 16 KILKENNY RD, so we must define a field width of 14 for the ADDRESS field to accommodate this address;

(c) the data type: **alphabetic** (letters only), **numeric** (numbers only) or **alphanumeric** (a combination of letters and numbers), **date** (dd/mm/yy), currency, logical (y/n). In our example the NAME field is alphabetic, the YEARS field is numeric and the ADDRESS field is alphanumeric.

We would now give our database program the following information about our personnel file:

FIELD	FIELD NAME	FIELD WIDTH	DATA TYPE
1	NAME	9	Alphabetic
2	ADDRESS	15	Alphanumeric
3	PHONE_NO	7	Numeric
4	SEX	1	Alphabetic
5	JOB	10	Alphabetic
6	YEARS	2	Numeric

This is the record structure for the file. The corresponding data entry screen is displayed below:

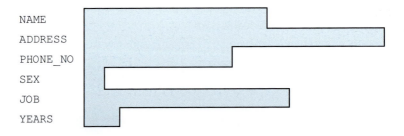

```
NAME
ADDRESS
PHONE_NO
SEX
JOB
YEARS
```

2. Entering data into the file

Once we have defined our data entry form, we must now enter data into the file. It is usually entered without punctuation.

It is important that data be entered consistently: in the YEARS field you must not enter '2' in one record and 'two' in the next. This can cause problems when you wish to search or sort the file later. You must take care at this stage, as incorrect data can be entered accidentally.

When you have entered all the data, the file can be displayed on the screen, or printed, and should appear as follows:

NAME	ADDRESS	PHONE_NO	SEX	JOB	YEARS
MURPHY P	6 GREENORE PK	4449234	M	SECRETARY	2
HOPKIRK L	16 KILKENNY RD	8349042	F	SECRETARY	3
MAHER K	56 MAIN ST	8899593	M	CHEF	0
GREENE A	55 WICKLOW RD	5231772	F	ACCOUNTANT	10
BURNS J	57 HAZEL RD	7783924	M	CHEF	2
OWENS M	56 ASHE ST	4931448	F	PHARMACIST	4

3. Editing the file

Once we have set up our file on computer, we can add new records or delete unwanted records. We can also change the contents of individual records in the file.

◼ Adding and deleting records

Let us assume that we have just received the following information about a person who is looking for a job:

Name	Address	Phone	Sex	Job	Years
McCann A	32 Shannon Park	8568264	M	Mechanic	7

We can select the command or option in our database program to add a new record to the file. A data entry form appears on the screen, and we simply enter the appropriate details. Let us also say that Kevin Maher finds a suitable job and no longer requires the agency's services. We can delete his record from the file by using the command or option to delete a record in our database program.

The file will now appear as follows:

NAME	ADDRESS	PHONE_NO	SEX	JOB	YEARS
MURPHY P	6 GREENORE PK	4449234	M	SECRETARY	2
HOPKIRK L	16 KILKENNY RD	8349042	F	SECRETARY	3
GREENE A	55 WICKLOW RD	5231772	F	ACCOUNTANT	10
BURNS J	57 HAZEL RD	7783924	M	CHEF	2
OWENS M	56 ASHE ST	4931448	F	PHARMACIST	4
MCCANN A	32 SHANNON PK	8568264	M	MECHANIC	7

◤ Changing the contents of records

Using the appropriate command or option, we can display a record and then delete or insert various items of information.

Let us say that Aisling Greene has moved to 68 Shannon Park, and her new telephone number is 8568234. Also, a mistake was made in the name field of the second record: the name should be Hopkins, not Hopkirk.

When we have made these changes, the file will appear as follows:

NAME	ADDRESS	PHONE_NO	SEX	JOB	YEARS
MURPHY P	6 GREENORE PK	4449234	M	SECRETARY	2
HOPKINS L	16 KILKENNY RD	8349042	F	SECRETARY	3
GREENE A	68 SHANNON PK	8568234	F	ACCOUNTANT	10
BURNS J	57 HAZEL RD	7783924	M	CHEF	2
OWENS M	56 ASHE ST	4931448	F	PHARMACIST	4
MCCANN A	32 SHANNON PK	8568264	M	MECHANIC	7

4. Searching the file

One of the really useful features of having files stored on a computer database is the ease and speed with which we can search for information. As records are numbered according to their position in a file, we can cause a particular record to be displayed. We can also display or print all those records that meet a certain condition or set of conditions.

◤ Searching for records by their position in the file

We can select the appropriate command or option to display record 3 in the personnel file:

RECORD NO.	NAME	ADDRESS	PHONE_NO	SEX	JOB	YEARS
3	GREENE A	68 SHANNON PK	8568234	F	ACCOUNTANT	10

◣ Searching for records using one condition

Let us say that Bestmatch Recruitment get a telephone call from a company's personnel officer looking for a secretary. We can search the file for the records containing details of secretaries. We follow these steps:

(a) select the option or command for searching the file

(b) choose the correct field for our search: the JOB field

(c) enter the job we are searching for: SECRETARY

(d) some programs may then require the user to give an 'execute' command to start the search.

The results of this search may appear as follows:

NAME	ADDRESS	PHONE_NO	SEX	JOB	YEARS
MURPHY P	6 GREENORE PK	4449234	M	SECRETARY	2
HOPKINS L	16 KILKENNY RD	8349042	F	SECRETARY	3

◣ Searching for records using more than one condition

We can obtain details of those people on our file who are female and who have more than three years' experience in their chosen career by carrying out the following steps:

(a) select the option or command for searching the file

(b) choose the field for our first search condition: the SEX field

(c) enter the sex for which we are searching: FEMALE

(d) choose the field for our second search condition: the YEARS field

(e) select the greater-than operand (>) and enter 3

(f) some programs may then require the user to give an 'execute' command to start the search.

Once the request has been carried out, the results may appear as follows:

NAME	ADDRESS	PHONE_NO	SEX	JOB	YEARS
GREENE A	68 SHANNON PK	8568234	F	ACCOUNTANT	10
OWENS M	56 ASHE ST	4931448	F	PHARMACIST	4

◣ Searching for records using variable symbols

Sometimes we may have to search a file without knowing the precise conditions under which we are performing the search. This can be done by using **variable symbols** (sometimes called 'wild cards'). These are characters (for example ? or *) that the program interprets as 'any character'.

Let us say that someone whose details are on the personnel file has just phoned the agency. The receptionist takes the caller's telephone number and assures her that the manager will return the call within the hour. The manager, however, loses the telephone number, but remembers the first three digits: 834. The database program will allow him to search the file for the details of any person whose telephone number starts with 834.

The steps taken to carry out this type of search on most database programs are as follows:

(a) select the option or command for searching the file

(b) choose the correct field for the search: the PHONE_NO field

(c) enter the portion of the data entry that we know: 834

(d) fill the remainder of the field with the variable symbol: ****

(e) some programs may then require the user to give an 'execute' command to start the search.

The result of this search on the personnel file will be displayed as follows:

```
HOPKINS L    16 KILKENNY RD    8349042    F  SECRETARY         3
```

5. Displaying selected fields

Another feature of a database program is its ability to display only a certain number of fields. This is useful when our records contain a large number of fields.

We may wish to display only the NAME, JOB and YEARS fields of all the records in the file. These are the steps we take:

(a) select the option or command that enables us to select the fields that we want displayed

(b) select the fields in the order in which we would like them displayed

(c) then select the command or option to execute the 'display selected fields' facility.

The result should appear as follows:

NAME	JOB	YEARS
MURPHY P	SECRETARY	2
HOPKINS L	SECRETARY	3
GREENE A	ACCOUNTANT	10
BURNS J	CHEF	2
OWENS M	PHARMACIST	4
MCCANN A	MECHANIC	7

It is possible to combine the 'display selected fields' and search facilities.

We may wish to display the NAME, ADDRESS and JOB fields of all those records belonging to the males on file. In order to carry this out we must:

(a) select the fields to be displayed: NAME, ADDRESS and JOB

(b) select the option or command for searching the file

(c) choose the field for the search condition: the SEX field

(d) enter the sex for which we are searching: MALE

(e) some programs may then require the user to give an 'execute' command to start the search.
The result should appear as follows:

NAME	ADDRESS	JOB
MURPHY P	6 GREENORE PK	SECRETARY
BURNS J	57 HAZEL RD	CHEF
MCCANN A	32 SHANNON PK	MECHANIC

6. Sorting the file

Another useful feature of our computer database is the ease with which we can sort the records. In this section we examine the following methods:

- alphabetical sorting
- numeric sorting
- reverse sorting
- multi-level sorting
- group sorting.

Most database programs would normally allow us to sort a file in the following way:

(a) select the option or command for sorting

(b) select the key field (this is a field chosen by the user on which sorting will be carried out)

(c) use the option or command to choose whether we wish to sort the records in ascending order (with text this is the same as alphabetical order) or descending order. The default setting in most database programs is in ascending order.

◪Alphabetical sorting

Let us assume that we wish to sort the records by name, in alphabetical order. The NAME field will thus be the key field. The results of this sort may be displayed as:

NAME	ADDRESS	PHONE_NO	SEX	JOB	YEARS
BURNS J	57 HAZEL RD	7783924	M	CHEF	2
GREENE A	68 SHANNON PK	8568234	F	ACCOUNTANT	10
HOPKINS L	16 KILKENNY RD	8349042	F	SECRETARY	3
MCCANN A	32 SHANNON PK	8568264	M	MECHANIC	7
MURPHY P	6 GREENORE PK	4449234	M	SECRETARY	2
OWENS M	56 ASHE ST	4931448	F	PHARMACIST	4

Numeric sorting

We can sort the file by number of years' job experience of each person. The YEARS field will be chosen as the key field. The sorted file will then appear as follows:

NAME	ADDRESS	PHONE_NO	SEX	JOB	YEARS
MURPHY P	6 GREENORE PK	4449234	M	SECRETARY	2
BURNS J	57 HAZEL RD	7783924	M	CHEF	2
HOPKINS L	16 KILKENNY RD	8349042	F	SECRETARY	3
OWENS M	56 ASHE ST	4931448	F	PHARMACIST	4
MCCANN A	32 SHANNON PK	8568264	M	MECHANIC	7
GREENE A	68 SHANNON PK	8568234	F	ACCOUNTANT	10

Reverse sorting

The file, as it appears above, is sorted in ascending order of number of years' job experience of each person. We can also sort the file in descending order, again using the YEARS field as the key field. The sorted file will now appear as:

NAME	ADDRESS	PHONE_NO	SEX	JOB	YEARS
GREENE A	68 SHANNON PK	8568234	F	ACCOUNTANT	10
MCCANN A	32 SHANNON PK	8568264	M	MECHANIC	7
OWENS M	56 ASHE ST	4931448	F	PHARMACIST	4
HOPKINS L	16 KILKENNY RD	8349042	F	SECRETARY	3
MURPHY P	6 GREENORE PK	4449234	M	SECRETARY	2
BURNS J	57 HAZEL RD	7783924	M	CHEF	2

Multi-level sorting

In our examples we have been sorting on one field: either the NAME field or the YEARS field. It is possible, however, to sort on a number of fields at the same time.

If we are sorting on two fields, the first field we select is the **primary sort field** and the second is the **secondary sort field**. We can now sort our file using the SEX field as the primary key field and the NAME field as the secondary key field. The result would be as follows:

NAME	ADDRESS	PHONE_NO	SEX	JOB	YEARS
GREENE A	68 SHANNON PK	8568234	F	ACCOUNTANT	10
HOPKINS L	16 KILKENNY RD	8349042	F	SECRETARY	3
OWENS M	56 ASHE ST	4931448	F	PHARMACIST	4
BURNS J	57 HAZEL RD	7783924	M	CHEF	2
MCCANN A	32 SHANNON PK	8568264	M	MECHANIC	7
MURPHY P	6 GREENORE PK	4449234	M	SECRETARY	2

As F comes before M in the alphabet, all the female entries are listed first, in alphabetical order, then the male entries in alphabetical order.

Group sorting

We can select a particular group of records from the file and display this group sorted on one or more fields. We may wish to have all records of those people who have more than two years' experience sorted alphabetically by name, and then displayed.

Some database programs may allow us to sort the file using the NAME field as the key field and then search the sorted file for all those people with more than two years' experience. Other programs may allow us to extract the records of those people with more than two years' experience and then sort these records into alphabetical order. The result in either case should appear as follows:

NAME	ADDRESS	PHONE_NO	SEX	JOB	YEARS
GREENE A	68 SHANNON PK	8568234	F	ACCOUNTANT	10
HOPKINS L	16 KILKENNY RD	8349042	F	SECRETARY	3
MCCANN A	32 SHANNON PK	8568264	M	MECHANIC	7
OWENS M	56 ASHE ST	4931448	F	PHARMACIST	4

7. Indexing the file

When we sort a database file, the records are physically sorted by the computer into the order required. We have seen, in an earlier example, that the records are numbered according to their position in the file.

NAME	ADDRESS	PHONE_NO	SEX	JOB	YEARS
BURNS J	57 HAZEL RD	7783924	M	CHEF	2
GREENE A	68 SHANNON PK	8568234	F	ACCOUNTANT	10
HOPKINS L	16 KILKENNY RD	8349042	F	SECRETARY	3
MCCANN A	32 SHANNON PK	8568264	M	MECHANIC	7
MURPHY P	6 GREENORE PK	4449234	M	SECRETARY	2
OWENS M	56 ASHE ST	4931448	F	PHARMACIST	4

We can get a print-out of the file sorted on the NAME field.

Many computer database programs offer an alternative to sorting, namely **indexing**. We can get a computer print-out of our unsorted file:

RECORD NO	NAME	ADDRESS	PHONE_NO	SEX	JOB	YEARS
1	MURPHY P	6 GREENORE PK	4449234	M	SECRETARY	2
2	HOPKINS L	16 KILKENNY RD	8349042	F	SECRETARY	3
3	GREENE A	68 SHANNON PK	8568234	F	ACCOUNTANT	10
4	BURNS J	57 HAZEL RD	7783924	M	CHEF	2
5	OWENS M	56 ASHE ST	4931448	F	PHARMACIST	4
6	MCCANN A	32 SHANNON PK	8568264	M	MECHANIC	7

If we index our file using the NAME field, the records themselves are not ordered. Instead, the numbers of the records are ordered in a small file called an 'index file'. As BURNS would head the list in alphabetical order, the first number in the index file would be 4, because this person's record is the fourth record in the file. The index file in this case would contain the following list of numbers: 4, 3, 2, 1, 6, 5.

When we activate this index file and then request a print-out, we would obtain the following:

RECORD NO	NAME	ADDRESS	PHONE_NO	SEX	JOB	YEARS
4	BURNS J	57 HAZEL RD	7783924	M	CHEF	2
3	GREENE A	68 SHANNON PK	8568234	F	ACCOUNTANT	10
2	HOPKINS L	16 KILKENNY RD	8349042	F	SECRETARY	3
6	MCCANN A	32 SHANNON PK	8568264	M	MECHANIC	7
1	MURPHY P	6 GREENORE PK	4449234	M	SECRETARY	2
5	OWENS M	56 ASHE ST	4931448	F	PHARMACIST	4

The records are printed according to the order of the numbers in the index file. Frequent database users rarely use sorting and prefer indexing, as index files can be activated very quickly. Sorting a large file can take some time.

Another advantage of using indexing rather than the sorting facility is that some database programs, when sorting a file, set up a completely new file and copy the records across to this new file in sorted order. We would then have two files containing exactly the same information stored on our disk – one sorted and one unsorted. In this case indexing is obviously preferable to sorting, as index files will take up a much smaller amount of disk space than sort files. The indexing facility is not available on all database programs.

8. Changing the record structure

Sometimes, after we have defined the record structure of a file and entered information into it, we may wish to change the record structure. This could be for one or more of the following purposes:

- adding a new field
- deleting an existing field
- changing the order of fields
- widening fields
- changing field names.

   The commands and techniques to change the record structure vary, depending on the database program you are using. As you proceed through this section you should check the appropriate command or technique to undertake a particular change to the record structure.

◪Changing the field width

The field width of the NAME field in our example was set at 9 in order to accommodate the longest name, which was HOPKINS L. The field is not wide enough, however, to allow us to include the first names. If we include the first name instead of the initial, Aisling Greene has the longest name: we need a field width of 14 to accommodate this name.

   When we have redefined the field width of the NAME field to 14 and edited the file to include the first names, it will appear as follows:

NAME	ADDRESS	PHONE_NO	SEX	JOB	YEARS
BURNS JOHN	57 HAZEL RD	7783924	M	CHEF	2
GREENE AISLING	68 SHANNON PK	8568234	F	ACCOUNTANT	10
HOPKINS LIZ	16 KILKENNY RD	8349042	F	SECRETARY	3
MCCANN AIDAN	32 SHANNON PK	8568264	M	MECHANIC	7
MURPHY DANIEL	6 GREENORE PK	4449234	M	SECRETARY	2
OWENS MARY	56 ASHE ST	4931448	F	PHARMACIST	4

◪Deleting a field from the record structure

As we have the telephone number of each person on file, there is little need for a field that includes the address. We will use the commands specific to our database program to delete this field from the record structure. The file would then appear as follows:

NAME	PHONE_NO	SEX	JOB	YEARS
BURNS JOHN	7783924	M	CHEF	2
GREENE AISLING	8568234	F	ACCOUNTANT	10
HOPKINS LIZ	8349042	F	SECRETARY	3
MCCANN AIDAN	8568264	M	MECHANIC	7
MURPHY DANIEL	4449234	M	SECRETARY	2
OWENS MARY	4931448	F	PHARMACIST	4

◤ Adding a new field to the record structure

As companies often phone the agency from various towns looking for staff in their own area, we might include a TOWN field for the hometown of each person on file. When we have set up this new field and included the appropriate details, our file would appear as follows:

NAME	TOWN	PHONE_NO	SEX	JOB	YEARS
BURNS JOHN	TRIM	7783924	M	CHEF	2
GREENE AISLING	NAVAN	8568234	F	ACCOUNTANT	10
HOPKINS LIZ	DROICHEAD NUA	8349042	F	SECRETARY	3
MCCANN AIDAN	MONAGHAN	8568264	M	MECHANIC	7
MURPHY DANIEL	CAVAN	4449234	M	SECRETARY	2
OWENS MARY	TRALEE	4931448	F	PHARMACIST	4

◤ Changing a field name

We can change the name of the field that includes each person's occupation from JOB to CAREER.

◤ Changing the order of fields

We may wish to move the YEARS field so that it appears second in the record structure. When we have made these final two changes to our record structure, our personnel file will now appear as follows:

NAME	YEARS	TOWN	PHONE_NO	SEX	CAREER
BURNS JOHN	2	TRIM	7783924	M	CHEF
GREENE AISLING	10	NAVAN	8568234	F	ACCOUNTANT
HOPKINS LIZ	3	DROICHEAD NUA	8349042	F	SECRETARY
MCCANN AIDAN	7	MONAGHAN	8568264	M	MECHANIC
MURPHY DANIEL	2	CAVAN	4449234	M	SECRETARY
OWENS MARY	4	TRALEE	4931448	F	PHARMACIST

◪Careful planning

The facilities for changing a record's structure are very useful but should be used sparingly. A prudent database user will always plan the record structure of a new file on paper before defining it on computer. A little early planning with field names and field widths will save a lot of alterations to the record structure later.

9. Performing mathematical operations

Two useful facilities offered by most database programs are:

(a) the ability to perform one of the four basic mathematical operations (add, subtract, multiply or divide) on the data items of two or more numeric fields and to place the result in another field

(b) the summation function.

◪Performing mathematical operations on data items

Set up the following file on your computer. It contains details of goods that are for sale at Jim's Electrical Superstore. The file consists of five records, and each record has four fields:

- ITEM: the name of the electrical item
- COST: its cost price
- QUANTITY: the number in stock
- RETAIL: its retail price.

The file's contents are as follows:

ITEM	COST	QUANTITY	RETAIL
WASHING MACHINE	360.00	7	520.00
REFRIGERATOR	390.00	3	560.00
DVD RECORDER	240.00	8	340.00
TELEVISION	450.00	4	650.00
VACUUM CLEANER	180.00	2	260.00

We can quite easily change the record structure to include two new fields:

- PROFIT: The data item in this field will be the profit obtained on the sale of one item, and can be obtained by the simple formula 'retail minus cost', which subtracts the contents of the COST field from the contents of the RETAIL field for each of the five records.
- VALUATION:The data item in this field will be the total value of all items of a particular type, for example the total value of all television sets. The valuation is obtained by a formula, 'cost multiplied by quantity', which multiplies the contents of the COST field by the contents of the QUANTITY field for each of the five records.

When you have set up the file containing the two fields, it should look like this:

ITEM	COST	QUANTITY	RETAIL	PROFIT	VALUATION
WASHING MACHINE	360.00	7	520.00	160.00	2520.00
REFRIGERATOR	390.00	3	560.00	170.00	1170.00
DVD RECORDER	240.00	8	340.00	100.00	1920.00
TELEVISION	450.00	4	650.00	200.00	1800.00
VACUUM CLEANER	180.00	2	260.00	80.00	360.00

◢ The summation function

Most database programs have a summation function, which allows us to sum fields. Let us say that someone wishes to buy all five of the items listed in the file. We can use the summation function to obtain the total value of the data items in the RETAIL fields of the five records. We get:

5 records summed on the RETAIL field
Total = €2,330.00

As we will see in the next section, the summation of fields can be carried out automatically when we generate reports.

10. Creating reports

A report is any meaningful information retrieved from a database and displayed or printed. Strictly speaking, all the output from the two files outlined in this chapter are reports. Most database programs, however, are equipped with a **report generator**. This is a facility that allows us to design the presentation of the output from a database file. The report generator can also total columns of numeric data automatically.

The following is a print-out of a report generated on the electrical shop file:

JIM'S ELECTRICAL SUPERSTORE VALUATION REPORT					
ITEM	COST	QUANTITY	RETAIL	PROFIT	VALUATION
WASHING MACHINE	360.00	7	520.00	160.00	2520.00
REFRIGERATOR	390.00	3	560.00	170.00	1170.00
DVD RECORDER	240.00	8	340.00	100.00	1920.00
TELEVISION	450.00	4	650.00	200.00	1800.00
VACUUM CLEANER	180.00	2	260.00	80.00	360.00
TOTAL		24			7770.00

▦ Summary

In this chapter we have examined the main facilities of a database program. Most of these facilities should be available on your program.

We have dealt with the simplest type of database, the **flat-file** database. This is one where all the files are treated individually by the program and are not linked in any way.

▦ Glossary of database terms

batch processing: the technique of updating a file at one time with all the transactions that have occurred in a given period.

database: a collection of related information about a subject, organised in a way that provides the means for retrieving and sorting the information, drawing conclusions and making decisions.

database management system (DBMS): a computer program used for creating databases and that provides the tools for inserting, retrieving, modifying and deleting information and for producing relevant reports from the database.

data entry form: a form layout on the screen that facilitates the entering of information into a database file. Only one record is displayed at a time, and the fields within each record are usually listed vertically.

field: a space for a specified piece of information in a record.

file: a collection of similar records.

fixed-length field: a field that is capable of holding a predetermined maximum number of characters.

fixed-length record: a record that is capable of holding a predetermined number of fixed-length fields.

flat-file database: a database in which all the files are treated individually by the program and are not linked in any way.

flat-file database program: a program that stores, organises and retrieves information from one file at a time.

index: a small file containing 'pointers' or information about the physical location of records in a database file. When searching or sorting, the database program uses the index rather than the full database.

microfiche: a form of microfilm in which documents are photographically reduced and copied onto small sheets of film.

microfilm: an information storage system in which documents are photographically reduced and copied onto 16 mm film strip.

multi-level sort: a sort that uses two fields, a primary sort field and a secondary sort field, to determine the order in which records are arranged.

multi-user system: a system that allows more than one person to have access to the database program and files at the same time.

programmable database: a database system that has its own programming language, allowing the user to structure files and reports according to specific needs.

random access: a method that allows the system to retrieve information by going directly to a specific part of a disk rather than having to go through all the preceding tracks and sectors.

real-time processing: the technique of updating a file when the operator is 'on-line' to the CPU and the updating is carried out immediately by the computer.

relational database: a database system that can link two or more files together through at least one common field. Such a program allows the user to update two or more linked files simultaneously in the same operation.

sequential file: a file in which the records are arranged in a particular order, usually ascending or descending order of key field.

serial file: a method in which the records in a file are not physically arranged in any particular order on a disk or tape.

sort: an operation that arranges data in a particular order.

variable-length field: a field whose length varies according to the contents of the field at a particular time.

variable-length record: a record in which the number of fields may vary from that of other records in the same file. Variable-length records usually consist of variable-length fields.

Chapter 3
Practical Database Assignments

These assignments are graded, and we advise that you work through them in the order in which they are given. **Note: You may enter the data given for each assignment into a new database table or file or you can download the database file containing the tables for each assignment (Microsoft Access format) from the Gill & Macmillan website at www.gillmacmillan.ie.**

▦ Guidelines for students

Unless the actual assignment specifies otherwise, the following guidelines apply.

1. The data entry screen

A properly formatted data entry screen must be created for each assignment.

- All fields must have suitable field names.
- There should be two fields per line on the data input screen. (In the case of an odd number of fields, the last field will obviously stand alone.)
- The input screen should have a centred title at the top.
- There is no need for borders or other effects.

2. Entering data

Care must be taken when entering data into a file and the following rules apply:

- Among the data types needed for fields in the assignments are text, number, currency, logical (yes/no) and date.
- Commas in numbers must not be entered, e.g. enter 10300 instead of 10,300.
- Currency amounts must be entered as values in numeric fields, e.g. enter 2.85 instead of €2.85.
- Where field names consist of two separate words, these should be joined by an underscore, e.g. Age Profile should appear as Age_Profile.

3. Creating reports

Assignment 12 onwards specifies the production of report formats.

- The field names used on data entry screens will suffice as column headings in reports.
- Unless specifically asked, do not perform any mathematical calculations on any numeric fields (e.g. averaging or totalling).

4. Using Microsoft Access

If you are using Microsoft Access, make a copy of the table and carry out the required edits on this copy.

◪ Functions and commands required

As you progress through these assignments you will need to check the commands, functions, icons and pull-down menus specific to your database program. You will also be practising commands and techniques learned in earlier assignments. (Note: If you do not have access to a printer, you can display the result of the task instead.)

The new work involved in each assignment is as follows:

ASSIGNMENT 1
- Creating a file
- Designing the data entry form
- Entering data
- Editing the contents of individual records
- Adding a new record
- Deleting an existing record
- Saving the file

ASSIGNMENT 2
- Consolidation assignment

ASSIGNMENT 3
- Consolidation assignment

ASSIGNMENT 4
- Searching on one condition

ASSIGNMENT 5
- Searching on two conditions

ASSIGNMENT 6
- Searching on three conditions
- Displaying selected fields for all records

ASSIGNMENT 7
- Combining the 'displaying selected fields' facility with a one-condition search

ASSIGNMENT 8
- Combining the 'displaying selected fields' facility with a two-condition search
- Sorting a file in alphabetical order on one field

ASSIGNMENT 9
- Sorting a file in ascending numerical order on one field
- Using the global replace facility

ASSIGNMENT 10
- Searching on four fields
- Sorting a file in descending numerical order on one field
- Organising a file on one field using the indexing facility (if possible)

ASSIGNMENT 11
- Deleting a field
- Inserting a new field
- Creating and saving a subset of a file

ASSIGNMENT 12
- Producing a report format

ASSIGNMENT 13
- Sorting a file chronologically
- Developing mailing labels

ASSIGNMENT 14
- Sorting on primary and secondary fields

ASSIGNMENT 15
- Modifying a report
- Producing a grouped report format

ASSIGNMENT 16
- Consolidation assignment

ASSIGNMENT 17
- Consolidation assignment

ASSIGNMENT 18
- Consolidation assignment

ASSIGNMENT 19
• FETAC Database Methods Sample Paper 1

ASSIGNMENT 20
• FETAC Database Methods Sample Paper 2

Assignment 1

You are required to set up a file containing information on eight students. The information on each student falls under the following six headings: name, age, sex, telephone number, area and class.

In database language you must set up a file of eight records, each record consisting of six fields. When defining the record structure, the field name and width for each field are as follows:

FIELD	FIELD NAME	WIDTH
1	Name	10
2	Age	2
3	Sex	1
4	Phone	7
5	Area	11
6	Class	3

Once you have set up your record structure **and** designed a suitable data entry screen with the heading 'Student Record', you should enter the following information into the file:

NAME	AGE	SEX	PHONE	AREA	CLASS
Maher R	17	M	5612431	Ballyfermot	LW1
Andrews K	16	F	2977116	Dundrum	AC2
Stephens G	18	F	8346002	Beaumont	LW1
O' Brien P	17	F	4977701	Rathgar	ST1
Byrne S	18	M	7679061	Sutton	CM1
Williams M	19	M	4511782	Kimmage	AC2
Conway C	16	F	8360890	Glasnevin	ST1
Doyle E	18	M	4566102	Crumlin	CM1

◣Carry out the following tasks:

Save:

   1. all the details to a file called STUDENT1.

Make the following alterations to the relevant records:

   2. Andrews is male and lives in Rathmines.

   3. Conway is 17 years old.

   4. E Doyle is a student in ST1 and not CM1.

Delete:

   5. P O'Brien's record from the file.

Add:

   6. the following information on a new student who has just joined the school: D Ryan, 16, male, 8453222, Cabra, LW1.

Save:

   7. this edited version of the file as STUDENT2.

Assignment 2

The following is a list of information on eight films that are available for rent from Leisure Video Ltd:

TITLE	CATEGORY	LEAD	LENGTH	CERT	PRICE
Miami Vice	Adventure	Colin Farrell	134	15	€5.25
Shrek	Animation	Shrek	90	12	€3.50
Million Dollar Baby	Drama	Morgan Freeman	131	15	€4.00
The Godfather	Drama	Marlon Brando	175	18	€2.50
Lord of the Rings	Fantasy	Elijah Wood	138	12	€5.25
Saving Private Ryan	War	Tom Hanks	170	15	€3.50
Legally Blonde	Comedy	Reese Witherspoon	96	12	€5.25
King Kong	Adventure	Naomi Watts	187	12	€4.00

The information on each film includes its title, category, leading actor or actress, running time, suitability certificate and rental cost. You are required to transfer this information to a database file on your computer. The record structure for the file is as follows.

FIELD	FIELD NAME	WIDTH
1	Title	19
2	Category	9
3	Lead	17
4	Length	3
5	Cert	2
6	Price	5

⬛ Carry out the following tasks:

Save:

1. the file as FILM1.

Make the following alterations to the relevant records:

2. *Miami Vice* is best described as an action film.
3. Hilary Swank played the leading role in *Million Dollar Baby*.
4. the running time for *Lord of the Rings* is 178 minutes.
5. the cost of renting *Legally Blonde* is only €3.50.
6. Leisure Video Ltd have withdrawn *The Godfather*. Erase the record on this film from the file.

Add:

7. The following information on two more films to the file:

TITLE	CATEGORY	LEAD	LENGTH	CERT	PRICE
Walk the Line	Drama	Joaquin Phoenix	136	12	€5.25
Love Story	Romance	Ali MacGraw	99	12	€2.50

Save:

8. this edited version of the file as FILM2.

Assignment 3

Getaway Travel Ltd, specialists in sun holidays, have just given you the following details on available bookings:

COUNTRY	RESORT	PRICE	DAY	TIME	FLIGHT	PLACES
Turkey	Kusadasi	645	Thursday	08:00	TK63	19
Portugal	Faro	810	Sunday	15:00	PO71	6
Spain	Marbella	590	Friday	00:30	SP16	0
Greece	Kos	775	Tuesday	06:30	GR95	3
Malta	Valetta	725	Friday	11:00	MA52	8
Spain	Salou	635	Sunday	18:00	SP23	12
Cyprus	Limassol	680	Saturday	09:30	CY48	2
Morocco	Agadir	615	Sunday	14:30	MO91	15

You are required to transfer this information to a database file on your computer.

⬛ Carry out the following tasks:

Save:

1. the file to disk as HOLIDAY1.

Make the following alterations to the relevant records:

2. the departure time for the Portuguese holiday should be 19:00.

3. the price of the holiday in Malta should only be €585.

4. there are only 8 places left on the Spanish holiday in Salou.

5. the holiday in Cyprus should be in Paphos and not Limassol.

6. the departure day for the Moroccan holiday should be Friday.

7. as the holiday in Marbella, Spain is fully booked, delete this record from the file.

8. information on two other holidays must be added to the file. The details are as follows:

COUNTRY	RESORT	PRICE	DAY	TIME	FLIGHT	PLACES
Greece	Corfu	660	Thursday	21:00	GR97	23
Portugal	Penina	785	Saturday	17:30	PO73	18

Save:

9. this edited version of the file to disk as HOLIDAY2.

Assignment 4

Express Couriers Ltd, based in Dublin, deliver items nationwide. Articles are classified as high (H), medium (M) or low (L) priority and are billed accordingly. Sandra Cosgrave, the managing director of the company, wishes to hold delivery details on a computer database file. You are requested to create the file and enter the following details:

ITEM	SENDER	LOCATION	RECIPIENT	COST	PRIORITY
Garden shed	Davy's DIY	Galway	P O'Dea	€42.00	M
Books	Reader's Heaven	Birr	T Dooley	€16.00	L
Wedding dress	Zoe's Boutique	Sligo	A Walsh	€50.00	H
Computer	Bits & Bytes Ltd	Galway	S O'Sullivan	€55.00	H
Dog kennel	Pet Mansions Ltd	Cork	G Dillon	€28.00	L
Satellite dish	DS Electrical Ltd	Dundalk	D McDonnell	€22.00	L
Contact lenses	Vision Care Ltd	Tralee	L Sheehy	€30.00	H
Cello	Endless Chords	Limerick	R Patterson	€36.00	M
Sunbed	Body Tones	Cork	O Hayes	€25.00	L
Safe	MD Security Ltd	Cavan	M O'Reilly	€45.00	H

Carry out the following tasks:

Save:

1. the file as COURIER1.

Make the following alterations to the relevant records:

2. Padraig O'Dea ordered a lawnmower and not a garden shed.

3. the charge for the delivery to Birr should be €19.00.

4. .the satellite dish is a high-priority delivery and the charge should be €42.00.

5. the cello is to be collected from Waltons.

6. the sunbed should be delivered to O Hynes in Tuam.

7. the computer delivery has been cancelled. Remove this record from the file.

Add:

8. the following details on a new delivery to the file:

ITEM	SENDER	LOCATION	RECIPIENT	COST	PRIORITY
Water cooler	Oasis Coolers	Galway	P Brogan	€65.00	H

Save:

9. this edited version of the file as COURIER2.

Display all the details of those deliveries:

10. which are high priority.

11. which go to Galway.

12. where the cost is less than €30.00.

Assignment 5

A hotelier who specialises in angling holidays has compiled information for her guests on all the lakes within 12 km of her hotel. She can give the name of any lake, its distance from the hotel, the presence of trout in the lake, the year it was last restocked with young fish, its floor type, its depth and the availability of boats.

The information available is as follows:

LAKE	DISTANCE	TROUT	RESTOCKED	LAKE FLOOR	DEPTH	BOAT HIRE
Tully	4.0	N	2006	Sand	10.2	N
Gulladoo	3.7	Y	2005	Sand	13.5	Y
Carrigallen	0.5	N	2006	Mud	8.5	N
Garadice	11.3	Y	2004	Sand	15.4	Y
Woodford	4.6	Y	2006	Mud	11.9	N
Glasshouse	2.6	Y	2005	Mud	10.3	Y
Keeldra	6.4	N	2004	Sand	9.6	N
Errew	13.8	Y	2006	Sand	13.0	Y
Killegar	3.2	N	2006	Mud	8.8	N
Cullies	4.4	N	2004	Mud	11.3	N

You are required to set up a database file on your computer containing the above information, using the headings given above as field names.

■Carry out the following tasks:

Save:

1. the file as LAKES1.

Make the following alterations to the relevant records:

2. The distance to Tully Lake, as given in the file, is by an old unapproved road. The actual distance from the hotel to this lake by the new road is 5.5 km, and this distance should be given in the file.
3. Trout are not present in Woodford Lake but are present in Cullies Lake.
4. Keeldra Lake was last restocked with young fish in 2006.
5. The maximum depth of Garadice lake has been measured incorrectly. Members of a visiting sub-aqua club have discovered an underwater channel with a depth of 24.3 m, and this must now be reflected in the file as the maximum depth of this lake.
6. Errew Lake is more than 12 km from the hotel and should not be listed. Erase this record from the file.
7. The hotelier, when compiling the information, overlooked an excellent trout lake that is only 7.2 km from the hotel. You must include its details in the file. The information is as follows:

LAKE	DISTANCE	TROUT	RESTOCKED	LAKE FLOOR	DEPTH	BOAT HIRE
Calloughs	7.2	Y	2006	Sand	14.1	Y

Save:

8. this edited version of the file as LAKES2.

Display all the details of those lakes:

9. where trout are present.
10. that have a lake floor of sand.
11. that are less than 4 km from the hotel and have boat hire.
12. that are more than 10 m deep and have a lake floor of mud.

Assignment 6

The marathon, a race over 26 miles, is held each year in a certain city. To aid efficient running of the event the organisers hold the following information on each entrant: the athlete's name, vest number, age, sex, club, wheelchair user (Y/N), number of previous marathons run and the athlete's personal best time in a marathon.

You are requested to set up a database file on computer containing the following details on ten marathon entrants using the headings given as field names:

ATHLETE	NUMBER	AGE	SEX	CLUB	WHEELCHAIR	MARATHONS	TIME
P Brady	6783	19	M	Cavan	N	1	3.2
O Murphy	2910	24	F	Wexford	N	5	2.8
K Nugent	3420	37	M	Portlaoise	Y	6	3.1
R O' Brien	8003	21	F	Santry	N	8	3.0
C Murtagh	4430	29	F	Trim	N	2	3.9
H Greene	7821	36	M	Drimnagh	N	11	2.7
S Daly	9926	44	M	Longford	N	6	3.3
R McCann	3418	18	F	Tuam	Y	4	2.9
F Lynch	1099	32	M	Santry	N	7	3.5
M Quinn	6225	23	F	Thurles	N	9	3.1

◼Carry out the following tasks:

Save:

1. the file as MARATHON.

Display all the details of the entrant(s) who:

2. have vest number 4430.
3. are from the Santry club.
4. are more than thirty years of age.
5. have personal best times of less than three hours.
6. are male **and** are a wheelchair user.
7. are more than thirty years of age **and** have a personal best time of less than three hours.
8. are female **and** have run more than five marathons.
9. are under twenty-five years of age **and** are not wheelchair entrants **and** who have run more than one marathon to date.
10. Display the Athlete, Age and Club fields **only** for all the entrants in the file.

Assignment 7

Benny's Books, a bookshop in Cavan town, opened its doors for business in 2006. Benny McCarthy, the proprietor, holds the following information on each book in stock:

- its title
- ISBN (International Standard Book Number)
- author's name
- publisher
- year of publication
- category to which the book belongs
- whether the book is hardback or not
- purchase price of the book.

Benny wishes to hold book details on a computer database file. You are employed to set up this file containing the information given below. You can use the headings given as field names.

TITLE	ISBN	AUTHOR	PUBLISHER	YEAR	CATEGORY	HARDBACK	PRICE
The Searchers	0-9811X	Long P	Macmillan	2001	Fiction	No	€11.99
Cooking for One	0-12925	Davis S	Cedar	2007	Cookery	Yes	€27.50
Driftwood	1-56227	Keogh R	Penguin	2003	Fiction	No	€6.50
Wood Turning	4-9188X	Smyth J	Macmillan	2006	DIY	Yes	€24.00
Saving Nancy	7-88912	Canvey L	Penguin	2002	Fiction	No	€7.80
Thai Cuisine	2-31716	Ying S	Cedar	2005	Cookery	No	€14.50
Spreadsheets	1-4599X	O'Neill S	Thornes	2006	Computer	No	€12.00
Nearly Home	3-71913	Anders L	Penguin	2005	Fiction	No	€8.99
Farmer Brown	2-45332	O'Brien R	Cedar	2006	Fiction	No	€8.50
Selling Online	1-2271X	Preneur E	Macmillan	2007	Computer	Yes	€22.00
Country Kitchens	5-88898	Laffey T	Penguin	2002	DIY	Yes	€9.99
Mama's Pasta	7-5919X	Graziani P	Thornes	2007	Cookery	Yes	€28.00

◨ Carry out the following tasks:

Save:

1. the file as BOOKS.

Display all the details of the book(s) that:

2. has the ISBN number 2-45332.
3. were published in 2002.
4. is categorised as fiction **and** costs more than €10.00.
5. are hardback **and** were published by Macmillan.
6. cost less than €10.00 **or** more than €15.00.
7. are categorised as fiction **and** were published before 2005 **and** cost less than €10.00.

Display:

8. the title, category and price of all books in the file.
9. the title, author, category and price of all computer books in the file.
10. the title, author, publisher and year of publication of all paperback books in the file.

Assignment 8

Leinster Coach Hire Ltd, established in 2006, offers carefree and cost-effective access to any part of the country. Each booking is recorded, at present, in the company's day log book. The following table shows the details of twelve separate bookings:

TO	PURPOSE	ORGANISER	DATE	GROUP	AGE PROFILE	COST	PREVIOUS USE?
Cork	Holiday	Greene P	04/10/07	22	1	€190.00	N
Knock	Pilgrimage	O' Connor K	15/09/07	83	5	€520.00	Y
Mosney	School tour	Daly T	14/06/07	38	3	€140.00	Y
Roscommon	Wedding	Cox D	18/08/07	14	2	€115.00	N
Killarney	Holiday	Cooney D	10/07/07	8	2	€85.00	Y
Blarney	Holiday	Mahon D	03/06/07	20	4	€175.00	N
Lough Derg	Pilgrimage	Galvin P	23/08/07	51	2	€330.00	N
Cavan	Fishing trip	Brennan M	25/07/07	12	2	€72.00	N
Belfast	School tour	Smyth J	28/06/07	60	3	€365.00	Y
Knock	Pilgrimage	Jones R	07/08/07	90	5	€600.00	N
Doolin	Field trip	Elsdon H	18/09/07	27	4	€280.00	Y
Galway	Holiday	Dunne C	18/08/07	9	1	€110.00	Y

Each booking shows:
- destination (to)
- purpose of the coach hire
- organiser
- date of proposed trip
- number in the group
- age profile of the passengers
- cost of the booking
- whether a previous booking has been made by the organiser.

The age profile is recorded using a 1–5 code system: 1 – senior citizens, 2 – adults, 3 – children, 4 – students and 5 – mixed. You are required to set up a database file on your computer containing the information in the table above. You should use the headings given in the table as field names.

◨ Carry out the following tasks:

Save:

1. the file as COACH.

Display all the details of the booking(s):

2. where there are more than ten in the group **and** the age profile of the intending passengers is adult.
3. that were made for August.
4. that are either pilgrimages **or** holidays.
5. that are neither pilgrimages **nor** holidays.
6. where there are more than fifty intending passengers in the group **and** the cost is less than €500.00 **and** where previous bookings have been made.
7. made for a group of senior citizens in October.

Display:

8. the destination, organiser, date and group details for any wedding bookings.
9. the destination, date and cost details for any bookings where the age profile of the group is either adult **or** mixed.

Sort:

10. the entire file in alphabetical order of the organiser's name.

Save:

11. this sorted file as COACH2.

Assignment 9

A maternity hospital holds the following information on new mothers:

- mother's name
- ward
- mother's age
- date of the birth
- sex of the baby
- weight of the baby in kilograms
- the number of children born to the mother
- PHI (private health insurance) (Y or N)
- attending doctor.

Set up a database file on your computer holding the details on the ten mothers listed below. You can use the headings given as field names.

MOTHER	WARD	AGE	DATE	SEX	WEIGHT	CHILD	PHI	DOCTOR
Mills D	St Peter's	22	3/9/07	F	2.9	1	Y	Dr Wilcox
O' Dea F	St Clare's	34	6/9/07	F	3.2	4	Y	Dr Evans
Willis P	St Anne's	29	6/9/07	M	3.0	1	N	Dr Evans
O' Hare Y	St Anne's	30	2/9/07	F	3.6	2	Y	Dr Kent
Sammon M	St. Anne's	41	3/9/07	M	2.9	5	Y	Dr Wilcox
O' Neill A	St Clare's	25	5/9/07	M	4.2	2	Y	Dr Kent
Molloy K	St Peter's	19	1/9/07	F	2.5	1	N	Dr Evans
Byrne L	St Anne's	33	5/9/07	M	3.7	1	Y	Dr Kent
Conway T	St Peter's	24	4/9/07	M	3.4	2	Y	Dr Kent
Quinn A	St Peter's	27	6/9/07	F	4.0	3	N	Dr Wilcox

◪ Carry out the following tasks:

Save:

1. the file as BABY1.

Replace:

2. the ward name St Peter's with St Mark's in the file by using the global replace facility of your database program.

Display all the details of the mother(s) who:

3. had baby girls and are in St Mark's ward.

4. are thirty years old or more **and** are being attended by Dr Kent.

5. had a baby girl weighing less than 4 kilograms on 6 September.

Sort:

6. the file into alphabetical order of mothers' names.

Save:

7. the sorted file as BABY2.

Display from the BABY2 file:

8. the name, age and attending doctor of those mothers who do not have private health insurance.

Sort:

9. the BABY2 file into ascending order of babies' weights.

Save:

10. this file as BABY3.

Display from the BABY3 file:

11. the name, ward, sex, weight and child details of those mothers whose new baby weighed 4 kilograms or less **and** who have more than one child.

Assignment 10

The Denver Pizza Company, established in 2006, supplies succulent American-style pizzas to homes all over Dublin. Nine items of information are held on each order received. Rick Baker, the owner of the company, wishes to transfer these order details to a computer database file. The information held on each order is as follows:

• customer's name and address
• the exact time that the order was placed
• the pizza type
• the pizza size – large (L), medium (M) or small (S)
• the base type – deep pan (DP) or light and crispy (LC)
• the number of toppings (Tpns) requested
• the price of the pizza

- whether or not the pizza was delivered.

Set up the database file on your computer containing the details in the table below. The headings in the table can be used as field names.

CUSTOMER	ADDRESS	TIME	PIZZA	SIZE	BASE	TPNS	PRICE	DELIVERY
O' Brien G	4 Seacliff Rd	18:33	Hawaiian	L	DP	8	€14.50	Yes
White M	51 Idrone Dr	17:51	Hot & Spicy	L	DP	3	€15.20	Yes
McCann F	3 Elkwood St	18:55	Mighty Meaty	S	LC	5	€8.50	No
Wilson H	15 Wood Ct	18:03	Full House	L	LC	4	€16.50	Yes
Brady A	9 Hill Gdns	18:24	BLT	M	LC	7	€9.90	Yes
McHugh M	121 Myrtle St	17:46	Veggie' s Delight	M	DP	3	€9.30	No
O' Reilly P	67 Russell Ave	18:15	Hawaiian	S	LC	8	€6.90	Yes
Foley K	19 Kincora Rd	16:40	Original	L	DP	5	€12.70	Yes
Cummins B	4 Church Ave	17:05	Bombay Double	S	DP	4	€7.70	No
Dowd P	22 Ludford Pk	18:37	Sicilian	S	LC	3	€7.20	Yes
Maher R	156 Barry Rd	17:30	Mighty Meaty	L	DP	6	€16.00	No
Colgan E	10 Hilltop St	16:51	Original	M	DP	5	€9.00	Yes

◪ Carry out the following tasks:

Save:

1. the entire file as PIZZA1.

Display all the details of the order(s) for any:

2. medium original pizza.
3. large pizzas with five toppings or less.
4. small pizzas delivered after 18:00.
5. large deep pan pizzas that were delivered and cost less than €16.00.

Sort:

6. the file into chronometric (time) order.

Save:

7. the sorted file as PIZZA2.

Display:

8. the customer's name and address, the pizza type and the order time for all light and crispy pizzas that were delivered.

Sort:

9. the file into descending order of pizza prices.

Save:

10. this sorted file as PIZZA3.

Display:
11. the customer's name, the pizza type, size and price for all orders listed except those for Hawaiian **and** Original pizzas.
12. using the indexing facility of your program (if possible), produce a display of the entire file organised in alphabetical order of customer names.
13. **save** the indexed file as PIZZA4.

Assignment 11

You are required to set up a database file containing information on the twelve countries listed below. The information on each country includes:
- the name of the country
- its population
- its area (in square kilometres)
- the capital city
- the principal language
- its unit of currency
- the highest point above sea level in metres (HP)
- the type of government (Govt)
- the main religion (Rel).

In the table, abbreviations have been used for the government types and main religions. The abbreviations for government types are as follows:
- constitutional monarchy – Cm
- federal republic – Fr
- constitutional republic – Cr
- Islamic republic – Ir
- multiparty republic – Mr.

The abbreviations for the religions are:
- Christianity – Ch
- Islam – Is
- Judaism – Ju.

You can use the headings in the table as field names.

COUNTRY	POPULATION	AREA	CAPITAL	LANGUAGE	CURRENCY	HP	GOVT	REL
Ireland	4,200,000	70,284	Dublin	English	Euro	1,041	Cr	Ch
UK	60,609,000	244,100	London	English	Pound	1,343	Cm	Ch
Germany	82,422,000	356,755	Berlin	German	Euro	2,963	Fr	Ch
USA	298,440,000	9,372,614	Washington	English	US dollar	6,194	Fr	Ch
Pakistan	165,803,000	796,095	Islamabad	Urdu	Rupee	8,611	Ir	Is
Brazil	188,078,000	8,511,965	Brasilia	Portuguese	Real	3,014	Fr	Ch
Israel	6,352,000	20,770	Jerusalem	Hebrew	Shekel	1,208	Mr	Ju
Argentina	39,921,000	2,766,889	Buenos Aires	Spanish	Peso	6,960	Fr	Ch
Iran	68,688,000	1,648,000	Tehran	Farsi	Rial	5,604	Ir	Is
Peru	28,302,000	1,285,216	Lima	Spanish	Nuevo sol	6,768	Cr	Ch
Morocco	33,241,000	458,730	Rabat	Arabic	Dirham	4,165	Cm	Is
Sweden	9,016,000	449,964	Stockholm	Swedish	Krona	2,111	Cm	Ch

◤Carry out the following tasks:

Save:

1. the file as COUNTRY1.

Display all the details of any:

2. non-English-speaking countries where Christianity is the main religion.
3. countries that are either constitutional or federal republics with populations of less than 100 million people.

Delete:

4. the field containing the details for the highest point above sea level from the file.

Insert:

5. a new field between the Currency and Govt fields to hold the per capita gross national product details for each country. The latter is expressed in US dollars. Use GNP as the field name.

Enter:

6. The following per capita GNP details for each country into the new field in each record:
   Ireland - $34,100, UK - $30,900, Germany - $29,800, USA - $42,000, Pakistan - $2,400, Brazil - $8,400, Israel - $22,300, Argentina - $13,700, Iran - $8,100, Peru - $6,100, Morocco - $4,300, Sweden - $29,800.

Sort:

7. the file into descending order of per capita GNP.

Save:

8. the sorted file as COUNTRY2.

Extract:

9. from the COUNTRY2 file all the details of countries whose per capita GNP is less than US $10,000.

Recall:

10. the original COUNTRY1 file to the screen.

Sort:

11. this file into alphabetical order of country names.

Save:

12. this sorted file as COUNTRY3.

Print:

13. the entire COUNTRY3 file.

Assignment 12

MountainView Business Park is home to twelve different companies. Pat Cash, the manager of the park, holds the following details on each company:

- *Company* – the company's name
- *Business* – its line of business
- *Owner* – the owner of the company
- *Established* – the year that the company was set up
- *Type* – whether it is a service (S) or manufacturing (M) company
- *Employees* – the number of staff
- *Premises* – whether the company's premises are owned (O) or rented (R)
- *Export* – whether the company exports its products (Y or N).

   You must enter the details in the table below into a database file using the italicised words above as field names.

COMPANY	BUSINESS	OWNER	ESTABLISHED	TYPE	EMPLOYEES	PREMISES	EXPORT
Absel Drilling	Concrete drilling	Stone D	2003	S	12	R	No
HomeWorld	Kitchens	Brady P	2007	M	7	O	No
Curtex Blinds	Window blinds	Curtain R	2005	M	21	O	Yes
Moo-moo Foods	Dairy products	O'Grady K	2003	M	43	O	Yes
Elegant Rooms	Interior design	Ashley A	2007	S	5	R	No
P Murtagh & Co.	Architects	Murtagh P	2001	S	9	O	No
Premier Ices	Ice cream	McCool R	2006	M	18	O	No
Cans and All	Recycling	Tidy D	2005	M	26	R	No
Which Way?	Brass signs	Knowles S	2006	M	8	R	No
Little Ones	Children's clothes	McEniff B	2005	M	35	O	Yes
EasyClean	Carpet cleaning	Waters B	2007	S	4	R	No
Jetwash	Pressure washers	Richards M	2007	M	15	R	Yes

◪ Carry out the following tasks:

Save:

1. the file as COMPANY1.

Display:

2. the company names and owners for all companies set up prior to 2007.

Insert:

3. a new telephone field after the owner field.

Enter:

4. the telephone number of each company: Absel Drilling – 21988, HomeWorld – 32751, Curtex Blinds – 30887, Moo-moo Foods – 21997, Elegant Rooms – 32880, P Murtagh & Co. – 20017, Premier Ices – 31634, Cans and All – 24119, Which Way? – 31772, Little Ones – 30955, EasyClean – 32859, Jetwash – 30910.

Sort:

5. the file into descending order of the number of staff employed.

Save:

6. the sorted file as COMPANY2.

Extract:

7. from the COMPANY2 file all the details of the non-exporting companies who own their own premises.

Print:

8. the query file from the previous question.

Recall:

9. the original COMPANY1 file to the screen.

Sort:

10. the file into alphabetical order of company name.

Save:

11. this sorted file as COMPANY3.

Create:

12. a report format, using the COMPANY3 file, that has the heading 'MountainView Business Park' and shows the company names, respective owners and respective numbers of employees.

Assign:

13. the name BUSPARK to the report.

Print:

14. the report.

Assignment 13

Ticketron Ltd take bookings for various entertainment events. Details of each booking are held on a record card. A blank record card looks like this:

```
                        TICKETRON LTD

   PERSON ................      ROAD......................
   AREA ..................      COUNTY ...................
   EVENT .................      VENUE ....................
   TYPE ..................      PRICE ....................
   DATE ..................      TICKETS ..................
   CREDIT CARD ........
```

The type field shows whether the event is a concert (C), a play (P) or a sporting (S) occasion. The credit card field shows whether the booking was made by credit card (Y/N). Set up a database file on your computer and enter the following details of eight separate bookings:

F Cahill	12 Farnham St
Cavan	Co. Cavan
WWE Smackdown	Point
S	€40.00
29/08/2007	1
N	

S Daly	65 Greenlea Rd
Terenure	Dublin 6
Snow Patrol	Millstreet
C	€45.00
07/07/2007	2
Y	

P Fox	34 Ennis Rd
Limerick	Co. Limerick
Sive	Abbey
P	€18.00
19/07/2007	2
Y	

A Hoey	9 Muirhevna Rd
Dundalk	Co. Louth
Madonna	Slane
C	€85.00
21/07/2007	1
Y	

P Keran	High St
Ballinamore	Co. Leitrim
Elton John	RDS
C	€70.00
08/09/2007	4
Y	

M Murphy	85 Glanmire Rd
Cork	Co. Cork
Big Maggie	Gaiety
P	€25.00
25/06/2007	3
Y	

P Nolan	22 Clogher Rd	J Quinn	8 Main St
Crumlin	Dublin 12	Clifden	Co. Galway
The Mai	Peacock	Feile	Pairc Ui Caoimh
P	€20.00	C	€100.00
26/08/2007	2	23/07/2007	2
Y		N	

◼Carry out the following tasks:

Save:

1. the file as TICKET1.

Organise (using the sort or indexing facilities):

2. the file into chronological (date) order.

Save:

3. the index or sorted file as TICKET2.

Extract:

4. from the organised file all the details of those bookings made by credit card for events in July.

Save:

5. this subset of the file as CCJULY.

Print:

6. the CCJULY file.

Recall:

7. the original TICKET1 file to the screen.

Sort:

8. the file into ascending order of event type (primary key) and ascending order of ticket prices (secondary key).

Save:

9. this sorted file as TICKET3.

Create:

10. a report format, using the TICKET3 file, that has the heading 'Ticketron Ticket Sales' and shows only the person, event, type, price and tickets fields. Do not total the currency or numeric fields.

Save:

11. this report as TICKETRP.

Re-sort:

12. the TICKET3 file into reverse chronological order.

Save:

13. the newly sorted file as TICKET4.

Develop:

14. suitable mailing labels (person, road, area and county) from the TICKET4 file with two labels across the page.

Save:

15. the mailing labels to a file called LABELS.

Print:

16. the mailing labels.

Assignment 14

Autoline Insure Direct PLC, based in Cork, provides car insurance for drivers of all ages. Details of each insured driver are currently held in paper files. A blank insurance card from the files would appear as follows:

```
┌─────────────────────────────────────────────────┐
│          AUTOLINE INSURE DIRECT PLC              │
│          DRIVER INSURANCE CARD                   │
│                                                  │
│   PERSON ..................   POLICY NO. ............│
│   CAR ......................   MODEL ...................│
│   REG. NO. ............   EXPIRY DATE ..........│
│   PREMIUM ............   CATEGORY ...............│
│   CLAIM .................   FULL LICENCE ..........│
└─────────────────────────────────────────────────┘
```

Two fields on this card require explanation:

- **Category** – the type of insurance bought. This may be fully comprehensive (Co), third party, fire and theft (Tt) or third party (Tp).
- **Claim** – whether the driver has claimed on a policy during the past five years (Y/N).

You are given the following details on eight different drivers that are insured with the company:

Mary Hughes	MP0987
Nissan	Almera
07-CN-559	12/09/2008
€722	Co
N	Y

Sean Silke	MO1009
Volkswagen	Golf
05-LS-6712	31/10/2008
€458	Tt
N	Y

Noel Murphy	MP7812
Toyota	Avensis
07-D-4599	02/09/2008
€1,239	Co
Y	Y

Kathy Nugent	SK2388
Renault	Clio
07-WX-1008	19/04/2008
€385	Tp
N	Y

Brenda Larkin	MO7661
Toyota	Yaris
06-MO-812	25/09/2008
€840	Tt
N	N

Eoin Moore	RD4556
Volkswagen	Passat
07-LM-88	15/08/2008
€550	Co
N	Y

James Keegan	SK9948
Ford	Focus
06-C-9120	30/09/2008
€1,085	Tt
N	N

Sandra Evans	MP8110
Nissan	Micra
05-KE-226	28/06/2008
€970	Co
Y	Y

Set up a database file on your computer and enter the details given. Your data entry screen should look identical to the record card shown on p. 100 (the border is optional).

◥ Carry out the following tasks:

Save:
1. the file as POLICY1.

Extract:
2. a subset of records from the file that consists of all policies that expire during September **or** October 2008.

Save:
3. this subset as SOPOLICY.

Sort:
4. the POLICY1 file into alphabetical order of category (primary key) **and** descending order of premium (secondary key).

Save:
5. the sorted file as POLICY2.

Extract:

6. a subset of records from the POLICY2 file that consists of all the details for drivers who have bought either third party **or** third party, fire and theft policies.

Save:

7. this new file as NONCOMP.

Produce:

8. a report format from the NONCOMP file showing all the fields with the heading 'Non Fully Comprehensive Policies'.

Save:

9. this report as POLRPT1.

Retrieve:

10. the POLICY1 file.

Sort:

11. this file into chronological order of expiry dates.

Save:

12. this sorted file as POLICY3.

Extract:

13. from the POLICY3 file all the details of policies on cars that were registered before 2007.

Save:

14. this subset to a new file called PRE07.

Produce:

15. a report format from the PRE07 file that has the heading 'Older Car Policies' and shows the driver's name, car, model, expiry date and premium only. This report should also show show average premium for the listed policies.

Save:

16. this report as OLDERCAR.

Print:

17. this latter report.

Assignment 15

Irish Estates Ltd provides details of farms for sale throughout Ireland. The following details are held on each farm:

- Auctioneer – handling the sale
- County – where the farm is located
- Code – each farm has a unique code
- Acres – number for sale

- Type – beef, dairy, mixed or tillage farm
- Price – seller's reserve price
- Lots – the farm may be divided into several lots
- Frontage – along the roadside (Fr)
- Dwelling house – on the land (Dw).

Set up a database file containing the details in the table below. The data input screen should have the centred title 'Irish Estates Ltd' and there should be three fields per line. Choose appropriate field names.

AUCTIONEER	COUNTY	CODE	ACRES	TYPE	PRICE	LOTS	FR	DW
Trim AgriSales	Meath	T244	8	Beef	€240,000	1	No	No
O' Shea Properties	Cork	O397	212	Dairy	€3,900,000	1	Yes	Yes
Cody & Daughter	Kilkenny	C098	103	Tillage	€3,100,000	2	Yes	Yes
Mahon Estates	Louth	M249	27	Beef	€625,000	1	Yes	No
Brady & Co.	Cavan	B884	77	Dairy	€1,550,000	1	Yes	No
McHale & Co.	Mayo	H452	68	Mixed	€1,100,000	2	Yes	Yes
O' Shea Properties	Kerry	O391	45	Mixed	€900,000	3	Yes	Yes
Mahon Estates	Meath	M230	12	Beef	€360,000	1	No	No
Wilson & Sons	Wexford	W348	52	Tillage	€1,170,000	2	Yes	No
Brady & Co.	Cavan	B763	32	Beef	€800,000	1	Yes	No
Green Acres Ltd	Tipperary	G091	150	Dairy	€350,000	1	Yes	Yes
Mahon Estates	Meath	M238	80	Dairy	€2,700,000	3	No	Yes

Carry out the following tasks:

Save:
  1. the file as FARM1.

Extract:
  2. from the file the county, acres, price and auctioneer fields **only** for any dairy farm listed.

Save:
  3. this subset as MILKFARM.

Print:
  4. the MILKFARM file.

Extract:
  5. from the original FARM1 file the county, acres, lots, dwelling house and price fields (in that order) for all non-dairy farms costing €1,000,000 or less.

Save:

6. this subset to a new file called NONMILK1.

Sort:

7. the NONMILK1 file into descending order of farm size (acres).

Save:

8. this sorted file as NONMILK2.

Produce:

9. a report format from the NONMILK2 file showing the acres and price fields. The report should have the centred heading 'Non-Dairy Farms'.

Save:

10. this report as FARMREP1.

Modify:

11. the report to include the dwelling house field.

Save:

12. this modified report as FARMREP2.

Recall:

13. the original FARM1 file to the screen.

Sort:

14. the file into alphabetical order of type (primary key) and descending order of price (secondary key).

Save:

15. this sorted file as FARM2.

Produce:

16. a *grouped* report format based on the type field from the file showing the type, price, auctioneer, county, acres and lots **only** for each farm listed. The report should have the centred heading 'Farms for Sale'.

Save:

17. this report as FARMREP3.

Print:

18. this latter report.

Assignment 16

Mayfield College provides a range of evening classes during the winter months. Elizabeth Gormley, the head of the evening school at Mayfield College, must hold the following details on each course:

- *Course*
- *Code*
- *Day*
- *Time*
- *Weeks* – duration of the course
- *Size* – number in class
- *Teacher*
- *Exam* – Y/N
- *Cost*
- *Room.*

Using the italicised words as field names, enter the details outlined in the following table into a database file:

COURSE	CODE	DAY	TIME	WEEKS	SIZE	TEACHER	EXAM	COST	ROOM
Spreadsheets	Ss	Wed	19:00-21:00	10	15	Flynn T	Yes	€220.00	C31
Accounting	Ac	Thu	19:00-20:30	20	25	Callow D	Yes	€565.00	A15
Typing	Ty	Mon	19:00-20:30	10	18	Cahill A	Yes	€99.00	S12
Psychology	Py	Mon	20:00-21:00	6	25	Watson B	No	€60.00	S19
Yoga	Yo	Tue	20:00-22:00	12	10	Wilson M	No	€135.00	Gym
Economics	Ec	Thu	19:30-21:00	20	20	Moore D	Yes	€499.00	A17
Spanish	Sp	Wed	19:00-21:00	15	15	O'Reilly K	No	€165.00	L04
Cookery	Co	Mon	19:00-21:00	8	12	Markey C	Yes	€199.00	K10
Aerobics	Ae	Thu	20:30-22:00	12	15	Wilson M	No	€150.00	Gym
Databases	Db	Mon	19:00-21:00	10	18	Flynn T	Yes	€235.00	C31

◣Carry out the following tasks:

Save:

1. the file as EVENING1.

Make the following alterations to the relevant records:

2. Desmond Callow takes his Accounting class in room A09.

3. Denise Moore's Economics class starts at 19:00 on Wednesday evenings.

4. Caroline Markey's Cookery class costs €179.

5. Michael Wilson's Aerobics class has been cancelled. Delete this record from the file.

Enter:

6. the following details on two new courses:

```
German        GE    THU    20:00-22:00  15    20    Kaltz M    Y  €165   L05
Law           LA    MON    19:00-21:00  18    25    Smyth J    Y  €485   A17
```

Erase:

7. the Code field from the file.

Enter:

8. a new field called Dept to show the department running the course and insert the following details for the relevant records:

COURSE	DEPT
Spreadsheets	Computer
Accounting	Business
Typing	Secretarial
Psychology	Fitness
Yoga	Fitness
Economics	Business
Spanish	Language
Cookery	Catering
Aerobics	Fitness
Databases	Computer
German	Language
Law	Business

Save:

9. this edited file as EVENING2.

Extract:

10. all the records for courses that are run on Monday evenings **and** cost less than €200.

Save:

11. this subset as MONCLASS.

Sort:

12. the EVENING2 file into alphabetic order of department (primary key) and descending order of cost (secondary key).

Save:

13. this sorted file as EVENING3.

Produce:

14. a report format using the EVENING3 file that has the heading 'Mayfield College – Evening Classes' and shows only the course, time, day, weeks and cost fields. The duration and cost fields must not be totalled on the report.

Save:

15. this report as CLASSRPT.

Print:

16. the report.

Assignment 17

The *Evening Echo*, Ireland's fastest-growing evening newpaper, carries twelve pages of classified advertisements. Mary McCarthy, the editor, holds nine different items of information on each classified advertisement in the paper:

- *Section* – under which the advertisement is placed
- *Description* – of item or service
- *Words* – number of words in the advertisement
- *Evenings* – number for which the advertisement is carried
- *Date* – of first printing
- *Name* – of person who placed the advertisement
- *Cost* – of placing the advertisement
- *Box no.* – reply (Y/N)
- *Payment* – credit card (Cc), cheque (Ch) or Cash (Ca).

Using the italicised words above as field names, produce a database file containing the details in the table below:

SECTION	DESCRIPTION	WORDS	EVENINGS	DATE	CUSTOMER	COST	BOX_NO	PAYMENT
Jobs	Personal Assistant	20	2	12/09/2007	Logan R	€26.00	Yes	Cc
Holidays	Kerry B&B	12	5	14/09/2007	Keegan M	€44.00	No	Ch
Pets	Pony	17	4	17/09/2007	Byrne A	€51.00	Yes	Cc
Lost & Found	Wallet	8	2	10/09/2007	Lawlor K	€15.00	Yes	Ch
Holidays	Sligo Hotel	30	3	18/09/2007	Silke D	€64.00	No	Cc
Equipment	Piano	25	2	13/09/2007	Evans H	€33.00	Yes	Ca
Pets	Dog	18	2	16/09/2007	Joyce C	€25.00	No	Ca
Jobs	Accountant	14	2	14/09/2007	Logan R	€21.00	Yes	Cc
Equipment	Gas Cooker	22	3	18/09/2007	Brogan A	€48.00	No	Cc
Pets	Budgie	14	4	15/09/2007	Conway T	€40.00	Yes	Ch
Pets	Cat	12	4	12/09/2007	O' Dea J	€32.00	Yes	Ca
Jobs	Chef	27	2	16/09/2007	Foley S	€34.00	Yes	Cc
Equipment	Bicycle	20	3	16/09/2007	Lynch B	€43.00	No	Ch
Holidays	Cavan Chalet	18	5	11/09/2007	O' Reilly P	€60.00	Yes	Cc

Carry out the following tasks:

Save:

1. the file as ADVERT1.

Make the following alterations to the relevant records:

2. the cost of advertising for the wallet in the **Lost & Found** section was only €12.00.
3. the piano was advertised in the **Music** section.
4. Susan Foley's advertisement was carried for three evenings, cost €48.00 and was paid for in cash.

Delete:

5. the record containing the details of an advertisement of a cat.

Save:

6. this edited version of the file as ADVERT2.

Extract:

7. all records of those advertisements that cost more than €40.00 and were paid for by credit card.

Save:

8. this subset as CCPAY.

Sort:

9. the ADVERT2 file into chronological order.

Save:

10. the sorted file as ADVERT3.

Produce:

11. a report format from the file using all the fields with the heading 'Evening Echo – Classifieds'. The cost field **only** must be totalled.

Save:

12. this report as ECHORPT1.

Sort:

13. the ADVERT3 file in ascending order of the number of **evenings** (primary key) and ascending order of **cost** (secondary key).

Save:

14. this sorted file as ADVERT4.

Produce:

15. a **grouped** report format (on evenings) from the file showing the evenings, cost, section, description, words and customer fields. The report should have the centred heading 'Customer Enquiries'. The report should also show the average cost of placing an advertisement and the average number of words in an advertisement.

Assignment 18

Computers Direct Ltd, owned by Sarah Turner, is a company that sells computers via the Internet to customers anywhere in Ireland. Sarah holds the following information on each computer in stock:

- type: whether the computer is a desktop or a notebook
- model: the computer model
- processor: the type of processor installed
- hard drive: the capacity of the hard drive (in gigabytes)
- memory: the size of the memory (in gigabytes)
- optical drive: the type of optical drive installed
- network card: whether there is a network card installed or not
- OS: the type of Windows operating system installed
- price: the purchase price of the computer.

Sarah wishes to hold the details on a computer database file. You are employed to set up this file containing the information given below. You can use the headings given as field names.

TYPE	MODEL	PROCESSOR	HARD DRIVE	MEMORY	OPTICAL DRIVE	NETWORK CARD	OS	PRICE
Notebook	Tiger 2X	Centrino	80	1	8 X DVD +/-RW	No	XP Pro	€1,199
Desktop	Panther SW	Pentium	160	1	16 X DVD +/- RW	Yes	XP Media Centre	€849
Desktop	Leopard QT	Pentium	250	2	16 X DVD +/- RW	Yes	Vista	€1,099
Desktop	Leopard MT	Celeron	100	1	CD/DVD Combo	No	XP Pro	€549
Notebook	Simba GR	Core Duo	60	1	8 X DVD +/-RW	Yes	Vista	€1,299
Desktop	Leopard TW	Core Duo	320	2	16 X DVD +/- RW	Yes	Vista	€1,549
Desktop	Panther VX	Viv-Pentium	250	1	8 X DVD +/-RW	No	XP Pro	€999
Notebook	Tiger 2Z	Centrino	120	1	16 X DVD +/- RW	Yes	Vista	€1,799
Desktop	Lion L5	Viv-Pentium	160	2	16 X DVD +/- RW	Yes	Vista	€1,849
Notebook	Tiger 2S	Celeron	60	1	CD/DVD Combo	No	XP Home	€499
Notebook	Simba GT	Viv-Pentium	160	2	16 X DVD +/- RW	Yes	Vista	€1,949
Desktop	Panther AM	Celeron	60	1	CD/DVD Combo	Yes	XP Pro	€399

◣Carry out the following tasks:

Save:

1. the file as COMPUTER.

Make the following alterations to the relevant records:

2. the Panther SW has an 8 X DVD +/- RW optical drive installed.
3. the Panther VX costs €1,049 and has a 280 GB hard drive.
4. the model name for the Simba GT should be Jaguar GR.

Save:

5. this edited version of the file as COMPUTER2.

Create subset(s) of the file showing:

6. all the details of desktop computers only.
7. all the details of computers costing less than €1,300 **with** the Vista operating installed.
8. The type, processor, hard drive, memory and price fields only of all computers that have a network card installed.
9. All the details of notebook computers sorted in alphabetical order of operating system (primary key) and descending order of price (secondary key).
10. the type, model, price and processor details (in that order) of computers that do not have a Celeron processor and cost less than €1,600. This subset should be sorted in alphabetical order of processor and ascending order of price.

Produce:

11. a report showing all the details of desktop computers. This report should have the heading 'Desktop Computers' and show the average cost of a desktop based on the prices listed. (Hint: The report should be based on the subset created in question 6.)

Save:

12. the report as DESKTOP.

Produce:

13. a report showing all the details of notebook computers sorted in alphabetical order of operating system (primary key) and descending order of price (secondary key). The report should have the heading 'Notebook Computers' and be grouped according to the operating system installed. (Hint: The report should be based on the subset created in question 9.)

Save:

14. the report as NOTEBOOK.

Assignment 19
FETAC Database Methods Sample Paper 1

◤Introduction

Ardara Crafts Distribution Centre collects articles, both handmade and machine-made, from craftspeople throughout a wide area, for sending on to buyers both overseas and within the country. Some of the articles sent in to the Centre are sent on as they are, because they are made for a single order, while other articles are divided up between a number of buyers. Michael Herrity, the manager of the centre, requires a database to be set up in order to facilitate the handling of the articles and to ensure that the correct articles go to make up the correct orders.

◤Task 1 (6 marks)

From the database structure provided in Figure 1, create a database to store the data provided in Figure 2, using appropriate field names and data types. Write out this structure and save the resulting database as **'CRAFTS'**.

NAME OF FIELD	DATA TYPE	WIDTH
Name of Worker	?	15
Address	?	25
Method by which Article was Made	?	8
Category of Article	?	11
Size	?	6
Colour of Article(s)	?	12
Quantity	?	3
Are Goods Part of Single Order ?	?	1

Figure 1

SUPPLIER	ADDRESS	HOW_MADE	CATEGORY	SIZE	COLOUR	QTY	SINGLE ORDER
Cashin Alma	Ardamin House, Sligo	Handmade	Pullover	M/L	Brown/Blue	12	Y
O' Neill Ian	24, Rock Road, Ardara	Machine	Shawl	M/L	Black/Brown	4	N
Clarke Anne	Glebe House, Carigoe	Handmade	Scarves	M/L	Red/Green	11	N
Buitlear Sean	Carraig Dubh, Ath an Ri	Handmade	Pullover	S/M/L	Grey/Green	8	Y
Fleming Sandra	Barton House, Ardara	Machine	Rug	M	Red/White	3	Y
Walsh Catriona	Rose Cottage, Beltra	Machine	Tablecloth	M/L	White	2	Y
Kinnear Martha	45, Carnlough Rd, Ardara	Machine	Bedspread	L	Red/Blue	3	N
O' Hare Enda	Clonagoe, Sligo	Handmade	Pullover	S/M	Red/Blue	9	N
Kernaghan Sean	Hill Farm, Killybegs	Machine	Socks	S/M	Blue/Grey	14	Y
O' Shea Aine	12, Tymon Way, Ardara	Handmade	Rug	M	Blue/Red	1	Y
Tormey Alan	Craft Shop, Portnoo	Handmade	Pullover	M/L	Brown/Black	7	N
O' Fiach Maire	Dronamore, Donegal	Handmade	Scarves	S/M/L	White/Brown	8	N

Figure 2

Task 2 (13 marks)

Using a suitable data input format screen, enter and save the data in Figure 2 into the database 'CRAFTS'.

Notes on data input format screen:

I. Where possible, there should be at least two fields and suitable field labels on each line of the data entry screen.
II. The entry screen should have a suitable centred heading.
III. No extra marks will be given for borders, highlighting, etc.

Task 3 (14 marks)

Mr Herrity requires labels for those deliveries from his suppliers which are **not** part of a single order, in order that he may identify who made the articles, using what method, to what category they belong, in what colour(s) they are provided and how many there are in each consignment.

(a) Extract a suitable subset of the master file for this purpose, saving it to a new file, NOTSING.

(b) Organise the file 'NOTSING' in ascending order of colour (primary key field) and descending method of manufacturing (secondary key field), and save this organised file or index as 'NOTSING2' for printing now or later.

(c) Develop suitable labels from the file 'NOTSING', for the purpose specified in the introduction to this task, placing at least two labels across the page, for printing now or later.

◥ Task 4 (6 marks)

Using the original database 'CRAFTS', develop a report format, containing all fields and all records, which will include a suitable report title, suitable column titles and a total for the quantities of articles, for printing now or later.

◥ Task 5 (11 marks)

(a) Make the following alterations to the database 'CRAFTS':
  I.   Delete the records for Ian O'Neill and Martha Kinnear.
  II. Change the colour of Anne Clarke's scarves from red/green to red/grey.
  III. Change the pullover from Enda O'Hare to a bedspread, and the quantity to 3 (three).

(b) Using the altered file 'CRAFTS' from 5(a), select only those records for suppliers who can provide articles in small sizes, using an appropriate search string, and save the results as 'CRAFTS2', for printing now or later.

(c) Select the fields containing the name of the suppliers, the manner in which the articles are made, the type of articles, the sizes supplied and the colours, from all the records in the altered file 'CRAFTS' from 5(a), and save as 'CRAFTS3' for printing now or later.

Assignment 20
FETAC Database Methods Sample Paper 2

◪ Introduction

The Casualty Department of St Paul's Hospital receives over 200 patients on a busy day. Patients will be present for a variety of reasons ranging from road traffic accidents (RTA) through to suspected heart attacks. As each patient arrives he/she is assigned to one of the consultants working in the Casualty Department. Upon examination the consultant will record the initial diagnosis and decide what further action should be taken. This action will be one of the following:

- admit the patient to one of the hospital's wards
- refer the patient to the X-ray department
- discharge the patient.

For the purpose of maintaining accounts, the hospital also needs to establish whether or not the patient is a member of VHI and to keep records of the charge for the consultation. This charge will be recorded as follows:

1. When the patient presents him/herself the charge is €40.
2. When the patient is taken to hospital by ambulance the charge is €100.

The patient may, of course, decide to pay all or part of the payment at the time he/she arrives. The amount recorded in the charge field is therefore the balance owed.

The Casualty Department wants to maintain these details on a database.

◪ Task 1 (4 marks)

From the database field layout provided in Figure 1, create a structure appropriate to the database package you are working with (for example, a database file structure in dBase or Table in Microsoft Access), to store the data provided in Figure 2, using appropriate field names and data types. Write out this structure on the form provided and save the structure with the name 'CASUALTY'.

NAME OF FIELD	DATA TYPE	WIDTH

Figure 1

◣Task 2 (8 marks)

Design and create a data input screen (FORM) and then use the data input screen to enter the sample data shown in Figure 2 into the database structure 'CASUALTY' created in task 1.

With regard to the data input screen you should follow these guidelines:

(a) All fields must have suitable field labels.

(b) The input screen should have a title on top and be centred.

(c) There is no need for borders or other effects.

Your invigilator will award marks to your screen design during the examination.

RECORD NUMBER	DATE	PATIENT'S NAME	ADDRESS	CONSULTANT	INITIAL DIAGNOSIS	VHI	CHARGE	ACTION TAKEN
00001	23/11/07	Bob Dunne	Wexford	Dr Davies	RTA	Y	100.00	X-RAY
00002	23/11/07	Steve Smith	Dublin	Dr Martin	Heart Condition	Y	40.00	ADMIT
00003	23/11/07	Jane Dawe	Dublin	Dr Byrne	Scalding	N	0.00	DISCHARGE
00004	24/11/07	Mark Roe	Galway	Dr Davies	RTA	Y	100.00	ADMIT
00005	24/11/07	Mary Murray	Sligo	Dr Martin	RTA	N	40.00	DISCHARGE
00006	24/11/07	Michelle Black	Dublin	Dr Martin	Heart Condition	Y	100.00	ADMIT
00007	25/11/07	Jenny Smith	Wexford	Dr Davies	RTA	Y	40.00	X-RAY
00008	25/11/07	Ruth Byrne	Cork	Dr Byrne	Heart Condition	N	40.00	ADMIT
00009	26/11/07	Martin Keane	Cork	Dr Davies	Unknown	N	100.00	ADMIT
00010	26/11/07	Pat Smith	Ballina	Dr Martin	Heart Condition	N	40.00	DISCHARGE

Figure 2

Note: In the case of the VHI field you may substitute Yes for Y and No for N if this is appropriate for the package that you are using.

Print the data set either now or at the end of the examination.

◣Task 3 (12 marks)

The accounts officer in St Paul's wishes to send invoices *only to those patients who have either been admitted to one of the hospital's wards or sent for X-ray.* You are asked to produce these mailing labels. For logistical reasons the accounts officer requests that the labels be printed in a particular sequence:

1. Ascending order on the consultant field (primary sort field).

2. Descending order on the charge field (secondary sort field).

Each label should show the date as well as the patient's name, address and record number. The actual printing of the labels can take place at the end of the examination if you so wish.

Task 4 (13 marks)

Before attempting tasks 4(a) through 4(d) below, make a copy of your original data set (entered at task 2) with the name 'CAQUERY'. Then, using this data set:

(a) Find and print (now or later) all records for patients who are members of the VHI. **Write the query condition you used on the listing.**

(b) Substitute all occurrences of the value €100.00 in the charge field with the value €80.00.

(c) Find and print (now or later) all records for patients who owe more than €50. **Write the query condition you used on the listing.**

(d) Delete all records for patients who have been discharged. **Print the resulting database now or later.**

Task 5 (13 marks)

Using the original database created in tasks 1 and 2, design and print a report that shows for all records the following fields (and in the order listed):

- patient's name
- patient's address
- consultant in attendance
- diagnosis
- action taken
- charge.

The report should be headed 'St Paul's CASUALTY Report' and should show the print date. Choose suitable titles for each field above. The Charge column should be totalled.

Database Structure Entry Form

Name: _____

Examination Number: _____

Date: _____

Chapter 4
Introduction to Spreadsheets

Introduction
What is a spreadsheet?

A spreadsheet is a screen image of a form or matrix made up of rows and columns in which automatic and interconnected calculations are made.

In 1978 an American business student named Dan Bricklin got very tired of adding columns of numbers and then adding them again and again when only a few changes had been made. He approached a programming friend for help in solving his problem, and they came up with a program called Visicalc, written for the Apple II computer. There are now many other spreadsheet programs available, such as Microsoft Excel, Lotus 1-2-3 and Quattro Pro. Most of these programs contain many new features.

What does a spreadsheet look like?

	A	B	C	D	E	F
1		CELL B1				
2						
3						
4						CELL F4
5						
6	CELL A6					
7						
8						
9				CELL D9		
10						
11						
12						
13						
14						
15						
16						
17						
18						
19						
20					CELL E20	

Each **column** in a spreadsheet is usually labelled with a letter, and each **row** with a number. The panel where a column and a row cross each other is a **cell**. Where column A and row 6 meet is cell A6; where column B and row 1 meet is cell B1.

A small spreadsheet might contain 200 rows and sixty columns; this means that it would have 12,000 cells. The size of a computer screen would not allow all these cells to be seen together: usually a screen can show about six columns and twenty rows at a time. Any movement outside or below the edge of the screen will mean losing the display of some information from the previous screen.

In fact, the display can be considered as a movable window that can view only one 'page' or screen of the spreadsheet at any time.

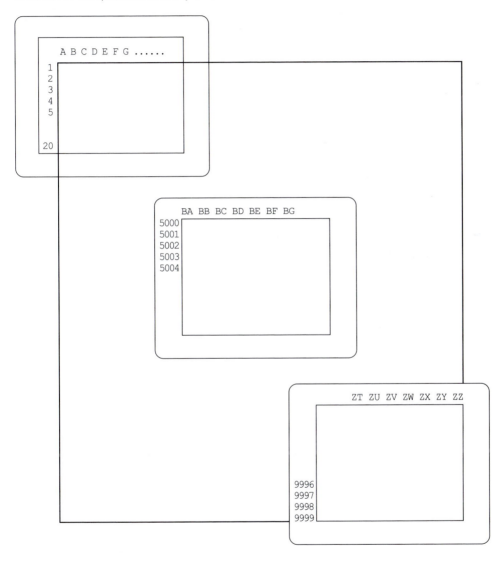

What can be put into a spreadsheet?

Any of three types of data can be entered in a cell: a value, a label or a formula.

A **value** (or 'numeric') is any number on which calculations can be performed. This excludes dates and times, numbers followed by units of measurement and numbers at the beginning of headings. Also, large numbers must be entered without the traditional comma (or, in modern practice, the space) used as the 'thousand marker', as this would prevent calculations being carried out on them; most spreadsheets, however, can add such markers to the results.

A **label** is any non-numeric data. Normally it is text used as headings, such as the labels INCOME, EXPENSES and PROFIT in the example below, but can also include numbers that are not used for calculation purposes, e.g. year headings.

A **formula** is any algebraic expression used for performing calculations on different cells. In cell C8 in the illustration below, +C5-C6 is a formula that subtracts the contents of cell C6 from the contents of cell C5. When a formula is typed into a cell, the result of the calculation is displayed in that cell, not the formula.

Remember to use the asterisk (*) as the multiplication sign, the stroke (/) for division and the circumflex (^) for 'to the power of', and to leave no spaces between numbers and signs.

	A	B	C	D
1	PROFIT STATEMENT, 2005 TO 2007			
2				
3		2005	2006	2007
4				
5	INCOME	100000	200000	400000
6	EXPENSES	50000	80000	170000
7				
8	PROFIT	+B5-B6	+C5-C6	+D5-D6

▓ Example 1

The following topics will be discussed using example 1 below:
1. Setting up the spreadsheet
2. Entering formulae
3. The summation function
4. Improving the appearance of the spreadsheet
5. Replication
6. Editing the spreadsheet
7. Considering 'what if?' situations
8. The 'logical if' function
9. Other facilities.

This example contains a record of personal income and weekly expenditure of a family for four weeks.

The only items entered directly are the wages and the various expenses during the week. All other totals and figures are worked out automatically.

	A	B	C	D	E	F
1	PERSONAL BUDGET	WEEK 1	WEEK 2	WEEK 3	WEEK 4	TOTAL
2						
3						
4	OPENING BALANCE	1000	1212.95	1461.25	1750.3	
5	WAGES	1100	1150	1138	1162	4550
6						
7	TOTAL MONEY	2100	2362.95	2599.25	2912.3	
8						
9	EXPENSES					
10						
11	CAR EXPENSES	50	65.1	40.3	55.75	211.15
12	FOOD	204.3	218.85	179.3	192.6	795.05
13	BILLS	65	115	130	165	475
14	ENTERTAINMENT	90	50	26.6	147.75	314.35
15	BANK SAVINGS	200	200	200	200	800
16	MORTGAGE	252.75	252.75	252.75	252.75	1011
17	MISC.	25	0	20	50	95
18						
19						
20	TOTAL EXPENSES	887.05	901.7	848.95	1063.85	3701.55
21	CLOSING BAL.	1212.95	1461.25	1750.3	1848.45	

1. Setting up the spreadsheet

In this example, column A contains labels that explain the contents of rows 4 to 21. The labels WEEK 1, etc. are column headings that identify which week the figures in the columns relate to.

The width of column A will have to be changed to accommodate the labels in it. This is done by giving the appropriate command or by moving the dividing line between two columns with the mouse pointer. Here the width is changed from the default setting of nine characters to eighteen characters wide. On most spreadsheets it is possible to change all or just one column width.

The labels in the example would be typed into the blank sheet first. Formulae will be used to calculate totals and closing and opening balances. The information on income and expenses would then be typed in each week.

The opening balance in week 1 is any spare money we have. For the other weeks it is the difference between the total we receive in a week and the total expenses, i.e. the previous week's closing balance.

2. Entering formulae

The TOTAL MONEY is the opening balance plus net wages (wages after tax). The formula in B7 would therefore be +B4+B5. (Remember that when a formula is entered in a cell it is the result that is displayed, not the formula.)

To total the expenses we must again use a formula in B20. This would be +B11+B12+B13+B14+B15+B16+B17.

The CLOSING BAL. is the difference between total income and total expenses this week. The formula to be typed in B21 therefore is +B7-B20.

The opening balance for week 2 will be the closing balance for week 1, so in C4 we enter the formula +B21.

For the next three weeks the formulae will be repeated, except for cell references. The formulae for week 2 are:

Cell C4: + B21

Cell C7: + C4 + C5

Cell C20: + C11 + C12 + C13 + C14 + C15 + C16 + C17

Cell C21: + C7 - C20

Similarly the formulae for week 3 will be:

Cell D4: + C21

Cell D7: + D4 + D5

Cell D20: + D11 + D12 + D13 + D14 + D15 + D16 + D17

Cell D21: . . .

Try working out the formulae for week 4 yourself.

Cell E4: . . .

Cell E7: . . .

Cell E20: . . .

Cell E21: . . .

Finally, the totals for the month are entered. The formula for total wages is B5+C5+D5+E5. This will be entered in cell F5. Similarly, the formula for total car expenses will be +B11+C11+D11+E11. This would be entered in cell F11. Try working out the formulae for the following cells:

Cell F12: . . .
Cell F13: . . .
Cell F14: . . .
Cell F15: . . .
Cell F17: . . .
Cell F20: . . .

3. The summation function

You may have noticed that the formulae in cells B20, C20, D20 and E20 are very long. They would be even longer if we had any more expenses.

We can use the summation or total function to add up whole columns or rows of numbers. Instead of typing all the parts of the formula, we only have to type in the first and last cell references. Using Microsoft Excel the formula in cell B20 would be =SUM(B11:B17); in Lotus 1-2-3 it would be @SUM(B11..B17). Similarly the formula in F5(+B5+C5+D5+E5) would be replaced with =SUM(B5:E5) or @SUM(B5..E5). Check your own spreadsheet program for the formula for this function. Write down on a page all the shorter summation formulae required to add up the rows and columns in this example.

Other mathematical functions are available on most spreadsheet programs, e.g. the 'average' function, which will find the mean of a range of numbers. Other mathematical functions available include sin, cos, tan, etc. More advanced financial and statistical functions are available on some spreadsheet programs.

4. Improving the appearance of the spreadsheet

Changing the format of numbers

You will notice that the money amounts in our example are very untidy in appearance. This is because all the numbers do not have the same number of decimal places. For money amounts of course this is usually two. If possible, the euro sign should be displayed in front of the amounts. A special command can be given to change the required range or group of numbers to this style, called 'currency format'.

Aligning the labels

You will also notice that the week labels are not exactly in line with the amounts below them. This is because numbers are automatically displayed **flush right** or aligned on the right (i.e. the last digit is at the extreme right of the cell), whereas text is automatically displayed **flush left** or aligned on the left (i.e. the first character of the label is at the extreme left of the cell). However, it is possible to change the alignment of any cell to flush right, flush left or centred.

Here we will give the command to change the week labels to flush right and change the money amounts to cash format. Our spreadsheet should now look like this:

	A	B	C	D	E	F
1	PERSONAL BUDGET	WEEK 1	WEEK 2	WEEK 3	WEEK 4	TOTAL
2						
3						
4	OPENING BALANCE	€1,000.00	€1,212.95	€1,461.25	€1,750.30	
5	WAGES	€1,100.00	€1,150.00	€1,138.00	€1,162.00	€4,550.00
6						
7	TOTAL MONEY	€2,100.00	€2,362.95	€2,599.25	€2,912.30	
8						
9	EXPENSES					
10						
11	CAR EXPENSES	€50.00	€65.10	€40.30	€55.75	€211.15
12	FOOD	€204.30	€218.85	€179.30	€192.60	€795.05
13	BILLS	€65.00	€115.00	€130.00	€165.00	€475.00
14	ENTERTAINMENT	€90.00	€50.00	€26.60	€147.75	€314.35
15	BANK SAVINGS	€200.00	€200.00	€200.00	€200.00	€800.00
16	MORTGAGE	€252.75	€252.75	€252.75	€252.75	€1,011.00
17	MISC.	€25.00	€0.00	€20.00	€50.00	€95.00
18						
19						
20	TOTAL EXPENSES	€887.05	€901.70	€848.95	€1,063.85	€3,701.55
21	CLOSING BAL.	€1,212.95	€1,461.25	€1,750.30	€1,848.45	

5. Replication

You will have noticed when entering the data in our example that there is a lot of repetitive typing of formulae. If you had to expand the model to accommodate fifty-two weeks, you would be very tired after typing in all the formulae! However, all spreadsheets allow you to 'replicate' or copy formulae or text from one area of the spreadsheet to another.

There are three levels of copying or replicating to begin with: straight copying, range copying and formula copying.

Straight copying

This is where one item (whether a number or label) is copied from one cell to another, and can be used when you want to avoid retyping names or headings. It is done by entering the appropriate command and the identification of the cells you want to copy from ('source cells') and copy to ('target cells').

Range copying

This involves entering the 'source range' of cells to be copied and the 'target range' of cells to be copied to.

Formula copying

There are three types of formula copying: **absolute**, where there is no change in the cell references when copied; **relative**, where the copied formulae change cell references according to their position; and **absolute and relative**, where some cell references in the formula do not change when copied and others do. For example, copying down a column:

ABSOLUTE	RELATIVE	ABSOLUTE-RELATIVE	RELATIVE-ABSOLUTE
A1*B1	A1*B1	A1*B1	A1*B1
A1*B1	A2*B2	A1*B2	A2*B1
A1*B1	A3*B3	A1*B3	A3*B1
A1*B1	A4*B4	A1*B4	A4*B1
A1*B1	A5*B5	A1*B5	A5*B1

(The formula to be copied is the first one in each column. Notice that only the row numbers change by one when copying relative cell references down a column.)

Copying across rows:

Absolute	A1*B1	A1*B1	A1*B1	A1*B1
Relative	A1*B1	B1*C1	C1*D1	D1*E1
Absolute-relative	A1*B1	A1*C1	A1*D1	A1*E1
Relative-absolute	A1*B1	B1*B1	C1*B1	D1*B1

(The formula to be copied is the first one in each row. Notice that only the column letter changes by one when copying relative cell references across a row.)

In the personal budget example above we could have copied most of our formulae. We could have typed the formula +B4+B5 in B7, then copied it across to C7, D7 and E7 using relative cell references, so that each cell reference would change across the row. This would be done by identifying B7 as the cell to copy from and the range C7 to E7 as the range to copy to.

If we were to copy B7 using absolute cell references or a combination of absolute and relative cell references, we would get incorrect totals. The results from the different alternatives would be:

COPY	FROM B7	TO C7	TO D7	TO E7
Absolute	=B4+B5	=B4+B5	=B4+B5	=B4+B5
Relative	=B4+B5	=C4+C5	=D4+D5	=E4+E5
Absolute-relative	=B4+B5	=B4+C5	=B4+D5	=B4+E5
Relative-absolute	=B4+B5	=C4+B5	=D4+B5	€2,850.30
Results	B7	C7	D7	E7
Absolute	2,100.00	2,100.00	2,100.00	2,100.00
Relative	2,100.00	2,362.95	2,599.25	2,912.30
Absolute-relative	2,100.00	2,150.00	2,138.00	2,162.00
Relative-absolute	2,100.00	2,312.95	2,561.25	2,850.30

Replication could also be used for the formulae in rows 20 and 21. For row 20 we would copy the formula from cell B20 to the cells in the range C20 to F20, using relative cell references. In the same way we would copy the formula in cell B21 (+B7-B20) to the cells in the range C21 to E21.

Copying with relative cell references could also be used for the formulae in column F, from cell F11 to the cells in the range F12 to F16.

◪ The importance of replication

It is the replication function that gives the computer spreadsheet its real power. Once the core or original formulae have been entered, it is only a matter of replicating them as far as the memory of your computer will allow. Spreadsheets can be constructed very quickly and easily using replication, which is their main advantage over manual systems. In our example we could expand the model to cover fifty-two weeks by simple replication of the formulae: no new formulae would need to be typed in.

6. Editing the spreadsheet

◪ Simple editing

If we want to change any information on the spreadsheet, we simply type over it or use the editing facility to insert or delete some characters. In this example we want to change the contents of cell A5 to read NET WAGES instead of WAGES. We will use the editing facility, type the word NET and then press [enter].

◤Inserting rows or columns

In our example we might decide to enter a blank row in row 9 to separate the expenses more clearly from other data on the sheet. To do this we use the appropriate command for inserting a row. The result will be that the present contents of row 9 will move down one row; all subsequent rows will also move down one row.

When we do this the computer automatically changes all formulae that are affected by the move. The formula for total expenses will change from @SUM(B11..B16) to @SUM(B12..B17), while the formula to calculate the closing balance will change from +B21 to +B22. In fact, most of the formulae in the spreadsheet will change because of the insertion of the row.

If we insert a new column, the information is moved across to the right, and again any formulae that are affected will change automatically.

Our spreadsheet will look like this after these two changes have been carried out:

	A	B	C	D	E	F
1	PERSONAL BUDGET	WEEK 1	WEEK 2	WEEK 3	WEEK 4	TOTAL
2						
3						
4	OPENING BALANCE	€1,000.00	€1,212.95	€1,461.25	€1,750.30	
5	NET WAGES	€1,100.00	€1,150.00	€1,138.00	€1,162.00	€4,550.00
6						
7	TOTAL MONEY	€2,100.00	€2,362.95	€2,599.25	€2,912.30	
8						
9						
10	EXPENSES					
11						
12	CAR EXPENSES	€50.00	€65.10	€40.30	€55.75	€211.15
13	FOOD	€204.30	€218.85	€179.30	€192.60	€795.05
14	BILLS	€65.00	€115.00	€130.00	€165.00	€475.00
15	ENTERTAINMENT	€90.00	€50.00	€26.60	€147.75	€314.35
16	BANK SAVINGS	€200.00	€200.00	€200.00	€200.00	€800.00
17	MORTGAGE	€252.75	€252.75	€252.75	€252.75	€1,011.00
18	MISC.	€25.00	€0.00	€20.00	€50.00	€95.00
19						
20						
21	TOTAL EXPENSES	€887.05	€901.70	€848.95	€1,063.85	€3,701.55
22	CLOSING BAL.	€1,212.95	€1,461.25	€1,750.30	€1,848.45	

Perhaps we forgot to include some expenses. In that case we would need to insert a new row and heading containing the new information. Let us say the forgotten expense was pocket money of €5 a week given to one of the children, and the information is to be inserted after the food expense. When this row is inserted, the formulae and amounts will change automatically to reflect this: for example, the total expenses formula for week 1 will now be @SUM(B12..B19).

The spreadsheet will look like this after inserting the new pocket money row:

	A	B	C	D	E	F
1	PERSONAL BUDGET	WEEK 1	WEEK 2	WEEK 3	WEEK 4	TOTAL
2						
3						
4	OPENING BALANCE	€1,000.00	€1,207.95	€1,451.25	€1,735.30	
5	NET WAGES	€1,100.00	€1,150.00	€1,138.00	€1,162.00	€4,550.00
6						
7	TOTAL MONEY	€2,100.00	€2,357.95	€2,589.25	€2,897.30	
8						
9						
10	EXPENSES					
11						
12	CAR EXPENSES	€50.00	€65.10	€40.30	€55.75	€211.15
13	FOOD	€204.30	€218.85	€179.30	€192.60	€795.05
14	POCKET MONEY	€5.00	€5.00	€5.00	€5.00	€20.00
15	BILLS	€65.00	€115.00	€130.00	€165.00	€475.00
16	ENTERTAINMENT	€90.00	€50.00	€26.60	€147.75	€314.35
17	BANK SAVINGS	€200.00	€200.00	€200.00	€200.00	€800.00
18	MORTGAGE	€252.75	€252.75	€252.75	€252.75	€1,011.00
19	MISC.	€25.00	€0.00	€20.00	€50.00	€95.00
20						
21						
22	TOTAL EXPENSES	€892.05	€906.70	€853.95	€1,068.85	€3,721.55
23	CLOSING BAL.	€1,207.95	€1,451.25	€1,735.30	€1,828.45	

7. Considering 'what if?' situations

When the spreadsheet is set up we can experiment with the data to consider the effect of different figure or policy changes. These are called 'what if?' calculations.

In the example above we could ask ourselves, what if we decided not to bring the car to work? This would mean we would only spend €20 a week on car expenses. All we would need to do is type over the amounts in the car expenses row with the new amount, €20. All the totals will be recalculated for us. Note the saving on the weekly balances.

Any number in the spreadsheet can be changed to see what effect it might have on our total budget. On a more complex example involving many thousands of calculations, this ability to recalculate is invaluable for decision-making.

Our spreadsheet will look like this after the car expenses are changed:

	A	B	C	D	E	F
		WEEK 1	WEEK 2	WEEK 3	WEEK 4	TOTAL
1	PERSONAL BUDGET	WEEK 1	WEEK 2	WEEK 3	WEEK 4	TOTAL
2						
3						
4	OPENING BALANCE	€1,000.00	€1,237.95	€1,526.35	€1,830.70	
5	NET WAGES	€1,100.00	€1,150.00	€1,138.00	€1,162.00	€4,550.00
6						
7	TOTAL MONEY	€2,100.00	€2,387.95	€2,664.35	€2,992.70	
8						
9						
10	EXPENSES					
11						
12	CAR EXPENSES	€20.00	€20.00	€20.00	€20.00	€80.00
13	FOOD	€204.30	€218.85	€179.30	€192.60	€795.05
14	POCKET MONEY	€5.00	€5.00	€5.00	€5.00	€20.00
15	BILLS	€65.00	€115.00	€130.00	€165.00	€475.00
16	ENTERTAINMENT	€90.00	€50.00	€26.60	€147.75	€314.35
17	BANK SAVINGS	€200.00	€200.00	€200.00	€200.00	€800.00
18	MORTGAGE	€252.75	€252.75	€252.75	€252.75	€1,011.00
19	MISC.	€25.00	€0.00	€20.00	€50.00	€95.00
20						
21						
22	TOTAL EXPENSES	€862.05	€861.60	€833.65	€1,033.10	€3,590.40
23	CLOSING BAL.	€1,237.95	€1,526.35	€1,830.70	€1,959.60	

8. The 'logical if' function

Is the profit this year greater than last year? Has the aeroplane been overloaded with luggage? The answers to these questions are either true or false. These are considered logical questions, i.e. those having true or false answers.

Most spreadsheet programs allow you to employ a formula to ask a question and generate a true or false response. The general pattern this formula takes is:

If (condition, true response, false response)

The function is very similar to the IF-THEN-ELSE command found in most programming languages.

In the example above we could get the computer to make a decision for us. For weeks 2, 3 and 4 we decided to save money based on the following criterion: *If the expenses of the previous week are less than €850, then we will save €200 for this particular week; otherwise we will not save anything for the week*. The first week's saving is entered as normal in cell B17, but the following formula is entered in cell C17 for week 2:

@IF(B22<850, 200,0) – Lotus 1-2-3 or =IF(B22<850,200,0) – Microsoft Excel

The formula can then be copied across the row for cells D17 and E17, using relative cell references. The spreadsheet will now look like this:

	A	B	C	D	E	F
1	PERSONAL BUDGET	WEEK 1	WEEK 2	WEEK 3	WEEK 4	TOTAL
2						
3						
4	OPENING BALANCE	€1,000.00	€1,237.95	€1,726.35	€2,030.70	
5	NET WAGES	€1,100.00	€1,150.00	€1,138.00	€1,162.00	€4,550.00
6						
7	TOTAL MONEY	€2,100.00	€2,387.95	€2,864.35	€3,192.70	
8						
9						
10	EXPENSES					
11						
12	CAR EXPENSES	€20.00	€20.00	€20.00	€20.00	€80.00
13	FOOD	€204.30	€218.85	€179.30	€192.60	€795.05
14	POCKET MONEY	€5.00	€5.00	€5.00	€5.00	€20.00
15	BILLS	€65.00	€115.00	€130.00	€165.00	€475.00
16	ENTERTAINMENT	€90.00	€50.00	€26.60	€147.75	€314.35
17	BANK SAVINGS	€200.00	€0.00	€200.00	€200.00	€600.00
18	MORTGAGE	€252.75	€252.75	€252.75	€252.75	€1,011.00
19	MISC.	€25.00	€0.00	€20.00	€50.00	€95.00
20						
21						
22	TOTAL EXPENSES	€862.05	€661.60	€833.65	€1,033.10	€3,390.40
23	CLOSING BAL.	€1,237.95	€1,726.35	€2,030.70	€2,159.60	

Notice that cell C17 now contains €0.00 as no money was saved in week 2 due to the fact that the expenses for week 1 (cell B22) were greater than €850. However, the savings for weeks 3 and 4 in cells D17 and E17 show €200, meaning that the expenses for the previous week in each case, i.e. cells C22 and D22, were less than €850. The expenses for week 4 (E22) exceed €850, so if the criterion was applied to week 5, no savings would take place in week 5.

'What if?' again
We could then ask the question, what would the situation be if we used the car again for work, but this time making use of the new saving policy? We would only have to change all car expense amounts back to the original figures: all the other calculations will be done for us, including the amount we would save each week. (Note that we will save nothing on the second and fourth weeks.)

	A	B	C	E	F	G
1	PERSONAL BUDGET	WEEK 1	WEEK 2	WEEK 3	WEEK 4	TOTAL
2						
3						
4	OPENING BALANCE	€1,000.00	€1,207.95	€1,651.25	€1,935.30	
5	NET WAGES	€1,100.00	€1,150.00	€1,138.00	€1,162.00	€4,550.00
6						
7	TOTAL MONEY	€2,100.00	€2,357.95	€2,789.25	€3,097.30	
8						
9						
10	EXPENSES					
11						
12	CAR EXPENSES	€50.00	€65.10	€40.30	€55.75	€211.15
13	FOOD	€204.30	€218.85	€179.30	€192.60	€795.05
14	POCKET MONEY	€5.00	€5.00	€5.00	€5.00	€20.00
15	BILLS	€65.00	€115.00	€130.00	€165.00	€475.00
16	ENTERTAINMENT	€90.00	€50.00	€26.60	€147.75	€314.35
17	BANK SAVINGS	€200.00	€0.00	€200.00	€0.00	€400.00
18	MORTGAGE	€252.75	€252.75	€252.75	€252.75	€1,011.00
19	MISC.	€25.00	€0.00	€20.00	€50.00	€95.00
20						
21						
22	TOTAL EXPENSES	€892.05	€706.70	€853.95	€868.85	€3,321.55
23	CLOSING BAL.	€1,207.95	€1,651.25	€1,935.30	€2,228.45	

9. Other facilities

Most spreadsheet programs have several other useful features, which we can use to make this application work more effectively.

◤ Quick cursor movement

It is possible on most spreadsheets to move directly to another cell. This is done by clicking on the cell or giving a command or using a function key. The name of the desired cell is requested and the cursor moves directly to that cell. This facility is very useful when using a very large spreadsheet.

Non-scrolling titles

Selected rows and columns can be fixed on the screen so that they do not scroll off when we move to another part of the spreadsheet. If we had the budget information for fifty-two weeks in our sample spreadsheet, we might need to fix column A so that the labels for each expense would be on display permanently as we go from column to column.

Printing part or all of the spreadsheet

Large spreadsheets can be printed on several sheets and the parts joined together. Selected parts of the spreadsheet can also be printed.

Only columns A and F in the example above might be required on paper, so that the total amount for each expense could be noted separately. This would require 'hiding' columns B through E. This would be displayed as follows:

	A	F
1	PERSONAL BUDGET	TOTAL
2		
3		
4	OPENING BALANCE	
5	NET WAGES	€4,550.00
6		
7	TOTAL MONEY	
8		
9		
10	EXPENSES	
11		
12	CAR EXPENSES	€211.15
13	FOOD	€795.05
14	POCKET MONEY	€20.00
15	BILLS	€475.00
16	ENTERTAINMENT	€314.35
17	BANK SAVINGS	€400.00
18	MORTGAGE	€1,011.00
19	MISC.	€95.00
20		
21		
22	TOTAL EXPENSES	€3,321.55
23	CLOSING BAL.	

Turning off automatic recalculation

When a new number is typed into a spreadsheet, the computer automatically recalculates all other cells affected by this change. But recalculation can take a considerable time on small computers. It is possible to turn off automatic recalculation until all changes have been made; then a command can be entered to recalculate.

Using the 'look-up' function

A range of cells that have codes and corresponding values in them can be searched with the 'look-up' function. This will return a value that relates to the code requested. This function is often used to produce invoices, where product codes are entered and the price per unit is 'looked up' by the computer.

Summary of the standard facilities of a spreadsheet program

- The cursor can be moved quickly to anywhere in the spreadsheet
- Rows and columns can be inserted in existing spreadsheets
- Rows and columns and ranges of data can be deleted
- Cell display can be changed to show different formats
- Single items or ranges of data can be copied
- Formulae can be copied or replicated
- Mathematical functions are available, e.g. sum, average, sin, cos, tan (on some spreadsheets other functions are available, such as financial and statistical functions)
- Editing facilities are available, both while information is being typed in and afterwards
- Column widths can be changed
- Data can be stored for later retrieval
- Part or all of the spreadsheet can be printed
- Logical decisions can be made on data using the 'if' function
- Coded data can be looked up using the 'look-up' function
- Non-scrolling rows and columns can be fixed on the screen when more than one screen of data is used
- Data in the spreadsheet can be protected to prevent further changes
- Some spreadsheets allow integration or links with other types of program, such as graphics and word-processor programs.

Creating a spreadsheet

Before typing in a spreadsheet, you should plan what you want to do. This will involve some of the following decisions:

1. What title will I give the spreadsheet?
2. What headings will I use for the rows and columns? These should be concise but descriptive.
3. Will I need to increase or decrease the width of a column, and by how much?
4. Which of the items will be labels and which values?

5. Where will I use a formula, and can I use a built-in function?
6. Can I replicate this formula? If so, will it be relative, absolute or a combination?
7. Should the data be displayed in a special format, e.g. currancy format, and where?
8. What file name will I use for the spreadsheet? This name will have to be concise but should remind you of the contents of the spreadsheet when retrieving it later.

⊞ Example 2

A more complex spreadsheet.

A small airline operates a twelve-seater aeroplane between Dublin and Knock. It wants to store passenger information on a spreadsheet. The following conditions apply:
1. The basic price of a ticket is €50.
2. There is VAT at 21 per cent on the basic price of all tickets (excluding discount).
3. There is a 10 per cent discount on the basic price of all tickets for children under twelve.
4. A passenger is charged an extra €1 for every 1 kg over the 20 kg luggage allowance. No VAT is charged on this extra charge.

The only items to be typed in are the passenger information and the standard data such as ticket price, penalty charge, etc. All other figures are to be automatically calculated by the spreadsheet through the use of formulae.

Questions

1. Set up a spreadsheet for a particular flight, including the following passenger information:

SEAT NO.	NAME	AGE	LUGGAGE (KG)
1	Brendan Bradley	45	17
2	Ciarán Collins	5	7
3	Denis Collins	11	9
4	Martin Collins	26	23
5	Aisling Doyle	42	18
6	Kevin Geraghty	7	14
7	Paul Hillery	35	21
8	Brian Laffey	17	16
9	Sean Byrne	27	10
10	Bernadette Ryan	10	20
11	Sheila Ryan	24	17
12	Deirdre WhITE	33	4

2. Use appropriate formulae and replication to show the ticket price discount, VAT and baggage penalty for each passenger. Use suitable headings.

3. Save the spreadsheet as AIR.

4. Produce a print-out of the entire spreadsheet.

◣Solution

Decide on the following before typing in data:

1. The title: KNOCK AIRLINES. This will be put into cells A1 and B1.

2. The following row headings will be used for the standard data in cells A2 to A5. Column A must be eleven characters wide. The figures will be put opposite this information in cells B2 to B5.

PRICE	50
VAT	21%
DISCOUNT	10%
PENALTY	1

3. Column headings will be needed for the following: SEAT NO., NAME [fifteen characters wide], AGE, PRICE, DISCOUNT, PRICE LESS DISCOUNT, VAT, PENALTY and TOTAL PRICE. The spreadsheet should now look like this:

	A	B	C	D	E	F	G	H	I	J
1	KNOCK AIRLINES									
2	PRICE	50								
3	VAT	21%								
4	DISCOUNT	1%								
5	PENALTY	1								
6										
7										
8	SEAT NO.	NAME	AGE	LUGGAGE	PRICE	DISCOUNT	PRICE-DIS.	VAT	PENALTY	TOTAL PRICE
9										
10	1	B BRADLEY	45	17						
11	2	C COLLINS	5	7						
12	3	D COLLINS	11	9						
13	4	M COLLINS	26	23						
14	5	A DOYLE	42	18						
15	6	K GERAGHTY	7	14						
16	7	P HILLERY	35	21						
17	8	B LAFFEY	17	16						
18	9	S BYRNE	27	10						
19	10	B RYAN	10	20						
20	11	S RYAN	24	17						
21	12	D WHITE	33	4						

4. Align all headings flush right.

5. All money amounts should be changed to currency format.

6. Decide on formulae. These will be:

E10: +B2. This must be copied down the column, using an absolute cell reference, as everybody has the same basic ticket price before other considerations are taken into account.

F:10 =IF(C10<12, E10*B4,0) – Microsoft Excel. All parts of this formula will be copied, using relative cell references, except B4, which should remain absolute down the column. (Note: B4 is an absolute cell reference in Excel.)

G10: +E10-F10. This will be copied down the column, using relative cell references. The formula simply subtracts the discount (if any) from the price.

H10: +G10*B3. G10 will be relative and B3 will be absolute when copied, as the VAT rate remains 21 per cent for all tickets.

I10: =IF(D10>20,(D10-20)*B5,0). All will have relative cell references, except B5 (the penalty amount, €1), which should be absolute. (D10-20) calculates the number of kilograms over the 20 kg limit.

J10: +G10+H10+I10. This gives the total price and should be copied using relative cell references. It includes the discounted price plus the VAT and penalty charge (if any).

The final spreadsheet should look like the following after the editing and copying discussed above:

	A	B	C	D	E	F	G	H	I	J
1	KNOCK AIRLINES									
2	PRICE	50								
3	VAT	21%								
4	DISCOUNT	1%								
5	PENALTY	1								
6										
7										
8	SEAT NO.	NAME	AGE	LUGGAGE	PRICE	DISCOUNT	PRICE-DIS.	VAT	PENALTY	TOTAL PRICE
9										
10	1	B BRADLEY	45	17	€50.00	€0.00	€50.00	€10.50	€0.00	€60.50
11	2	C COLLINS	5	7	€50.00	€5.00	€45.00	€9.45	€0.00	€54.45
12	3	D COLLINS	11	9	€50.00	€5.00	€45.00	€9.45	€0.00	€54.45
13	4	M COLLINS	26	23	€50.00	€0.00	€50.00	€10.50	€3.00	€63.50
14	5	A DOYLE	42	18	€50.00	€0.00	€50.00	€10.50	€0.00	€60.50
15	6	K GERAGHTY	7	14	€50.00	€5.00	€45.00	€9.45	€0.00	€54.45
16	7	P HILLERY	35	21	€50.00	€0.00	€50.00	€10.50	€1.00	€61.50
17	8	B LAFFEY	17	16	€50.00	€0.00	€50.00	€10.50	€0.00	€60.50
18	9	S BYRNE	27	10	€50.00	€0.00	€50.00	€10.50	€0.00	€60.50
19	10	B RYAN	10	20	€50.00	€5.00	€45.00	€9.45	€0.00	€54.45
20	11	S RYAN	24	17	€50.00	€0.00	€50.00	€10.50	€0.00	€60.50
21	12	D WHITE	33	4	€50.00	€0.00	€50.00	€10.50	€0.00	€60.50

This spreadsheet could be used again and again by the airline. The person operating the spreadsheet would enter the standard information, including name, age and weight of luggage, and all other figures would be calculated automatically.

Also, the formulae would not need to be changed when ticket prices and other variables changed. For example, if the rate of VAT were to change, the operator would only have to change the actual rate in cell B4: no formulae would need to be altered.

▦ Graphing the data

Most spreadsheet programs allow users to present numerical data on a spreadsheet in graph form.

▦ Example 3

There are currently 402 students enrolled at Leeside College. The following table shows the numbers of students taking the various courses offered at the college:

COURSE	NUMBER
Accounting	62
Catering	98
Computing	75
Hairdressing	46
Marketing	37
Secretarial	84

The bar graph

Peter Connolly, the college principal, has asked us to produce a bar graph of the data shown in the table. We follow these steps:

1. Enter the data onto a spreadsheet.
2. Select the cells containing the data.
3. Choose the **Create Chart/Graph** command or icon.
4. Indicate where the graph should appear on the spreadsheet.
5. Specify the graph type (bar).
6. Add a graph title.
7. Add labels for the x and y axes.

   The bar graph should appear as follows:

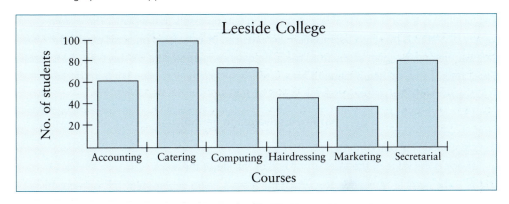

If the data to be graphed is changed, the bar graph will automatically reflect the changes.

The pie graph

In a similar manner, we can produce a pie graph to show the percentage of students taking each course. No axes labels are required. We have, however, included a graph title and a legend; the latter is a key that identifies the items shown on the graph by colour, hatch pattern or symbol.

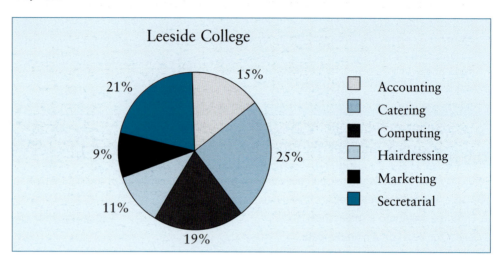

▦ Financial matters

Depreciation

Depreciation is the cost to a business of wear and tear on assets that it owns. There are a variety of methods by which depreciation amounts can be calculated on items purchased. One popular method is known as the fixed-declining balance method. The DB function, in Microsoft Excel, returns the real depreciation of an asset for a specific period using the fixed-declining balance method. The syntax of the function is as follows:

$$=DB(cost,salvage,life,period)$$

1. *Cost* is the initial cost of the asset.
2. *Salvage* is the value of the asset at the end of the life of the asset.
3. *Life* is the number of periods over which the asset is being depreciated. This is frequently known as the useful life of the asset.
4. *Period* is the period for which you want to calculate the depreciation. It must be in the same units as life (e.g. years).

▦ Example 4

Conor Lawlor has just purchased a new car costing €40,000. The estimated life of the car is
twelve years. It has been decided that the salvage value of the car in twelve years' time will
only be €5,000. Conor asked us to produce a spreadsheet to show the depreciation on the car
at the end of each year for the first ten years. The completed spreadsheet appears as follows:

	A	B
1	Depreciation Analysis	
2		
3	Item Purchased =	Car
4	Estimated Life (yrs) =	12
5	Initial Cost =	€40,000.00
6	Salvage Value =	€5,000.00
7		
8	Year	Depreciation
9		Amount
10	1	€6,360.00
11	2	€5,348.76
12	3	€4,498.31
13	4	€3,783.08
14	5	€3,181.57
15	6	€2,675.70
16	7	€2,250.26
17	8	€1,892.47
18	9	€1,591.57
19	10	€1,338.51

The depreciation amounts displayed in column B were obtained as follows:
(a) The formula, =DB(B5,B6,B4,A10), was entered in cell B10.
(b) It was then copied into the range of cells B11:B19.
(c) Notice that the heading 'Depreciation Analysis' has been increased in size and centre
   aligned across cells A1 and B1.

Loan repayments

Lending agencies frequently use spreadsheets to calculate loan repayments. The PMT function,
available on most spreadsheet programs, returns the payment for an investment based on
periodic, constant payments and a constant interest rate.

The syntax of this function in Microsoft Excel is:

=PMT(rate,nper,-pv)

1. *rate* is the loan interest rate
2. *nper* is the number of payment periods
3. *pv* is the loan amount.

   Make sure that you are consistent about the units you use for specifying *rate* and *nper*. If *rate* is per year then *PMT* returns the number of payments per year and *nper* is the number of years.

Example 5

Patricia O'Leary wishes to borrow €30,000 from the EasyLoan Building Society. Patricia asked us to produce a spreadsheet showing the monthly repayments over the twenty-five year term of the loan for four different interest rates (7%, 8%, 9% and 10%). Our completed spreadsheet is now shown:

	A	B
1	Loan Repayments	
2		
3	Years =	25
4	Months =	300
5	Loan =	€30,000.00
6		
7	Interest	Monthly
8	Rate	Repayment
9	7%	€212.03
10	8%	€231.54
11	9%	€251.76
12	10%	€272.61

   The monthly repayment amounts displayed in column B were obtained as follows:
(a) The formula, *=PMT(A9/12,B4,-B5)*, was entered in cell B9.
(b) It was then copied into the range of cells B10:B12.
   As the monthly repayments were required, the rate (i.e. the contents of cell *A9*) was divided by twelve to maintain consistency with the number of repayment periods (i.e. the contents of cell *B4*).

Investment venture

Investors must frequently decide between investing in new ventures or leaving the money on deposit in the bank or building society. A measure of the potential of an investment venture is to compare the projected income with bank interest earnings. Current spreadsheet programs offer the user an efficient means of making this comparison through the use of the net present value (NPV) function.

The syntax of this function in Microsoft Excel is:

$$=NPV(rate, range\ of\ values)$$

The function returns the net present value of an investment based on a series of periodic cashflows, *range of values* and a discount rate equal to *rate*. The cashflow periods must be equally spaced in time.

▦ Example 6

Gerard Clarke, the owner of Breffni Farm Machinery Ltd, is considering investing €1 million in his business. This amount of money must be invested in full at the outset. The projected sales from it are expected to last from 2007 to 2010 inclusive. The corresponding sales for each successive year are €300,000, €500,000, €900,000 and €1,200,000. The Thrifty Building Society, however, are offering 15% interest on all deposits over €750,000. Gerard has asked us to advise him on whether he should go ahead with the venture or simply deposit the money with the building society. We have produced the following spreadsheet to aid Gerard in his decision:

	A	B	C	D	E
1	Farm Machinery Ltd				
2					
3	Projected Sales				
4					
5	Investment	2007	2008	2009	2010
6	€1,000,000.00	€300,000.00	€500,000.00	€900,000.00	€1,200,000.00
7					
8	Interest Rate Given =	15%			
9					
10	Net Present Value =	€1,916,809.90			
11	Bank Savings Return =	€1,749,006.25			

The initial investment and the current interest rate are displayed in cells A6 and B8, respectively. The projected incomes from sales over the four-year period have been entered in the range of cells B6:E6.

The net present value, displayed in cell B10, was obtained by entering the formula: *=NPV(B8,B6:E6)*. The bank savings return, displayed in cell B11, was obtained by entering the formula *=A6*1.15^4* (the initial investment plus the compound interest earned). The spreadsheet shows that the return on the investment venture would be better than the deposit earnings at the building society in this particular case.

▦ Using macros

Macro basics

A macro is a sequence of specially phrased instructions which, when executed, will accomplish a specific task or set of tasks. Macros are frequently used to automate tedious and time-consuming work. A macro is normally assigned a name and a short-cut key; when either is invoked (called upon), the macro is executed.

Let us say that we wish to alter a numeric display in a cell on a Microsoft Excel spreadsheet to currency format. We would follow these steps:

1. Place the cell pointer in the appropriate cell
2. Choose the *Number* option from the *Format* menu
3. Select *Currency* from the category list presented
4. Choose the exact currency format required.

A macro to automate this procedure, when produced, would appear as follows:

MACRO	COMMENT
Money (m)	Macro name and key
=FORMAT.NUMBER("€0.00")	Change to currency format
=RETURN()	End of macro

The macro is executed by pressing CRTL+m (Windows version).

Creating a macro

Most current spreadsheet programs offer the user two methods by which a macro can be created:

(a) building a macro manually
(b) recording a macro.

Building a macro manually

The processing of building a macro manually can normally be broken down into six separate stages:

1. Planning
2. Entering
3. Documenting
4. Naming
5. Executing
6. Saving.

An editing stage may also be required if the macro is not executing properly.

▦ Example 7

The Adair Arms Hotel offers excellent accommodation to visitors. Each week Karen O'Brien, the hotel manageress, produces a Visitor Category Card using the spreadsheet program on her computer. A completed card is shown below:

A	B	C
Adair Arms Hotel		
Guest Category		
	Home	Foreign
Business	27	8
Holiday	31	62
Other	23	11

We will now create a macro, using Microsoft Excel, to produce a template based on the above table. When the macro is executed, the following details should appear on the spreadsheet:

	A	B	C
1	Adair Arms Hotel		
2			
3	Guest Category		
4		Irish National	Non-Irish National
5	Business		
6	Holiday		
7	Other		

Planning

The following fifteen instructions will go to make up the macro:

NUMBER	INSTRUCTION REQUIRED
1	Move the cell pointer to cell A1
2	Enter "Adair Arms Hotel"
3	Move the cell pointer to cell A3
4	Enter "Guest Category"
5	Move the cell pointer to cell A5
6	Enter "Business"
7	Move the cell pointer to cell A6
8	Enter "Tourism"
9	Move the cell pointer to cell A7
10	Enter "Other"
11	Move the cell pointer to cell B4
12	Enter "Irish National"
13	Move the cell pointer to cell C4
14	Enter "non-Irish National"
15	End macro

Entering

Each of the instructions outlined above should have a corresponding macro instruction. The instructions must be entered, using the appropriate syntax, onto a Microsoft Excel macro sheet. The macro sheet is almost identical in appearance to a spreadsheet. The default column widths, however, are a little wider on a macro sheet than those on a spreadsheet.

Documenting

Documenting a macro involves adding comments to explain its purpose and/or its mode of execution. These comments are essential for anyone using a macro that was created by someone else.

Naming

The macro is then assigned a name and/or key. Microsoft Excel users place the name and key in the cell above the first macro instruction. The precise command is then given to associate the macro name and key with the list of instructions. We will assign 'template' and 't' as the name and key of our macro.

Our completed macro should appear as follows:

```
Macro                              Comments

template (t)                       Macro name and key
=SELECT(!A1)
=FORMULA("Adair Arms Hotel")       This macro creates a data entry template for the
=SELECT(!A3)                       Adair Arms Hotel to show the number of
=FORMULA("Guest Category")         home and foreign guests in each guest
=SELECT(!A5)                       category who stayed at the hotel.
=FORMULA("Business")
=SELECT(!A6)
=FORMULA("Tourism")
=SELECT(!A7)
=FORMULA("Other")
=SELECT(!B4)
=FORMULA("Irish National")
=SELECT(!C4)
=FORMULA("non-Irish National")
=RETURN()
```

Executing

When the macro name or key is invoked, the macro instructions are carried out. Our macro may be executed by pressing the 'CTRL' and 't' keys simultaneously.

Saving

Most current spreadsheet programs allow users to save new macros to a central macro library. This means that a macro originally produced for application on a particular spreadsheet may be used while working on other spreadsheets.

Recording a macro

Macros can also be produced by using the macro recording facility of a spreadsheet program. This facility allows the user to record keystrokes and mouse selections as macro instructions. The latter can then be assigned a name and/or key and can be executed as a macro. Creating macros in this way has a number of advantages:

- it is less time consuming
- the macros are error-free
- complex macros can be produced by novices.

Interactive macros

Interactive macros pause during execution and allow the user to enter input before execution resumes.

▦ Example 8

We will now create an interactive macro to convert any number of inches to centimetres. The macro will pause during execution and allow the user to enter the number of inches.

- Measurements required: 1 inch = 2.54 centimetres

Our macro will consist of twelve instructions:

NUMBER	INSTRUCTION REQUIRED
1	Move the cell pointer to the A1 cell
2	Enter "Length Conversion"
3	Move the cell pointer to the A3 cell
4	Enter "Inches ="
5	Move the cell pointer to the B3 cell
6	Pause for input
7	Move the cell pointer to the C3 cell
8	Enter "Centimetres ="
9	Widen column C to 13 to fit the label 'Centimetres ='
10	Move the cell pointer to the D3 cell
11	Enter a formula to multiply the contents of cell B3 by 2.54
12	End the macro

A fully documented macro, in Microsoft Excel, to carry out the instructions above should appear as follows:

Macro	Comments
Length (l)	**Macro name and key**
=SELECT(!A1)	
=FORMULA("'Length Conversion")	This macro converts any number of inches
=SELECT(!A3)	to the equivalent number of centimetres.
=FORMULA("Inches =")	
=SELECT(!B3)	
=FORMULA(**INPUT("",1)**)	The highlighted instruction pauses execution
=SELECT(!C3)	of the macro and 'expects' input.
=FORMULA("'Centimetres =")	
=COLUMN.WIDTH(13)	
=SELECT(!D3)	
=FORMULA(!B3*2.54)	
=RETURN()	

▦ Conclusion

Spreadsheets are extremely powerful and useful analytical tools. They are used by people in many different occupations, including accountants, statisticians, engineers and scientists. They are easy to use, and complex spreadsheets can be constructed quickly by using replication and the many built-in functions and facilities we have discussed.

In the next chapter you will have an opportunity to practise using spreadsheets by working through the different assignments.

▦ Glossary of spreadsheet terms

absolute cell reference: a cell reference that does not adjust or change when a formula is copied to another cell.

alignment: the cell formatting function that controls the position of labels within a cell.

automatic recalculation mode: a feature whereby cell values are recalculated every time any cell relating to those values is changed.

block: a series of adjacent cells manipulated as an entity; also called a 'range'.

built-in functions: ready-to-use formulae that perform mathematical, statistical and logical calculations, e.g. the summation function.

currency format: a value format in which a number is displayed with two decimal places and usually with a euro sign and thousand markers.

cell: a rectangle formed by the intersection of a row and a column and in which numbers, labels and formulae can be entered and edited.

cell address: a code used to identify a cell by specifying the row and column, e.g. B34.

cell format: the way in which values and labels are displayed in a cell; the more common formats for numbers include integer format, currency format and exponent format; common formats for labels are flush right, flush left and centred.

cell pointer: a rectangular highlight that indicates the current cell, in the same way that the cursor indicates the current position in text.

cell reference: a cell address when used in a formula, e.g. A1 and A10 in the formula @SUM(A1..A10).

cell type: the classification of a cell according to whether it contains a label, a value or a formula.

centred: a label format in which the text is halfway between the left and right edges of the column.

column: a vertical series of cells running the full length of the spreadsheet, and usually identified by a letter or letters.

exponent format: a value format in which a number is displayed in the form of a real number between 1 and 9 multiplied by 10 to the power of the appropriate integer.

flush left: a label format in which the text is aligned with the left-hand edge of the column.

flush right: a label format in which the text is aligned with the right-hand edge of the column.

formula: an algebraic expression that defines the relationship between two or more values, using cell references to represent the values or formulae they contain, e.g. +A2+B7.

integer format: a value format in which a number has no decimal fraction.

label: any non-numeric data in the spreadsheet.

non-scrolling titles: a function that allows rows or columns to remain fixed on the display when the rest of the screen scrolls out of view; also called 'fixed titles'.

real format: a value format in which a number includes a decimal fraction.

relative cell reference: a cell reference that is adjusted or changed when a formula is copied to another cell.

replication: the function that allows labels, values and formulae to be copied to another part of the spreadsheet (also called 'copying').

rounding error: the difference between the exact number and the displayed number.

row: a horizontal series of cells running across the full breadth of the spreadsheet, and usually identified by a number.

spreadsheet: a screen image of a form or matrix made up of rows and columns in which automatic and interconnected calculations are made.

spreadsheet program: the computer program needed to set up a spreadsheet and to allow the use of commands, formulae and special functions.

value: any arithmetic quantity in the spreadsheet.

'what if?' analysis: the manipulation of data so that numeric variables are changed to show the effect of different policies.

window: a rectangular frame in the display that allows other parts of the spreadsheet to be viewed on the same screen.

Chapter 5
Practical Spreadsheet Assignments

These assignments are graded, and we advise that you work through them in the order in which they are given. **Note: You may enter the data given for each assignment onto a new spreadsheet or you can download the spreadsheet (labels and values only) in Excel format for each assignment from Gill & Macmillan's website at www.gillmacmillan.ie.**

◥Functions and commands required

As you progress through these assignments you will need to check the commands, functions, icons and pull-down menus specific to your spreadsheet program. You will also be practising commands and functions learned in earlier assignments. (Note: If you do not have access to a printer you can display a preview of the print-out on the screen.)

The following points should be noted:

- When entering data on amounts of money, do not add the '€' sign as the data item will then be treated by the spreadsheet program as a label. Spreadsheet cells holding details on amounts of money should be formatted to currency display.
- Once constructed, some of the larger spreadsheets in the later assignments may not be entirely visible on the screen. You will need to 'freeze titles' and/or hide certain columns as required.

The new functions and commands encountered in successive assignment are as follows:

ASSIGNMENT 1
- Entering data onto a spreadsheet
- Altering the column width
- Changing the contents of a cell
- Deleting the contents of a cell
- Saving a spreadsheet
- Exiting the system

ASSIGNMENT 2
- Recalling a spreadsheet
- The summation function
- Replicating a formula
- Aligning headings

ASSIGNMENT 3
- Inserting a new column
- Inserting a new row
- Finding the average of a row
- Formatting a range of value to whole number format

ASSIGNMENT 4
- Consolidation assignment

ASSIGNMENT 5
- Multiplying the contents of two cells
- Formatting a range of cells to currency display

ASSIGNMENT 6
- The maximum, minimum and count functions
- Deleting a row of data

ASSIGNMENT 7
- Arithmetic formulae

ASSIGNMENT 8
- Absolute and relative cell references

ASSIGNMENT 9
- Consolidation assignment

ASSIGNMENT 10
- Producing a pie graph
- Producing a bar graph

ASSIGNMENT 11
- Producing a line graph
- Producing a grouped bar graph

ASSIGNMENT 12
- The 'IF' function – one condition
- The date function
- Sorting rows into alphabetical order

- Protecting cell contents
- Printing the entire spreadsheet

ASSIGNMENT 13
- The 'IF' function – two conditions using AND
- Sorting rows into numerical order
- Copying cell displays
- Printing selected columns

ASSIGNMENT 14
- The 'IF' function – nested conditions
- Manual recalculation
- Hiding cell contents
- Printing selected rows

ASSIGNMENT 15
- Aligning main heading
- Header and footer

ASSIGNMENT 16
- The horizontal look-up function
- Altering cell and font colours
- Hiding entire columns

ASSIGNMENT 17
- The vertical look-up function

ASSIGNMENT 18
- Consolidation assignment

ASSIGNMENT 19
- Financial functions – NPV, PMT and DB

ASSIGNMENT 20
- Simple macros

ASSIGNMENT 21
- FETAC Spreadsheet Methods Sample Paper 1

ASSIGNMENT 22
- FETAC Spreadsheet Methods Sample Paper 2

Assignment 1

The following spreadsheet shows the numbers of different makes of cars sold by Kells Motors for the first three months of the year.

	A	B	C	D
1	Kells Motors			
2	Car	Jan	Feb	Mar
3	Makes			
4	BMW	15	10	8
5	Ford	31	22	17
6	Mercedes	12	11	9
7	Renault	20	18	14
8	Toyota	27	21	15

◩ **Carry out the following tasks:**

Enter:

1. the data as shown onto a spreadsheet.

Alter:

2. the width of column A to best accommodate Kells Motors.

Delete:

3. the contents of cell A3.

Change:

4. the contents of cell D6 to 8.

Save:

5. the spreadsheet as **CAR1** to your disk.

Close

6. the file.

Assignment 2

◤**Carry out the following tasks:**

Load:
1. the **CAR1** file from your disk.

Enter:
2. the label *Total* in cell E2.
3. the correct formula in cell E4 to calculate the sum of the values in cells B4 to D4 inclusive.

Replicate:
4. the formula in cell E4 to cells E5, E6, E7 and E8.

Enter:
5. the label *Total* in cell A9.
6. the correct formula in cell B9 to calculate the sum of the values in cells B4 to B8 inclusive.

Replicate:
7. the formula in cell B9 to cells C9 and D9.

Align:
8. the labels in the range of cells B2:E2, i.e. Jan, Feb, Mar and Total, to the right.

Save:
9. the spreadsheet as **CAR2** to your disk.

Close:
10. the file.

Assignment 3

◤**Carry out the following tasks:**

Load:
1. the file **CAR2** from your disk.

Insert:
2. a new column titled *Apr* between the *Mar* and *Total* columns.

Enter:

3. Enter the following data into this new *Apr* column:

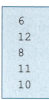

Amend:

4. the totals to take account of this new insertion.

Insert:

5. a new row titled *Honda* between the *Ford* and *Mercedes* rows.

Enter:

6. the following data into this new *Honda* row:

Honda	20	17	15	12

Amend:

7. the totals, where necessary, to take account of this new insertion.

Insert:

8. the label *Average* in cell G2.

Enter:

9. a formula in cell G4 to calculate the average monthly sales of BMW cars.

Replicate:

10. the formula in cell G4 to the range of cells G5:G9.

Format:

11. the numbers in the average column to whole number format (no decimals).

Save:

12. the file as **CAR3** to your disk.

Close:

13. the file.

Assignment 4

The following table shows student results in four tests. The maximum mark possible for each test is 10; the minimum possible is 0.

TEST RESULTS				
Student	Test 1	Test 2	Test 3	Test 4
J Kelly	9	9	7	8
S Nicholl	0	8	5	4
O Browne	2	7	7	7
M Carey	9	10	8	7
C Smyth	9	7	8	9
E Quinn	3	6	0	0
U Daly	3	6	5	3
F Murphy	9	10	8	5

You are required to enter the details in the table onto a spreadsheet.

◪Carry out the following tasks:

Add a new:

1. *Overall Marks* column to show the total marks obtained by each student in all four tests.
2. *Average Marks* column to show the average mark for each student in the four tests. (Hint: Use the average function.)

Amend:

3. the marks for J. Kelly, O. Browne and F. Murphy in test 3 to 9, 9 and 10, respectively.
4. the mark for S. Nicholl in test 4; it should be 7.

Add:

5. a new *Test Average* row to show the average mark for each test.

Format:

6. the marks in the *Average Marks* column and in the *Test Average* row to number format (one decimal place).

Save:

7. the spreadsheet as RESULTS.

Assignment 5

The following table shows the cone sales for seven different flavours of ice cream at Mel's Ice Cream Parlour over a five-day period:

MEL'S ICE CREAM PARLOUR					
Flavour	Mon	Tue	Wed	Thu	Fri
Caramel	18	24	11	19	14
Choc Chip	27	33	25	20	29
Mint	5	4	9	13	8
Orange	12	9	7	5	4
Pistachio	8	11	12	10	13
Strawberry	22	31	17	22	34
Vanilla	35	20	28	25	37

You are required to enter this data onto a spreadsheet.

Carry out the following tasks:

Save:

1. the spreadsheet as ICE1.

Add:

2. a column after Friday's data to show the total sales of each ice cream flavour over the five-day period.

Insert:

3. a column between Friday's data and total sales.

Enter:

4. in the new column the following ice cream sales for Saturday: Caramel – 20, Choc Chip – 26, Mint – 17, Orange – 6, Pistachio – 17, Strawberry – 28, Vanilla – 31. Amend the totals formulae to take account of this insertion.

Add:

5. a column after the *total sales* column to show the *cone cost* for each ice cream flavour. Caramel – €1.40, Choc Chip – €1.65, Mint – €1.50, Orange – €1.35, Pistachio – €1.45, Strawberry – €1.30 and Vanilla – €1.25. (Note: When entering the costs, do not type the € symbol, i.e. 1.4 instead of €1.40.)

6. a total income column after cone cost to show the total income generated over the week for each ice cream flavour.

Enter:

7. a formula, in the appropriate cell, to show the total income for the week at Mel's Ice Cream Parlour.

Format:

8. the cone cost and total income columns to currency format.

Save:

9. the spreadsheet as ICE2.

Assignment 6

The table below shows the sales commission of seven salespeople who sell different products for Annex Ltd. The salespeople are paid their commission at the end of a three-month period.

ANNEX LTD					
COMMISSION PAYMENTS					
Name	EE No	Qtr 1	Qtr 2	Qtr 3	Qtr 4
A Behan	901	1575	2951	108	2905
B Collins	264	712	2215	1306	3556
C Daly	745	2478	2428	2561	1761
A Nolan	256	397	2272	647	2970
A Sheils	633	1422	2400	1203	2413
T Timmons	908	1780	567	675	3598
J Wynne	353	3359	3671	1904	1866

Enter the details shown in the table onto a spreadsheet.

◥ **Carry out the following tasks:**

Change:

1. the name C. Daly to C. Davis.
2. the amount for J. Wynne for the second quarter to 1536.25.

Insert:

3. a new *Division* column between the employee number (EE No) and the first-quarter details to give the following division names:

   A. Behan: Paper

   B. Collins: Equipment

   C. Davis: Paper

   A. Nolan: Stationery

   A. Shiels: Equipment

   T. Timmons: Stationery

   J. Wynne: Paper

Alter:

4. the width of the *Division* column to accommodate the longest entry.

Add:

5. a new *Total Commission* column to show the total commission for each salesperson for the four quarters.
6. a *Bonus* column to show the end-of-year bonus payable to all salespeople; those in the Paper Division are to get €300 extra; all other divisions get a bonus of €200.
7. a *Commission Earnings* column to show the total commission plus bonus for each salesperson.
8. a new *Commission Payable* row to display the total commission issued in each quarter.

Insert:

9. (preserving the alphabetical order of employee names) a new row containing the following details for G Ennis, who joined the Equipment Division of the company in the third quarter:

Name	EE No	Qtr 1	Qtr 2	Qtr 3	Qtr 4
G Ennis	449	0	0	2007	3458

Add:

10. a new row that shows the average commission issued in each quarter.
11. a new row that shows the maximum commission issued in each quarter (hint: use the maximum function).
12. a new row that shows the minimum commission issued in each quarter (hint: use the minimum function).
13. a new row that shows the total number of salespeople (hint: use the count function).

Delete:

14. the row containing A. Nolan's details.

Format:

15. all money amounts to currency format (no cents).

Save:

16. the spreadsheet as EARNINGS.

Assignment 7

The table below shows the present and previous electricity meter readings for ten different customers. ESB Customer Supply wishes to calculate the bill for each customer based on this data.

ELECTRICITY BILLS		
COMPANY NAME	PREVIOUS READING	PRESENT READING
S Andrews	35839	36428
H Brennan	13538	14011
A Connors	20153	21042
P Conway	28603	29256
K Deegan	32568	33410
D Martin	42398	43117
S O' Brien	15644	16585
J Penrose	22715	23510
J Quinn	9638	10263
J Shaw	17988	18346

The cost of one unit of electricity is currently €0.13.

You must enter the details as shown in the table onto a spreadsheet.

◣Carry out the following tasks:

Add:

1. a Units Used column to show the number of units of electricity used by each customer.
2. a Unit Cost column to show the cost of one unit of electricity, i.e. all of the cells opposite customer names in this column will contain 0.13.
3. a Units Charge column to show the total cost of the units used by each customer.
4. a Standing Charge column. The current standing charge for each customer is e8.55, i.e. all of the cells in this column will contain 8.55.
5. a Total Amount column to show the total amount for each customer (hint: units charge + standing charge).
6. a VAT Payable column. VAT is calculated as 13.5 per cent of the total amount for each customer.
7. an Amount Payable column to show the total amount payable by each customer.

Insert:

8. the following details on Lisa Gleeson's account, preserving the alphabetical order of the customers' surnames:

Previous	Present
Reading	Reading
23488	24064

Obtain:

9. the amount payable by Lisa.

Format:

10. the columns containing money amounts to currency display (to two decimal places).

Align:

11. the labels in columns B to J to the right.

Save:

12. the spreadsheet as **BILL1**.

Print:

13. the entire spreadsheet centred horizontally and vertically on the page. The print-out should be in landscape orientation.

Assignment 8

Carrigallen Mart holds livestock sales every week. The table below shows the monthly sales of cattle, pigs and sheep for the past year:

MONTH	CATTLE	PIGS	SHEEP
January	1466	2621	1121
February	1839	3819	1619
March	2844	1726	2144
April	4525	1341	3282
May	2193	1716	2792
June	1153	1205	1844
July	1008	1017	1102
August	1796	1914	1219
September	4377	2838	1372
October	5542	3561	2611
November	3829	4219	2433
December	2081	4532	1518

You are required to enter these details onto a suitably titled spreadsheet.

Save:

1. the spreadsheet as MART1.

Insert:

2. a row, labelled *Total Sold,* beneath the December details.

Enter:

3. formulae into this row to obtain the total number of each animal type sold during the year.

Insert:

4. a new column after each of the three livestock columns.

Label:

5. these three new columns – Cattle (%), Pigs (%) and Sheep (%), respectively.

Obtain:

6. the percentage of each animal type sold each month as a fraction of the total sales for that particular animal type for the year. (Hint: Each formula will have absolute and relative cell references.)

Format:

7. these three percentage columns to percentage format (one decimal place).

Add:

8. a new column, labelled Total Livestock, after the last column on the spreadsheet showing the total number of livestock sold each month and obtain the total for the year.

9. a new column, labelled Total Livestock (%), after the Total Livestock column showing the percentage of livestock sold each month as a fraction of the yearly total. This column should also be formatted to display percentages (one decimal place).

Save:

10. the spreadsheet as MART2.

Assignment 9

Riversdale Farms Ltd supply fresh vegetables to a number of greengrocers in the Dublin area. The table below shows the number of kilograms of carrots, onions, parsnips and tomatoes delivered to ten different greengrocers' shops on a particular day:

RIVERSDALE FARMS LTD				
SHOP	CARROTS	ONIONS	PARSNIPS	TOMATOES
J Bean & Sons	80	40	65	50
Cabbage Patch	65	45	40	85
Get Fresh	120	75	70	100
Just In	75	80	30	75
Lentils & Co	90	45	25	70
Picked Today	50	70	40	45
Salad Days	85	35	15	30
SpringFresh Ltd	110	90	100	85
The Runner Bean	70	20	45	55
Vegworld	60	50	10	40

You must enter these details onto a suitably titled spreadsheet.

◤ Carry out the following tasks:

Save:

1. the spreadsheet as VEG1.

Insert:

2. a new column after each of the four weight columns.

Label:

3. these new columns – *Carrots (€), Onions (€), Parsnips (€)* and *Tomatoes (€),* respectively.

Insert:

4. two new rows between the spreadsheet heading and the column headings.

Enter:

5. the following price details into the two new rows:

VEGETABLE	CARROTS	ONIONS	PARSNIPS	TOMATOES
Price/kg	€1.28	€0.82	€2.05	€1.60

Enter:

6. appropriate formulae into the four new price columns to calculate the total cost of each vegetable type bought by each individual shop. (Hint: Each formula will have absolute and relative cell references.)

Insert:

7. a column, labelled *Total Price,* after the *Tomatoes (€)* column, showing the total cost of all four vegetable types for each shop.
8. a new row, labelled *Overall Income,* below the bottom row on the spreadsheet, showing the total income generated from sales of all four vegetable types to all ten shops.

Format:

9. all columns containing money details to currency format.

Save:

10. this spreadsheet as VEG2.

Assignment 10

◪Task 1

The table below shows the number of students in a class who achieved various grades in an examination.

EXAMINATION RESULTS	
Result	Number
Distinction	4
Merit	6
Credit	9
Pass	7
Fail	4

Enter the data given onto a spreadsheet.

Produce:

1. a pie graph of the examination results shown. The graph should have:
   - *Examination Results* as its title
   - a legend (colour code for the segments)
   - the actual values (data labels) placed beside each segment.

Save:

2. the spreadsheet and graph as **GRADES** to your disk.

The table below shows the numbers of personal computers sold by a company during the first six months of the year.

COMPUTER SALES	
Month	Sales
Jan	73
Feb	85
Mar	97
Apr	68
May	59
Jun	75

Enter the data given onto a spreadsheet.

Produce:

1. a column (bar) graph of the monthly computer sales. The graph should have:
- a chart title – *Computer Sales*
- an x-axis title – *Month*
- a y-axis title – *Unit Sales.*

Save:

2. the spreadsheet and graph as **COMGRAPH** to your disk.

Print:

3. the graph only.

Assignment 11

◥ Task 1

The table below shows a company's profits in millions of euro over a five-year period.

COMPANY PROFITS	
Year	Profit (€, mn)
2003	3.1
2004	4.5
2005	4.8
2006	5.0
2007	5.6

Enter the data given onto a spreadsheet.

Produce:
   1. a line graph of the annual profits.

Add:
   2. the following text to the graph:
- chart title – *Company Profits*
- x-axis – *Year*
- y-axis – *Profits (in € Millions).*

Save:
   3. the spreadsheet as **PROFITS** to your disk.

Print:
   4. the graph.

Copy:
   5. the graph from the original to a new worksheet.

Alter:
   6. the y-axis scale to start at '3' on the graph in the new worksheet.

Re-save:
   7. the spreadsheet as **PROFITS2**.

Print:
   8. the graph, centred horizontally and vertically on the page.

◪Task 2

The table below shows the numbers of packets of three different cereals sold at a store during the year.

CEREAL SALES			
Month	Muesli	Cornflakes	Porridge
Jan	115	67	213
Feb	141	80	198
Mar	122	97	155
Apr	139	120	91
May	94	179	48
Jun	86	230	32
Jul	102	214	22
Aug	113	182	34
Sep	122	133	48
Oct	105	101	78
Nov	122	92	119
Dec	133	78	156

Enter the data given onto a spreadsheet.

Produce:

1. a line graph showing the sales trends of the three cereals listed during the year.

Add:

2. the following text to the graph:
   - main heading – *Cereal Sales*
   - x-axis – *Months*
   - y-axis – *Unit Sales.*

   The graph should include a legend showing a different colour for each cereal given.

Save:

3. the spreadsheet and graph as **CEREALS** to your disk.

Close:

4. the file.

◪Task 3

The table below shows the numbers of guests of differing nationalities who stayed at the Russell Hotel over a three-year period.

	A	B	C	D
1	Russell Hotel - Guest Numbers			
2				
3	Nationality	2005	2006	2007
4				
5	American	2900	1800	900
6	British	2400	4200	5000
7	French	1900	1800	1600
8	German	1500	1100	700
9	Other	2200	2600	3800

Enter the data given onto a spreadsheet.

Produce:
1. a column (bar) graph depicting the numbers of foreign guests who stayed at the Russell Hotel over the three-year period.

Add:
2. the following text to the graph:
   - main heading – *Russell Hotel Guests 2005–2007*
   - x-axis – *Nationality*
   - y-axis – *Tourist Numbers.*

3. a legend to the graph showing a colour for each year. The graph should also have data values over each column.

Save:
4. the spreadsheet and graph as **TOURISTS**.

Print:
5. the graph.

Assignment 12

Mac's Tool Hire Company, set up by Susan MacMahon in 1996, provides a wide range of electrical and mechanical tools suitable for use by the professional builder or the DIY enthusiast. A 25 per cent discount is offered on all equipment hired for more than two weeks. Susan needs your expertise in using a spreadsheet program to help in the preparation of customer invoices. You must transfer the following invoice details to a spreadsheet:

MAC'S TOOL HIRE COMPANY

CUSTOMER INVOICE: SEAN MURPHY

Tool Hired	Weekly Cost	Weeks Hired
Skill Saw	€15.00	2
Drill	€12.00	4
Cement Mixer	€225.00	5
Electric Plane	€33.00	1
Generator	€75.00	1
Rotovator	€66.00	3
Roofing Torch	€24.00	4
Compressor	€54.00	1
Pressure Washer	€81.00	2
Floor Edger	€39.00	3

◨ Carry out the following tasks:

Save:

1. the spreadsheet as TOOLS1.

Add:

2. a *Total Cost* column showing the total cost of hiring each item listed.
3. a *Discount Given* column showing the discount, if any, available on each item. (Hint: Use the IF function.)
4. an *Actual Cost* column showing the amount payable on each item.
5. three rows below the last row of data showing:
   (a) the total of actual costs for all items listed *(Total Bill)*
   (b) the VAT payable at 21 per cent on the bill *(VAT Payable)*
   (c) the total amount payable by the customer *(Amount Payable)*.

Insert:

6. a row beneath the row containing the customer's name.

Enter:

7. today's date in this new row. (Use the appropriate date function.)

Sort:

8. the rows containing the equipment details into alphabetical order of equipment name.

Protect:

9. all cells containing formulae.

Save:

10. the spreadsheet as TOOLS2.

Print:

11. the entire spreadsheet.

Assignment 13

Bethany Travel Ltd specialises in organising pilgrimages for Irish parishes to a number of shrines in Europe and the Holy Land. The following table shows booking details for last week:

PARISH NAME	PILGRIMAGE DESTINATION	GROUP SIZE	TICKET COST
Ballinteer	Medjugorje	72	€799.00
Clifden	Fatima	29	€619.00
Drumshambo	Fatima	16	€619.00
Ennis	Rome	25	€899.00
Gorey	Lourdes	38	€669.00
Gort	Medjugorje	50	€799.00
Killeshandra	Lourdes	33	€669.00
Kimmage	Lourdes	85	€669.00
Mostrim	Fatima	20	€619.00
Navan	Fatima	12	€619.00
Omagh	The Holy Land	19	€949.00
Thurles	Lourdes	27	€669.00

(Table title: BETHANY TRAVEL LTD)

A 20 per cent reduction was given to parish groups where the pilgrimage destination was not Lourdes **and** the group consisted of more than thirty people, otherwise a 10 per cent reduction was given.

A 5% government tax was levied on all bookings.

You must enter the details in the table onto a suitably titled spreadsheet.

◤Carry out the following tasks:

Save:

1. the spreadsheet as PILGRIM1.

Add:

2. a Group Cost column showing the total ticket costs for each parish group.
3. a Group Reduction column showing the total reductions for each parish group. (Hint: Use a compound IF statement.)
4. a Govt Tax column showing the total government tax levied on each parish group. (Hint: This is calculated on the group cost.)
5. a Group Total column showing the actual amount paid by each parish group after the appropriate reduction was made and the government tax levied.
6. an Individual Cost column showing the actual amount paid by each member of the parish group.

Sort:

7. the rows on the spreadsheet into descending order of parish group size.

Copy:

8. the details displayed in the *Parish Name* column and the corresponding details in the *Individual Cost* column to Columns L and M, respectively, on the spreadsheet.

Protect:

9. all cells containing formulae.

Save:

10. this spreadsheet as PILGRIM2.

Print:

11. the contents of columns L and M.

Assignment 14

Ashton Electrical Ltd, based in Cork, is one of Ireland's leading importers of electrical goods. The company supplies electrical shops throughout the country with a wide variety of modern domestic appliances. A new shipment of goods is due at the company's warehouses next week and it has been decided to hold a sale in order to clear the existing stock.

The following percentage reductions are available during the sale of existing stock:

Individual items costing:

€500 or less – 20 per cent

between €500 and €800 – 25 per cent

€800 or more – 30 per cent

The company's fleet of lorries delivers the goods to the individual shops. If the delivery distance is more than twenty miles then the charge is €3.00 per mile, otherwise the charge is €2.00 per mile.

J.D. Abbot, the head of sales at Ashton Electrical, has employed you for the sale period to produce customer invoices on a spreadsheet. The following incomplete invoice has just been given to you:

```
ASHTON ELECTRICAL LTD
Customer: Harry Murphy & Co        Address: 4 Main St, Athlone
Date:       Today's Date           Delivery Distance: 32

Electrical              Usual      Units
Item                    Price      Bought

Cooker                 €669.00        5
Deep Fat Fryer          €82.00       18
Dishwasher             €819.00        3
DVD Recorder           €340.00       10
Fridge Freezer         €555.00        6
Microwave              €234.00        9
Stereo                 €485.00        7
Television           €1,800.00        4
Vacuum Cleaner         €225.00       12
Vented Dryer           €725.00        2
Washer Dryer           €849.00        7
Washing Machine        €522.00        3
```

Enter the invoice details given onto a spreadsheet. Use the appropriate function to include today's date.

◼ Carry out the following tasks:

Save:

1. the spreadsheet as SALE1.

Add:

2. a *Total Price* column showing the total price of all the units bought of each item **before** any sales reduction.

3. a *Reduction Available* column showing the total reduction on all the units bought of each item. (Hint: Use a nested IF statement.)

4. a *Total Sale Price* column showing the total price of all the units bought of each item **after** the sales reductions are made.

5. a *Total Charge* row beneath the bottom row of the spreadsheet showing a total for the *Total Sales Price* column.

6. a *VAT Payable* row showing the VAT due on this invoice (VAT is charged at 21 per cent).

7. a *Delivery Charge* row showing the total cost of delivering the items listed to Harry Murphy & Co. (Hint: Use a simple IF statement.)

8. a *Total Amount Payable* row showing the actual amount payable on this current delivery to Harry Murphy & Co.

Save:

9. the file as SALE2.

Switch:

10. to manual recalculation mode.

Make:

11. alterations to the contents of the appropriate cells to take account of the following:
    - four dishwashers and nine vacuum cleaners were bought
    - the usual price of a washer dryer is €819.

Switch:

12. to automatic recalculation mode.

Sort:

13. the rows containing the item details into descending order of *Total Sales Price.*

Protect and hide:

14. the contents of all cells containing formulae.

Save:

15. the spreadsheet as SALE3.

Print:

16. the cell displays for the *Total Charge, VAT Payable, Delivery Charge* and *Total Amount Payable* rows only.

Assignment 15

Anne Wright of Wright Homes estate agency in Trim, Co. Meath wishes to give her non-first-time property buyers the true cost of purchasing a property. Anne tells her customers that the actual cost of a home is:

purchase price + stamp duty + legal fees + surveyor's fee

Stamp duty is a tax, calculated as a percentage of the purchase price, which is paid to the government on property purchases. For non-first time buyers, the following table shows the different property price brackets and the corresponding percentages.

STAMP DUTY BRACKETS	
Up to €127,000	0%
€127,000–€190,500	3%
€190,501–€254,000	4%
€254,001–€317,500	5%
€317,501–€381,000	6%
€381,001–€635,000	7.5%
Over €635,000	9%

Anne estimates:

- the legal fees to be 1 per cent of the purchase price of any property

- that the surveyor's report costs €1,000 on all properties in excess of €500,000, otherwise the fee is €500.

Anne gives you the following table showing details of properties sold to non-first-time buyers during the past month.

WRIGHT HOMES		
Name	Property Type	Purchase Price
Martha Brennan	House	€485,000
Pat Canavan	House	€950,000
Jim Foy	Site	€105,000
Eithne Foley	Apartment	€185,000
Stephen Hughes	House	€242,000
Lillian McElwaine	Apartment	€375,000
Joyce Moran	House	€310,000
Tom Phillips	House	€520,000
John Stephens	House	€1,200,000
Fred Walsh	Apartment	€177,000

You are required to enter the property details shown in this table onto a spreadsheet.

◤Carry out the following tasks:

Save:
1. the spreadsheet as PROPERTY1.

Add:
2. a *Stamp Duty* column showing the stamp duty for each property listed. (Hint: Use a nested IF statement.)
3. a *Legal Fees* column showing the legal fees incurred on the purchase of each property listed.
4. a *Surveyor's Report* column showing the cost of the report for each property listed. (Hint: Use a basic IF statement.)
5. an *Actual Price* column showing the actual price of each property listed.

Format:
6. all money amounts to currency format (no cents).

Align:

7. the main heading centrally over the columns.

8. the labels in all columns, with the exception of those in columns A and B, to the right.

Sort:

9. the rows containing the property details into ascending order of actual price.

Protect and hide:

10. he contents of all cells containing formulae.

Insert:

11. your own name and today's date as a header and footer, respectively, on the spreadsheet.

Save:

12. the spreadsheet as PROPERTY2.

Print:

13. the spreadsheet in landscape format, ensuring that it is centred horizontally and vertically on the page.

Assignment 16

CareFree Car Rentals, established in 2005, has given you the following table showing rental details for ten tourists who have hired cars from the company:

CAREFREE CAR RENTALS					
Daily Car Hire Rates					
Category	A	B	C	D	E
Rate	€150.00	€95.00	€80.00	€65.00	€50.00
Customer Name	Car Type	Car Category	Days Hired		
Pierre Almont	Opel Astra	C	8		
Maria Bonetti	Ford Fiesta	D	5		
Daniel Davies	VW Passat	B	4		
Keith Frazier	Renault Clio	D	9		
Petra Lamvelt	Toyota Avensis	B	4		
Ida Luff	Mazda 6	B	6		
Shari McKenzie	Opel Corsa	E	7		
Carlo Ponti	Nissan Primera	B	8		
Sven Stonson	BMW 5	A	4		
Hillary Wallace	VW Golf	C	6		

You are required to enter the details shown in the table onto a spreadsheet.

◤ Carry out the following tasks:

Save:

1. the spreadsheet as CARHIRE1.

Choose:

2. suitable contrasting background and foreground colours, e.g. yellow on dark blue, for the range of ten cells containing the daily rates for each category of car.

Add:

3. a **Basic Cost** column showing the basic cost of car rental for each of the customers listed. (Hint: Use the horizontal look-up function.)

4. an **Extra Days Reduction** column showing the reduction amount, if any, that each customer receives. This reduction amount of €10.00 per day is given for each extra day that a car is rented over the standard five-day rental period. (Hint: Use a simple IF statement.)

5. an **Amount Payable** column showing the actual rental payable by each customer after the correct reduction, if any, has been made on the basic cost.

Save:

6. the spreadsheet as CARHIRE2.

Switch:

7. to manual recalculation mode.

Make the following alterations to the appropriate cells:

8. the daily car rental costs have increased by €5.00 for all categories.

9. the VW Passat and Toyota Avensis were hired for three and seven days, respectively.

10. The reduction amount has been increased to €12.50 per day for each extra day that a car is rented over the standard five-day rental period.

Switch:

11. to automatic recalculation mode.

Hide:

12. all columns except the **Customer Name** and **Amount Payable** columns.

Save:

13. the spreadsheet as CARHIRE3.

Print:

14. the customer names and corresponding amounts payable from the two columns that are visible on the spreadsheet. This print-out should show column and row identifiers.

Assignment 17

The Corn Mill Theatre in Carrigallen, Co. Leitrim caters for a wide range of theatrical tastes. The current play running at the theatre is John B. Keane's *Sive.* The table below shows the audience attendances in the four different categories for the three areas of the theatre for last evening:

CORN MILL THEATRE – AUDIENCE RECEIPTS			
Audience Category	Base Level	Lower Circle	Upper Circle
Adult	51	35	42
Child	14	22	27
Student	28	19	23
Unwaged	20	12	17

You are required to enter the details shown in the table onto a spreadsheet.

◥ Carry out the following tasks:

Save:

1. the spreadsheet as THEATRE1.

Insert a column labelled:

2. *Base Level (€)* after the *Base Level* column.
3. *Lower Circle (€)* after the *Lower Circle* column.
4. *Upper Circle (€)* after the *Upper Circle* column.

Insert:

5. eight rows between the spreadsheet heading and the column headings.

Enter:

6. the following details concerning ticket prices into the new rows. (Use the correct date function to enter today's date):

TODAY'S DATE			
Ticket Prices			
	Base Level	Lower Circle	Upper Circle
Adult	€12.00	€15.00	€18.00
Child	€5.00	€6.50	€8.00
Student	€7.50	€10.00	€13.00
Unwaged	€9.00	€12.00	€15.50

The details from this table can be used as a look-up table.

Enter:

7. formulae in the three new columns to calculate the receipts taken in the various audience categories for each section of the theatre. (Hint: Using the ticket price details in the look-up table and the attendance figures, construct the formulae using the vertical look-up function).

Add:

8. a column, labelled *Total Receipts*, showing the total receipts taken in each of the four audience categories for the whole theatre.

Insert:

9. a formula in the appropriate cell to show the total receipts taken for last evening.

Add:

10. a column, labelled *% Receipts*, showing the percentage of total receipts taken in each of the four audience categories.

Format:

11. the display, in this latter column, to percentage format (one decimal place).

Copy:

12. the cell displays in the *Audience Category* and *% Receipts* columns to the L and M columns, respectively.

Protect and hide:

13. the contents of all cells containing formulae.

Save:

14. the spreadsheet as THEATRE2.

Produce:

15. a pie graph, titled *Corn Mill Theatre – Audience Receipts,* showing the percentage breakdown of audience receipts.

Save:

16. the graph as CORNMILL.

Print:

17. the graph.

Assignment 18

Wheel World Ltd, a shop specialising in the sale of new bicycles and cycling accessories, has been in existence for over twenty years. Susan Kelly, the owner of the shop, provides a hire purchase method of payment to any customer who has just bought a new bicycle at the shop. Different rates of interest are charged depending on the number of agreed monthly payments. The interest payable is calculated as a percentage of the cost of the bicycle. The interest rate categories are as follows:

Monthly Payments	2	6	10	12	18	24
Interest Rate	0%	3%	6%	7%	10%	15%

If the customer uses Susan's hire purchase method of payment, an initial deposit must be paid. The deposit is calculated as 20 per cent of the cost on all bicycles over €350, otherwise the deposit payable is only 15 per cent of the cost of the bicycle.

Susan has given you the following details on ten new customers who have opted for her hire purchase system:

CUSTOMER NAME	BICYCLE MAKE	BICYCLE COST	NUMBER OF PAYMENTS
Sandra Allen	Falcon 65	€270.00	10
Seamus Cullen	Townsend G5	€240.00	6
John Dunne	Alexa MB4	€500.00	2
Marie Higgins	President CX	€590.00	24
Linda Logan	Alexa MB1	€420.00	12
Martin Murphy	Saracen 96	€320.00	18
Noel O' Brien	Falcon 105	€620.00	10
Carol O' Gorman	Marlboro DT	€450.00	2
Brian Ryan	Diamond 109	€290.00	6
Margaret Tracy	Saracen 98	€380.00	12

Enter the details in this table onto a suitably titled spreadsheet.

◪ Carry out the following tasks:

Save:

1. the spreadsheet as CYCLE1.

Insert:

2. two new rows between the spreadsheet title and the column titles.

Enter:

3. the details on monthly payments and interest rates outlined earlier into the two new rows.

Add:

4. an *Interest Payable* column showing the actual amount of interest due on each purchase. (Hint: Use the most suitable look-up function in the construction of the formula.)
5. a *Total Payable* column showing the actual amount of money that each customer must pay.
6. a *Deposit Due* column showing the deposit that must be paid by each customer. This is calculated on the total payable.

7. a *Monthly Amount* column showing the actual amount of money that must be paid monthly by each customer **after** the initial deposit has been paid.

Save:

8. the spreadsheet as CYCLE2.

Change:

9. the interest rates, in the look-up table, for 2, 6, 10, 12, 18 and 24 monthly payments to 5 per cent, 10 per cent, 15 per cent, 20 per cent, 25 per cent and 30 per cent, respectively.

Copy:

10. the details in the **Customer Name** column and the corresponding details in the *Interest Payable* column to the K and L columns, respectively.

Protect and hide:

11. the contents of all cells containing formulae.

Save:

12. the spreadsheet as CYCLE3.

Produce:

13. a bar graph of the details in columns K and L. The graph should have a suitable title and should show the customer names along the x-axis and the interest payable amounts along the y-axis.

Save:

14. the graph as INTEREST.

Print:

15. the graph.

Assignment 19

Section A – Investment venture

Mervyn Richardson, the owner of Jetwash Ltd, is considering an investment venture costing €250,000 which must be paid in advance. The projected sales from the venture, expected to last for 2005, 2006 and 2007, are €120,000, €140,000 and €160,000, respectively. Mervyn wishes to know if it is better to invest in the venture or to leave the money in the bank at the current interest rate of 12 per cent over the same period.

You must enter the details given below onto a spreadsheet.

```
                        JETWASH LTD

  Projected Sales

  Investment              2005            2006            2007
  €250,000.00         €120,000.00     €140,000.00     €160,000.00

  Interest Rate Given =    12%

  Net Present Value =
  Bank Savings Return =
  Worthwhile Investment =
```

Carry out the following tasks:

Enter a formula in the cell to the right of:

1. the *'Net Present Value ='* label to show the net present value of the investment at a rate of 12 per cent. (Hint: Use the NPV function in constructing the formula.)
2. the *'Bank Savings Return ='* label to show the compound interest that the money would earn over the same period.
3. the *'Worthwhile Investment ='* label to show whether the investment is worthwhile or not (Yes/No). (Hint: The investment is worthwhile if the net present value is greater than the bank savings return.)

Save:

4. the spreadsheet as JETWASH.

Section B – Mortgage repayments

Patrick Doyle, the manager of the EasyLoan Building Society, wishes to produce a mortgage repayments table to show the monthly repayments on a €150,000, €200,000 and €250,000 mortgage. The table must show repayments for varying interest rates (from 3 per cent to 5 per cent increments of 0.5 per cent). All mortgages are for twenty years.

You are required to enter the details in the following incomplete table onto a spreadsheet.

```
                   EASYLOAN BUILDING SOCIETY

                       Monthly Repayments Table

  Loan Term
  Years                            20
  Months                           240

          Interest Rate        €150,000    €200,000     €250,000
              3.0%
              3.5%
              4.0%
              4.5%
              5.0%
```

Carry out the following tasks:

Enter:

1. suitable formulae in the appropriate cells to show the monthly repayment for each mortgage amount and interest rate. (Hint: Use the PMT function in constructing the formulae.)

Save:

2. the spreadsheet as MORTGAGE.

Print:

3. the spreadsheet, showing the actual formulae used.

Section C – Depreciation

Office Machines Ltd supplies businesses nationwide with a range of modern office equipment. Sean O'Gorman, the managing director, is interested in the amounts of depreciation on equipment over a number of years.

Sean has given you the following incomplete table showing details of an autoprinter that has just been sold by the company:

OFFICE MACHINES LTD			
Equipment Sold = Autoprinter		Cost =	€40,000.00
Estimated Life (yrs) = 8		Salvage Value =	€5,000.00
Year Number	Depreciation Amount	Cumulative Depreciation	Net Book Value

You are required to enter these details onto a spreadsheet.

Carry out the following tasks:

Enter:

1. the values 1 to 8 in the eight cells beneath the Year Number column heading.
2. a formula in the Depreciation Amount column to calculate the depreciation at the end of the first year. (Hint: Use the DB function, i.e. the fixed-declining balance function.)

Copy:

3. this formula down the column to show the depreciation amounts for years 2 to 8.

Enter suitable formulae in the:

4. Cumulative Depreciation column to show the total depreciation on the autoprinter at the end of each year.
5. Net Book Value column to show the actual value of the printer at the end of each year.

Save:

6. the spreadsheet as PRINTER.

Print:

7. the spreadsheet showing the actual formulae used.

Assignment 20

Section A

Produce:

1. a macro that widens a column to 'best fit' the longest entry.

Save:

2. the macro as COLWIDEN.

Section B

Produce:

1. a macro that, upon execution, produces the following template:

	A	B	C	D
1	Claire's Cake Shop			
2				
3	Cake	Day 1	Day 2	Day 3
4				
5	Carrot			
6	Cheese			
7	Coffee			

Save:

2. the macro as CAKESHOP.

Section C

Produce:

1. an interactive macro that accepts any number of euro and returns the equivalent amounts of US dollars and UK pounds. Use the following exchange rates:
   €1.00 = $1.28 = £0.67

Save:

2. the macro as MONEY.

When the macro is executed and €25 is entered, you should obtain the following:

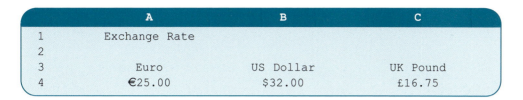

	A	B	C
1	Exchange Rate		
2			
3	Euro	US Dollar	UK Pound
4	€25.00	$32.00	£16.75

Assignment 21
FETAC Spreadsheet Methods Sample Paper 1
Task 1 (30 marks)

1. Set up the spreadsheet and input the data as shown in Figure 1.
   a. Align main heading (Hi-Tech Production) and subheading (Production Report – January 2007) centrally over the data.
   b. Set column widths to appropriate values.
   c. Column 1 heading and values should be centrally aligned.
   d. Column 2 heading and values should be left aligned.
   e. Column 3, 4, 5 and 6 headings and values should be right aligned.
   f. The profit figures should be the profit for the quantity produced in each factory and should be calculated values.
   g. The values in columns 4, 5 and 6 should be displayed in currency format.
   h. The *Total:* and *Total Profit:* should be calculated values. They should be aligned and displayed in the same format as the column in which they appear.
2. Insert the labels *Name:, Examination No:* and *Date:* in the positions indicated and insert the appropriate information after each.
3. Save the spreadsheet under the filename TASK1, for printing now or later. (The print-out should show borders – row/column labels.)

```
                        Hi-Tech Productions


                 Production Report    -    January 2007


                       Factory         Unit         Unit
                       Production    Production    Selling
     No. Factory       Quantity         Price        Price      Profit


       1  Clondalkin      2500         €2.80       €4.80
       2  Santry          3400         €2.50       €4.60
       3  Cork            2800         €3.00       €4.90
       4  Galway          2300         €2.60       €5.20
       5  Limerick        4400         €3.20       €5.30
       6  Athlone          800         €2.80       €4.60
       7  Sligo           1800         €2.90       €5.10
       8  Waterford       3500         €3.00       €5.00
       9  Dundalk         2700         €3.30       €5.20


                   Total:                   Total Profit:


  Name:
  College:
  Date:
```

Figure 1

◣Task 2 (25 marks)

1. Input the additional information shown in Figure 2.
   a. Change the month in the subheading to *February*.
   b. Insert an extra column where required.
   c. Insert the heading *Royalty Fee* in the new column and align to the right.
   d. Re-align the main and subheadings centrally over the data.
   e. The *Royalty Fee* should be calculated on the following basis and displayed in the
      column as a percentage (i.e. 6 per cent, 4 per cent, 2 per cent): if the production quantity
      is greater than 2000, then the royalty fee is 6 per cent; if the quantity is between 1000
      and 2000 inclusive, then the royalty fee is 4 per cent and if the quantity is less than 1000,
      then the fee is 2 per cent.
   f. The *Royalty Fee* should be displayed in percentage format and right aligned.
2. Reposition the *Total Profit:* heading.
3. Recalculate the profit on the following basis: the royalty fee is a percentage of the **Unit
   Selling Price** and reduces the profit by that amount.
4. Save the spreadsheet under the filename TASK2, for printing now or later. (The print-out
   should show borders – row/column labels.)

```
                              Hi-Tech Productions


                   Production Report      -      January 2007


                           Factory          Unit          Unit
                           Production    Production    Selling    Royalty
        No.    Factory     Quantity         Price        Price       Fee    Profit


         1     Clondalkin     2500          €2.80        €4.80
         2     Santry         3400          €2.50        €4.60
         3     Cork           2800          €3.00        €4.90
         4     Galway         2300          €2.60        €5.20
         5     Limerick       4400          €3.20        €5.30
         6     Athlone         800          €2.80        €4.60
         7     Sligo          1800          €2.90        €5.10
         8     Waterford      3500          €3.00        €5.00
         9     Dundalk        2700          €3.30        €5.20


                     Total:                            Total Profit:
      Name:
      College:
      Date:
```

Figure 2

◩ Task 3 (35 marks)

1. Input the additional information shown in Figure 3.

   a. Change the month to *March*.

   b. Delete the *Athlone, Sligo, Waterford* and *Dundalk* factories from the spreadsheet.

   c. Insert the **Blackrock** factory into the spreadsheet.

   d. Change the production quantities as shown.

   e. Insert the headings *Spare Capacity:* and *Value of Spare Capacity:* in the positions shown.

   f. Insert an extra column for the *Factory Production Capacity* and place this heading in the position shown.

   g. Right align the new column and heading.

   h. Re-align the main and subheadings centrally over the data.

   i. Insert the table: *No., Manager* and *Capacity* in the position shown and fill in the information in the table, aligned as in Figure 3.

2. Use the look-up function to insert the *Factory Production Capacity* for each factory in the *Factory Production Capacity* column, from the table in (1) above.
3. Calculate the total production capacity and place it in the position indicated at the bottom of that column.
4. The *Spare Capacity* should be the difference between the sum of the factory production capacities and the sum of the factory production quantities.
5. The *Value of Spare Capacity* should be calculated using the selling price only.
6. Sort the spreadsheet into alphabetical order on the *Factory* names.
7. Save the spreadsheet under the filename TASK3, for printing now or later. (Make two print-outs of TASK3 to show (1) values and (2) formulae and cell references.)

```
                        Hi-Tech Productions


              Production Report     -     March 2007


                    Factory        Factory         Unit      Unit
                    Production      Production   Production   Selling   Royalty   Profit
     No.  Factory   Capacity        Quantity       Price      Price      Fee


     6    Blackrock                   5000         €2.30     €5.10
     1    Clondalkin                   900         €2.80     €4.80
     2    Santry                      1800         €2.50     €4.60
     3    Cork                        3200         €3.00     €4.90
     4    Galway                      2300         €2.60     €5.20
     5    Limerick                    3500         €3.20     €5.30


          Total:                                             Total Profit:


     Spare Capacity:

                                                             Value of Spare
                                                                 Capacity:


          No.             1           2           3           4          5          6
          Manager:    M. Murphy   P. Doyle    J. Daly    B. Walsh   H. Byrne   N. Cleary
          Capacity:     4000        4500        4000        3000      4500       6000


     Name:
     College:
     Date:
```

Figure 3

1. Produce a bar graph from spreadsheet TASK3 to show the quantities produced in each factory:
   a. The quantities should be taken from the *Factory Production Quantity* column.
   b. The bar graph should have the heading *Production Quantities*.
   c. The x-axis should show the factory name under each bar and have the word *Factory* as the x-axis label.
   d. The y-axis should show the quantities in figures and have the word *Quantity* as the y-axis label.
2. Save the bar graph under the filename GRAPH (either separately or as part of the spreadsheet TASK3), for printing now or later.

Assignment 22
FETAC Spreadsheet Methods Sample Paper 2

▧Task 1 (30 marks)

William's Grain Merchants

Daily Grain Intake

(Date)

Cust. Code	Product	Weight (Tonne)	Price per Tonne	Bonus per Tonne	Total Price
225	Wheat	12.6	€102.00		
106	Barley	15.3	€95.00		
357	Wheat	21.7	€102.00		
246	Wheat	11.6	€102.00		
341	Oats	9.5	€90.00		
128	Barley	18.3	€95.00		
207	Oats	7.9	€90.00		

Totals:

Name:
Exam No:

Figure 1

1. Set up the spreadsheet and input the data as shown in **Figure 1**.
   a. Align the main heading **(William's Grain Merchants)** and the subheading **(Daily Grain Intake)** centrally over the data.
   b. Insert today's date, in the cell marked **(Date)**, from the computer clock.
   c. Set column widths to appropriate values.
   d. Column headings and contents should be as shown.
   e. Column headings and contents should be aligned as shown.
   f. All monetary values should be displayed in currency format, with two places of decimals.
2. The **Bonus per Tonne** should be displayed as €5.00 if the weight is less than 15 tonnes and €7.50 if the weight is 15 tonnes or over.
3. Calculate **Total Price** as **Price per Tonne** plus **Bonus per Tonne** multiplied by the **Weight** and display in the column under the heading Total Price.
4. Calculate the **Totals** for Weight and Total Price, using the SUM function, and display in the **Totals:** row, in the appropriate column.
5. Insert your name and centre name in the second column, beside the appropriate label.
6. Save the spreadsheet under the filename **REPORT1**, for printing now or later. The print-out should show borders (row/column identifiers).

Task 2 (5 marks)

```
                           William's Grain Merchants


                             Daily Grain Intake
(Date)


Cust.     Customer                Moisture    Weight   Price per    Bonus      Total
Code        Name      Product     Content     (Tonne)    Tonne    per Tonne    Price


225                   Wheat         24%        12.6
106                   Barley        18%        15.3
357                   Wheat         21%        21.7
246                   Wheat         20%        11.6
341                   Oats          15%         9.5
128                   Barley        19%        18.3
207                   Oats          13%         7.9


                                 Totals:


    Code:     106     128         207         225       246        341        357
    Name:   P. Daly A. Doyle    H. Jones    P. Coyle  J. Murphy  R. Dunne   W. Wise


    Name:

Exam No:
```

Figure 2

1 Input the additional information as shown in **Figure 2**.
   a. Insert two extra columns, one between the Cust. Code and Product columns and the second between the Product and Weight columns.
   b. Insert the heading **Customer Name** in the position shown and align as shown.
   c. Insert the values in the **Moisture Content** column and display as shown.
   d. Delete the values in the **Price per Tonne** column.
   e. Move the **Totals:** side heading one column to the right.
   f. Insert three extra rows between the Totals: row and your name.
   g. Insert the table **Code:** and **Name:** in the position shown and fill in the information in the table, aligning as shown.

2 a. Use the look-up function to insert the **Customer Name** from the table in 1g, into the column under the **Customer Name** column heading.

   b. Align the **Customer Names** to the left of the column.

3 a. Use the IF function to display the correct value in the **Price per Tonne** column, based on the following information:

   • Wheat €103.00 per tonne

   • Barley €97.00 per tonne

   • Oats €92.00 per tonne.

   b. Display the Price per Tonne in currency format, whole euro only (i.e. no decimal places).

4 Save the spreadsheet under the filename **REPORT2**, for printing now or later. The print-out should show borders (row/column identifiers).

◥ **Task 3 (35 marks)**

			William's Grain Merchants					
			Daily Grain Intake					
(Date)								
Cust. Code	Customer Name	Product	Moisture Content	Weight (Tonne)	Price per Tonne	Bonus per Tonne	Total Price	Collection Charge
225		Wheat	24%	12.6				
106		Barley	18%	15.3				
357		Wheat	21%	21.7				
246		Wheat	20%	11.6				
341		Oats	15%	9.5				
128		Barley	19%	18.3				
207		Oats	13%	7.9				
			Totals:					
				Average Price per Tonne:				
				Average Collection Charge per Tonne:				

Code:	106	128	207	225	246	341	357
Name:	P. Daly	A. Doyle	H. Jones	P. Coyle	J. Murphy	R. Dunne	W. Wise
Col. Charge:	2.0%	1.5%	3.0%	2.5%	1.5%	0.5%	3.5%

Name:

Exam No:

Figure 3

1. Input the additional information as shown in Figure 3.
   a. Insert the column heading **Collection Charge** to the right of the **Total Price** column and align as shown.
   b. Insert two extra rows between the **Totals:** row and the **table**.
   c. Insert the heading **Average Price per Tonne:** in the position shown and right align.
   d. Insert the heading **Average Collection Charge per Tonne:** in the position shown and right align.
   e. Insert an extra row between the table and your name at the bottom of the spreadsheet.
   f. Insert the side heading **Col. Charge:** and associated data in the table as shown.
   g. Ensure that the main heading and subheading are centrally aligned across all column headings.
2. a. Delete the data from the **Bonus per Tonne** column.
   b. Use the IF function to display the correct value in the **Bonus per Tonne** column, based on the following information:
      i. If the Moisture Content is greater than 23 per cent, then the Bonus per Tonne is *minus* €3.00 (i.e. -€3.00 or €[3.00]).
      ii. If the Moisture Content is greater than or equal to 20 per cent, but less than or equal to 23 per cent, then the Bonus per Tonne is *minus* €2.00 (i.e. -€2.00 or €[2.00]).
      iii. If the Moisture Content is less than 20 per cent, then the Bonus per Tonne is €5.00.
3. Calculate the collection charge using the look-up function to take the rate from the **Col. Charge** in the table multiplied by the **Total Price**, and display as € with two decimal places.
4. Calculate the average price per tonne and insert it in the **Total Price** column beside the heading **Average Price per Tonne:**.
5. Calculate the weighted average collection charge per tonne and insert it in the **Collection Charge** column beside the heading **Average Collection Charge per Tonne:**.*
6. **Sort** the spreadsheet in alphabetical order on the **Cust. Code**.
7. Save the spreadsheet under the filename **REPORT3** for printing now or later. Produce two print-outs of REPORT3 to show **(i) values** and **(ii) formulae and cell references**, both with borders (row/column identifiers).

*This should be calculated as the average of the individual collection charges **per tonne** for each customer.

Task 4 (10 marks)
1. Produce a macro which will perform the following tasks on REPORT3. (NB: Do and run/execute the macro on REPORT3.)
   a. Delete the values from the Cust. Code column.
   b. Delete the values from the Product, Moisture Content and Weight (Tonne) columns.

c.   Insert the date from the computer clock in the cell marked (Date).

2 Save the macro under the name NEWDAY (either separately or as part of the spreadsheet
   – REPORT3), for printing now or later.

◼Printing

Printing may be carried out after the time allocation for the examination, but no alterations
may be made to the saved files.

The following printouts are required:

1. Print-out of REPORT1, complete with border (row/column identifiers).

2. Print-out of REPORT2, complete with border (row/column identifiers).

3. Print-out of REPORT3, to show all *values* complete with border (row/column identifiers).

4. Print-out of REPORT3, to show all *formulae* and cell references.

5. Print-out of the Macro.

Chapter 6
Computer Applications Projects

▦ Introduction

The production of a good project demands the use of expressive and creative abilities as well as an understanding of how to use a particular computer program. Many students erroneously believe that they must be 'tapping away' on their computer keyboards for the entire duration of a project. A builder will only commence work on a house after he has received detailed house plans from an architect. Similarly, a project idea must be planned accurately and written up as an in-depth design. This project design must then be marked by your teacher **before** you embark on implementing the design using a computer program. In short, your tools during the design phase of your project are pen and paper and **not** a computer equipped with a particular applications program. It is recommended that you spend twice as much time on project design as you do on implementing the design on your computer.

▦ A project idea

The starting point is a period of quiet reflection to decide on a suitable topic for the project. Sources of project ideas are many and varied; some popular sources are:
- your work experience **(do not use real data)**
- hobbies.

A good guide to the suitability of an idea for a database project is to ask yourself the following questions:
- *Will the completed project be useful to others?*
- *How many fields will go to make up a record?*
- *Are all the fields relevant?*
- *Can suitable queries and reports be generated?*

Some popular topics for database projects include:

Club membership	Concert bookings
Employee details	Car rental
Dentistry patients	Student profiles
Product orders	Restaurant reservations
Shop stocks	Veterinary surgery – pet details

Similarly, a good guide to the suitability of an idea for a spreadsheet project is to ask yourself the following questions:

- *Will the completed project be useful to others?*
- *Will the final spreadsheet be easy to use?*
- *How many rows and columns will go to make up the spreadsheet?*
- *Will cumbersome formulae be required? (If so, it may not be a suitable project idea.)*

Some popular topics for spreadsheet projects include:

Employee salaries	Customer invoices
Cashflow projections	Insurance quotes
Pension schemes	Sales analysis
Stock re-ordering	Equipment hire
Budget forecasting	Loan repayments

A golden rule is to keep the project specifications before you while you work on the project.

▓ Producing a database project

This can be broken down into three distinct phases: the design phase, the implementation phase and the conclusion phase.

Design phase

A database project design should include:

1. An outline of the problem to be solved, including document analysis, e.g. data capture forms
2. Identification of:
   - record structure
   - relevant key fields for sorting and/or indexing the file
   - likely queries, reports and labels to be generated.
3. Design of the data entry screen layout (ideally this should be based on the data capture form to aid data entry).

Implementation phase

During this phase, a computer equipped with a suitable database program is required. Hard copy will obviously be produced using a printer. Ability to carry out the following should be demonstrated:

1. Create the record structure and data entry screen
2. Input data accurately

3. Modify the structure and amend data
4. Handle a variety of data types
5. Query the database on a variety of data types
6. Organise the data on different field types
7. Create relevant reports and labels.

Conclusion phase

The conclusion should include an evaluation of the project in terms of:
1. Its usefulness
2. All necessary modifications
3. Any likely improvements.

Common questions

How big should my database file be?
The completed database file should contain at least five fields and a minimum of twenty-five records.

What field types should I use?
Field types should consist of at least character, numeric and one other (e.g. date or logical).

Should I generate query files?
Two relevant queries should be produced as a minimum. Each resulting query file should contain at least four records. One of the queries should contain a logical operator (e.g. AND, OR, NOT).

Must the file be sorted?
The file must be sorted on a minimum of two separate fields and two printouts should be produced using the appropriate report format.

What should the finished project look like?
It should be of a professional standard, typed and bound, within the constraints of the equipment available.

▦ Producing a spreadsheet project

This can also be broken down into the same three distinct phases.

Design phase

A spreadsheet project design should include:
1. A concise description of the problem and a proposed solution, identifying a source of data.

2. Identification of:
   - input data
   - the processing required (in words)
   - output data generated.

   An example of each should be given.
3. Design of the screen layout, which should be based on a data capture form.
4. Specification of:
   - data format (e.g. alignment, currency, decimal places)
   - column widths
   - data to be hidden, frozen and or protected.

Implementation phase

During this phase, a computer equipped with a suitable spreadsheet program is required. Again, hard copy will obviously be produced using a printer. Ability to carry out the following should be demonstrated:

1. Create the spreadsheet
2. Print the spreadsheet
3. Print the spreadsheet showing formulae
4. Change a variable and print the altered spreadsheet.

Conclusion phase

The conclusion should include an evaluation of the project in terms of:

1. Its usefulness
2. All necessary modifications
3. Any likely improvements.

Common questions

How big should my spreadsheet be?
It is generally accepted that the completed spreadsheet should contain enough data to fill a monitor screen.

How complex should my formulae be?
This depends greatly on the problem which you are solving. The FETAC spreadsheet project guidelines suggest that a simple IF function should be included in at least one column of formulae as the basic minimum.

What should the finished project look like?
It should be of a professional standard, typed and bound, within the constraints of the equipment available.

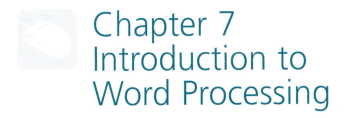

Chapter 7
Introduction to
Word Processing

A word processor is a program that makes it possible to use a microcomputer for entering, storing and manipulating text.

In typing a document we usually make some mistakes: spelling errors, missing or duplicated words and paragraphs in the wrong order, or even omitted. A word processor allows us to correct these errors and to make any other changes before the document is printed. It also allows us to store a copy of the document onto disk and to recall it later and edit it as required.

Facilities of a word processor

In this chapter we will examine the following facilities of a word processor:

1. Elementary editing: deleting and inserting
2. More advanced editing: moving text
3. Enhancing the appearance of a document
4. The 'find and replace' facility
5. Setting tabs
6. Stored paragraphs
7. Merge printing
8. Other facilities.

1. Elementary editing: deleting and inserting

Patrick Matthews is secretary to the managing director of a company that manufactures building insulation: Cavityfoam Enterprises Ltd. He produces all documents on his microcomputer, which is equipped with a word processor program.

This is the first draft of a document describing the company and its products:

Cavityfoam Enterprises Ltd was founded in 1981 by JohnHall and Fionnuala O'Connor. The aim of the company was to produce good-quality home insulation products at a competitive price.

The company initially employed only twelve people. As markets were quickly established, the number of people employed by the firm grew rapidly. In 1985 the company employed forty-three people, and by 2005 the work force numbered ninety-eight.

In response to a need in the market, the company directors decided to branch into factory farm building insulation products. John Hall spent nine months in Toronto observing the mannufacture and testing of Canadian insulation products.

Today Cavityfoam enterprises Ltd is one of Ireland's leading companies in the manufacture of insulation building products. The Company employs 265 people, and last year's profits were £1.7 million.

Fionnuala now edits this first draft. There are standard ways of indicating what changes are to be made: the most important of these are shown here.

Cavityfoam Enterprises Ltd was founded in 1981 by John⌄Hall and Fionnuala O'Connor. The aim of the company was to produce good-quality home insulation products at a competitive price.

The company initially employed |only| twelve people. As markets were quickly established, the number of people employed by the |firm| *company* grew rapidly. In 1985 the company employed forty-three people, and by 2005 the work⌣force numbered ninety-eight.

In response to a need in the market, the company directors decided to branch into factory⌃*and* farm building insulation products. John Hall spent nine months in Toronto observing the man⌃ufacture and testing of Canadian insulation products.

Today Cavityfoam ＿enterprises Ltd is one of Ireland's leading companies in the manufacture of ⌐insulation⌐ building⌐ products. The Ⓒompany employs 265 people, and last year's profits were £1.7 million.

⊢⊣ Delete a word	≡ Change from lower case (ordinary letters) to capitals
company ⊢⊣ Substitute a word	⌐⌐ Transpose (swap) words
Y Insert a space between words	≢ or ◯ Change from capitals to lower case
⋏ Insert a character or word	⌣ Close up (remove a space)
/ Delete a character	

New text can be inserted into a document by moving the cursor to the correct position and simply typing the text. Unwanted text can be deleted by positioning the cursor at the appropriate place and giving one of the delete commands. Word processors have commands to delete a character, word, line or block of text.

The word processor will rearrange the text after you have edited a line so that the remainder of the text will move forwards or back to fill the space.

The corrected text will now appear as follows:

Cavityfoam Enterprises Ltd was founded in 1981 by John Hall and Fionnuala O'Connor. The aim of the company was to produce good-quality home insulation products at a competitive price.

The company initially employed twelve people. As markets were quickly established, the number of people employed by the company grew rapidly. In 1985 the company employed forty-three people, and by 2005 the workforce numbered ninety-eight.

In response to a need in the market, the company directors decided to branch into factory and farm building insulation products. John Hall spent nine months in Toronto observing the manufacture and testing of Canadian insulation products.

Today Cavityfoam Enterprises Ltd is one of Ireland's leading companies in the manufacture of building insulation products. The company employs 265 people, and last year's profits were £1.7 million.

---

2. More advanced editing: moving text

The managing director has asked Patrick to draw up a letter to the wholesalers who stock Cavityfoam products. The letter should tell them of future price increases on some products and of the development of a new insulation material suitable for bungalows. Here is his draft:

Dear Wholesaler,

We regret to inform you that, because of spiralling raw material costs, we have increased the price of some products. Our very popular Astrofoam has been increased from €11.75 to €12.50 per cubic metre. Our insulation foam for farm buildings, Agrifoam, has been increased from €8.50 to €9.20 per cubic metre. The company has decided to extend its guarantee from ten to fifteen years on all of its insulation products. This fact should be made clear to the retailers, as our largest competitors only guarantee their products for seven years.

We are introducing a new insulation product called Bungafoam onto the market. This is suitable for bungalows, and is competitively priced at €11.50 per cubic metre.

Our sales representative will be calling on you on 28 March. He will furnish you with all the details of our other insulation products and will accept your order this month.

I wish to remind you of our 5 per cent discount on all products that are paid for in full on the delivery date.

I am confident that you will continue to stock the Cavityfoam range of insulation products.

Yours faithfully,

Fionnuala O'Connor
Managing Director

Fionnuala feels that some changes need to be made to this letter.

- Paragraph 2 should be moved so that it becomes the first paragraph of the letter. This is achieved by marking the paragraph to be moved and positioning the cursor at the new position in the document. The command to move a marked block of text must then be given.
- One paragraph should be divided into two. The paragraph that starts 'We regret to inform you . . . ' should be split at the point that begins 'The company has decided to extend . . .' This is achieved by inserting two carriage returns (pressing the 'enter' key twice) at the appropriate position in the text.
- Two separate paragraphs should be joined together. The paragraph that starts 'Our sales representative will be calling . . . ' and the one that starts 'I wish to remind you . . . ' should be run together. This is achieved by deleting the carriage returns between the paragraphs.

Fionnuala marks the draft with the following symbols:

Dear Wholesaler,

Ⓐ We regret to inform you that, because of spiralling raw material costs, we have increased the price of some products. Our very popular Astrofoam has been increased from €11.75 to €12.50 per cubic metre. Our insulation foam for farm buildings, Agrifoam, has been increased from €8.50 to €9.20 per cubic metre. Ⓑ The company has decided to extend its guarantee from ten to fifteen years on all of its insulation products. This fact should be made clear to the retailers, as our largest competitors only guarantee their products for seven years.

We are introducing a new insulation product called Bungafoam onto the market. This is suitable for bungalows, and is competitively priced at €11.50 per cubic metre.

Our sales representative will be calling on you on 28 March. He will furnish you with all the details of our other insulation products and will accept your order this month.
Ⓒ I wish to remind you of our 5 per cent discount on all products that are paid for in full on the delivery date.

I am confident that you will continue to stock the Cavityfoam range of insulation products.

Yours faithfully,

Fionnuala O'Connor
Managing Director

A: Move text to new position

B: Start new paragraph

C: Run-on (not a new paragraph)

The letter will appear as follows after all these changes have been made:

Dear Wholesaler,

We are introducing a new insulation product called Bungafoam onto the market. This is suitable for bungalows, and is competitively priced at €11.50 per cubic metre.

We regret to inform you that, because of spiralling raw material costs, we have increased the price of some products. Our very popular Astrofoam has been increased from €11.75 to €12.50 per cubic metre. Our insulation foam for farm buildings, Agrifoam, has been increased from €8.50 to €9.20 per cubic metre.

The company has decided to extend its guarantee from ten to fifteen years on all of its insulation products. This fact should be made clear to the retailers, as our largest competitors only guarantee their products for seven years.

Our sales representative will be calling on you on 28 March. He will furnish you with all the details of our other insulation products and will accept your order this month. I wish to remind you of our 5 per cent discount on all products that are paid for in full on the delivery date.

I am confident that you will continue to stock the Cavityfoam range of insulation products.

Yours faithfully,

Fionnuala O'Connor

Managing Director

It is obvious that these changes could not have been carried out on an ordinary typewriter without retyping the whole document.

3. Enhancing the appearance of a document

Most word processors offer the user a number of features to enhance the appearance of the text, although these should be used sparingly in business documents, especially by a beginner. They include:

- changing the font and font size
- centring and underlining key words and phrases
- altering the line spacing
- setting new margins and rearranging text accordingly.

◤Changing the font and font size

Word processors allow the use of different fonts. A font is a set of characters with a consistent and identifiable typeface. Each font has a name which you can use to select the font and apply it to text. Times New Roman and Dom Casual are examples of fonts. Further examples of common fonts are given in the table. The size of the font, known as the point size, can also be changed, as shown in the table.

TABLE OF COMMON FONTS		
10 point size	12 point size	16 point size
Times	Times	Times
Caslon 540	Caslon 540	Caslon 540
Stone Serif	Stone Serif	Stone Serif
Futura Book	Futura Book	Futura Book
Brush Script	Brush Script	Brush Script
Bodoni	Bodoni	Bodoni
Helvetica	Helvetica	Helvetica
Baskerville	Baskerville	Baskerville
Freestyle Script	Freestyle Script	Freestyle Script
Optima	Optima	Optima

◤Centring and underlining

Centring a line means moving it so that it is halfway between the left and right margins, making it stand out more clearly. This is very commonly used for headings.

Underlining a section of text means that a continuous line will be printed under this area.

Word processors also allow selected words to be printed in **bold type**.

To enhance a piece of text using one of these features, the text is usually first marked, and then the command to centre, underline or change to bold must be given.

Word processors also have a feature called **justification**, where the shorter lines of a document are spread out towards the right margin to make all the lines the same length (as in this paragraph). In business documents this is rarely an improvement over ordinary ('flush left') alignment, and it is never appropriate for letters.

The default setting on most word processors for justification is off (i.e. flush left alignment), and for line spacing is 1. These settings can be altered by using the correct commands before text is entered. It is also possible to alter justification and line spacing settings after the text has been entered: the text can then be realigned to the new settings.

Patrick has prepared a statement describing the company's plans for overseas expansion. He has centred the heading at the top of the document and changed its font (Caslon 540) and size (11.5 pt) , and he has also used bold type, italics and underlining for key phrases:

New Project

Cavityfoam Enterprises Ltd has decided to open a <u>new plant at Reims in France for the production of building insulation materials</u>. The outlay is projected to be £7.8 million, and at first the plant will employ thirty-five people. The town council has given **approval** for the construction of the factory, and it is hoped that production at the new plant will start in eighteen months. This venture will allow *Cavityfoam Enterprises* to gain a foothold in the European market for insulation products.

◢Altering the line spacing

The amount of spacing between the lines can also be altered on your word processor. Letters and statements for publication in newspapers often have 'double line spacing' – with approximately the depth of another line of type between each line – as printers prefer to receive text in this form.

◢Setting new margins

The managing director may wish to have the statement submitted to the local newspaper for publication in the next edition. Newspapers sometimes like text for publication to be formatted in newspaper style. Patrick can reset the margins on his word processor to allow a maximum line width of 5 cm, as well as changing to double line spacing and justifying the text (straight right and left margins). Centring, underlining and other enhancements are not used.

The document would now appear as follows:

> New project
>
> Cavityfoam Enterprises Ltd has decided to open a new plant at Reims in France for the production of building insulation materials. The outlay is projected to be €7.8 million, and at first the plant will employ thirty-five people. The town council has given approval for the construction of the factory, and it is hoped that production at the new plant will start in eighteen months. This venture will allow Cavityfoam Enterprises to gain a foothold in the European market for insulation products.

4. The 'find and replace' facility

Sometimes you may have used a word in the course of typing a document and then decide to replace it with another. A word processor offers you a facility with which you can replace one word with another, at one place in the document or at every occurrence of that word in the document.

In the document above, Patrick has used the word 'plant' three times. He can easily replace it with the word 'factory' by using the 'find and replace' facility on his word processor. The document would now appear as follows:

The 'find and replace' facility also allows you to replace entire phrases with alternative phrases. The length of phrase permitted may be limited, however.

> New project
>
> Cavityfoam Enterprises Ltd has decided to open a new factory at Reims in France for the production of building insulation materials. The outlay is projected to be €7.8 million, and at first the factory will employ thirty-five people. The town council has given approval for the construction of the factory, and it is hoped that production at the new factory will start in eighteen months. This venture will allow Cavityfoam Enterprises to gain a foothold in the European market for insulation products.

5. Setting tabs

All keyboards have a 'tab' key (short for 'tabulation'). When this key is pressed the cursor will jump a number of spaces horizontally. This saves the inconvenience of continually using the space bar to get to a certain position in the text.

There are a number of positions or 'tabs' already set at equal distances across the line. We can abandon these, however, and set our own tabs. This is an essential facility when we want to enter text in columns.

Tabs can be set quite easily on a word processor. You can change the number of tabs and their positions, thus varying the widths of columns and the space between them.

Patrick has been asked to list the prices of Cavityfoam products for the last three years in columns. The document appears as follows:

PRODUCT	2005	2006	2007
Agrifoam	7.80	8.50	9.20
Astrofoam	10.50	11.75	12.50
Bungafoam	–	–	11.50
Chip carpet	4.99	5.50	5.50
Floor seal	3.60	4.20	4.20
Mason tiles	1.80	2.20	2.20
Shedfoam	7.20	7.20	7.20

Patrick realises that the columns are too close together. He resets the tabs to adjust the distances between the columns. The document would now appear as follows:

PRODUCT	2005	2006	2007
Agrifoam	7.80	8.50	9.20
Astrofoam	10.50	11.75	12.50
Bungafoam	–	–	11.50
Chip carpet	4.99	5.50	5.50
Floor seal	3.60	4.20	4.20
Mason tiles	1.80	2.20	2.20
Shedfoam	7.20	7.20	7.20

An alternative is to set up a table. The gridlines on the table can be set to on or off. The main advantage of the table is that it can be easily changed.

An example of a table is given below (gridlines are set on):

PRODUCT		2005		2006		2007
Agrifoam		7.80		8.50		9.20
Astrofoam		10.50		11.75		12.50
Bungafoam		—		—		11.50
Chip carpet		4.99		5.50		5.50
Floor seal		3.60		4.20		4.20
Mason tiles		1.80		2.20		2.20
Shedfoam		7.20		7.20		7.20

6. Stored paragraphs

One of the most useful features of a word processor is the ability to store frequently used paragraphs in separate files on disk. When we are entering text into a file on our word processor we can copy one of the stored paragraphs into the file as required.

Many letters and documents produced on word processors are the result of 'pasting together' a number of stored paragraphs (sometimes called 'boilerplate paragraphs'). Cavityfoam Enterprises Ltd interviewed five suitably qualified people for two positions in the quality control department. The interview board has made its selection and has asked Patrick to send letters to the applicants, telling them of the board's decision. Patrick will store the following paragraphs in separate files on disk:

[Paragraph 1]
We should like to thank you for attending for interview on Thursday last. We were very impressed by your qualifications and experience.

[Paragraph 2]
We wish to offer you the position of quality control assistant. Please confirm your acceptance of the position as soon as possible so that we can organise a suitable date for a medical examination. We look forward to hearing from you.

[Paragraph 3]
We are, however, unable to offer you a position with our company at the present time. We wish you every success in your future career.

[Paragraph 4]
Yours faithfully,

Fionnuala O'Connor
Managing Director

Patrick can open individual documents on his word processor and use these paragraphs to compose appropriate letters.

Two of the applicants for jobs were Anne Breen and John Cuddy. Anne's efforts have been successful; John, however, has been unsuccessful. Both applicants will receive appropriate letters. The texts of these letters are as follows.

◥Letter 1: Comprising stored paragraphs 1, 2 and 4

18 June 2007

Ms Anne Breen
4 Oakwood Road
Castlebawn, Co. Donegal

Dear Ms Breen,

We should like to thank you for attending for interview on Thursday last. We were very impressed by your qualifications and experience.

We wish to offer you the position of quality control assistant. Please confirm your acceptance of the position as soon as possible so that we can organise a suitable date for a medical examination. We look forward to hearing from you.

Yours faithfully,

Fionnuala O'Connor
Managing Director

◪Letter 2: Comprising stored paragraphs 1, 3 and 4

18 June 2007

Mr John Cuddy
31 Eskermore Terrace
Castlebawn, Co. Donegal

Dear Mr Cuddy,

We should like to thank you for attending for interview on Thursday last. We were very impressed by your qualifications and experience.

We are, however, unable to offer you a position with our company at the present time. We wish you every success in your future career.

Yours faithfully,

Fionnuala O'Connor
Managing Director

The other three applicants would receive replies identical to one or other of the above letters.

This method of composing letters and documents from a set of stored paragraphs is widely used by people who use word processors as a central part of their work. A lawyer's secretary may store on disk a range of paragraphs relating to contracts and other legal documents. Different sets of paragraphs can then be combined in a document, depending on the nature of the contract being drawn up.

7. Merge printing

One of the most powerful features of a word processor is the merge printing facility. This allows you to draw up a **source file**, which usually consists of a single document or letter containing **variables**. The precise information to be included instead of the variables is entered in a **data file**. When you invoke merge printing, the various sets of data from the data file are merged into copies of the source file.

The managing director of Cavityfoam Enterprises Ltd has asked Patrick to send letters to wholesalers in three regions – south-west, south-east, and central – informing them of a demonstration of the new insulation product, Bungafoam. The details of the demonstration in each region are as follows:

REGION	TIME	DATE	VENUE
South-west	2 p.m.	3 April	Whiterock Hotel
South-east	3 p.m.	5 April	Silver Swan Hotel
Central	2 p.m.	10 April	Kilmore Hotel

Patrick would enter a source file in his word processor like the one shown below:

19 March 2007

Dear Wholesaler,

You are invited to a demonstration of our new insulation product for bungalows, called Bungafoam, at &time& on &date& in the &hotel&. This demonstration is for the benefit of all wholesalers in the &area& region.

There will be time after the demonstration for a discussion on the product. Any opinions or criticisms of the product will be welcome.

We look forward to seeing you at the demonstration.

Yours sincerely,

Fionnuala O'Connor
Managing Director

Patrick would then set up a data file and include the times, dates, hotels and regions in a manner similar to that outlined below.

> 2 p.m., 3 April, Whiterock Hotel, south-west
> 3 p.m., 5 April, Silver Swan Hotel, south-east
> 2 p.m., 10 April, Kilmore Hotel, central

You should check the exact format on your particular word processor for variables in the source file and for data in the data file.

When Patrick invokes the merge printing facility, the details from the data file will be merged with the source file, and three separate documents will be produced for the three regions. The three letters should appear as follows:

◤Letter 1: South-west region

19 March 2007

Dear Wholesaler,

You are invited to a demonstration of our new insulation product for bungalows, called Bungafoam, at 2 p.m. on 3 April in the Whiterock Hotel. This demonstration is for the benefit of all wholesalers in the south-west region.

There will be time after the demonstration for a discussion on the product. Any opinions or criticisms of the product will be welcome.

We look forward to seeing you at the demonstration.

Yours sincerely,

Fionnuala O'Connor
Managing Director

▶ Letter 2: South-east region

19 March 2007

Dear Wholesaler,

You are invited to a demonstration of our new insulation product for bungalows, called Bungafoam, at 3 p.m. on 5 April in the Silver Swan Hotel. This demonstration is for the benefit of all wholesalers in the south-east region.

There will be time after the demonstration for a discussion on the product. Any opinions or criticisms of the product will be welcome.

We look forward to seeing you at the demonstration.

Yours sincerely,

Fionnuala O'Connor
Managing Director

19 March 2007

Dear Wholesaler,

You are invited to a demonstration of our new insulation product for bungalows, called Bungafoam, at 2 p.m. on 10 April in the Kilmore Hotel. This demonstration is for the benefit of all wholesalers in the central region.

There will be time after the demonstration for a discussion on the product. Any opinions or criticisms of the product will be welcome.

We look forward to seeing you at the demonstration.

Yours sincerely,

Fionnuala O'Connor
Managing Director

8. Other facilities

Other commonly used facilities include the use of columns, frames, clip art and bullet points, as shown in the following sample.

Information Technology in Schools

Computers and related technologies have greatly changed our society and our world. We have now truly reached the information age. Computers are now poised to promote revolutionary change in our educational systems. This change may be compared to changes wrought by books. IT has similar characteristics. Books empower people who know how to read. In the same way, schools of the future will place major emphasis on helping all students to read IT.

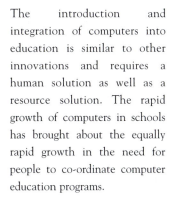

Recently, there has been a worldwide metamorphosis; having computers in schools is now seen as a service to the whole school and not just as a specialist subject. This specialist focus of the past had the undesirable effect of constraining wider curricular development in IT in other subjects, and denied the majority of pupils any substantial access to IT as a tool for learning.

More and more people are coming to realise that the current educational system is not adequate to the challenge of the information age. Emphasis is now shifting from a focus on the computer itself, to a focus on learning environments that are facilitated by computers. This change of focus has put major demands on schools to change in order to facilitate this challenge of integration. Massive amounts of money have been spent on the purchase of hardware and software. However, this has not solved the problem of true integration of computers into the curriculum. Major barriers to integration have

been identified, such as school structure, teachers' attitudes, teacher support, teacher training, lack of policy, lack of time and co-ordination.

The introduction and integration of computers into education is similar to other innovations and requires a human solution as well as a resource solution. The rapid growth of computers in schools has brought about the equally rapid growth in the need for people to co-ordinate computer education programs.

Most schools go through stages in their progression on to full integration. These stages are:

- **Innovation:** Just one or two members of staff exploring the educational use of IT.
- **Fire lighting:** Attempts are being made to get more staff involved, and someone, perhaps an IT co-ordinator, has been identified.
- **Promotion:** Serious attempts to engage large numbers of staff, where it is seen as an important element in the school development plan.
- **Growth:** As result of promotion the school faces serious demands for resources, staff development.
- **Co-ordination:** Associated with collaboration across the school about IT experiences.
- **Integration:** Methods of work have been established, most subjects using IT extensively for teaching.

⊞ Applications of word processing

Almost any application requiring the manipulation of text can be handled efficiently with a word processor. Only a few of the most common applications are described here.

Standard letters

These are letters containing the same information that are sent to many customers. With the merge printing facility the letters can be 'personalised', i.e. the name and address of the customer can be added to the letter. Matching envelope labels can also be printed.

Contracts and agreements

Most legal contracts contain standard information. When a solicitor's secretary prepares a contract, some of these paragraphs can be read into the document by using the stored paragraphs facility. The paragraphs need only be typed in once and can then be used any number of times.

Reports

Reports usually require a variety of styles of presentation. Some of the various text enhancement facilities can be used here, as well as the ability of most word processors to read text into the report from other sources, e.g. from a spreadsheet or database.

Mailshots

These are regular advertising leaflets posted to a compiled list of customers. The information may need to be changed from time to time, and word processor editing facilities will help here. More importantly, the word processor will produce printed labels showing the name and address of each customer.

Regularly updated lists

Lists of all kinds that require regular updating can be produced, such as price lists, directories, customer lists, inventories and catalogues.

⊞ Advantages of word processor use

We have already examined many of the advantages of word processors in the creation and editing of documents of all kinds. Some of the most important advantages are summarised here.

Storage of text

The ability to store and retrieve text means that it can be used again, either exactly as first used or with changes. Magnetic and optical storage media are also less bulky and easier to retrieve than paper copies.

Time savings

The ability to edit easily, both while entering text and subsequently, means a very significant saving in time, which is of great importance to a business.

Quality

The layout and general appearance of documents can be enhanced by changing typefaces, margins, alignment and line spacing, as well as by other enhancement features, particularly if a high-quality printer such as a laser printer is available.

Security

Confidential documents are easily protected on word processor files, which can be secured against accidental viewing or changing by use of the 'protect' tab on diskettes or programmed to require a password to permit viewing or changing them. Magnetic media can be easily stored in fireproof safes.

Ease of use

Most word processor programs are easy to operate and learn. Good programs have a key that provides on-screen help when you are entering text.

Disadvantages of word processor use

Despite their many advantages, word processors have a number of drawbacks that should also be taken into account.

Cost

Business-quality computers and peripherals can be expensive, and the rapid pace of technological change can make systems obsolete very quickly and frequent updates are required.

Staff training

Staff must be trained to use the computers and the word processor programs. Equipment and programs will need to be upgraded occasionally and the staff retrained in their use. This can be a considerable cost for a business.

Poor checking

Because so many editing facilities are available during the typing of text, there may be a temptation to be less thorough in correcting the final print-out.

Health

There is some evidence that prolonged use of monitors and keyboards can have adverse physical effects (e.g. eye strain, migraine) and repetitive strain injury (RSI).

⊞ Conclusion

In this section we have examined the main features of a word processor, and we hope that you will work through all the assignments in the next chapter on your own equipment and using your own programs. The word processor is by far the most widely used computer application, and the ability to operate one is essential in many occupations as the trend away from the use of typewriters continues.

⊞ Questions

Multi-choice questions

1. Word processing is:
   (a) the sending of text from a microcomputer to a large mainframe computer for processing
   (b) the use of microelectronic equipment to increase the amount of work carried out by office staff in a given time
   (c) the use of microelectronic equipment to enter, edit and store text
   (d) the use of microelectronic equipment to eliminate errors in writing
2. Centred text in a document may help to highlight:
   (a) text that has to be moved
   (b) the start of a new section
   (c) text that contains errors
   (d) where we must justify the text
3. Which of the following could be carried out just as efficiently using a typewriter as using a word processor?
   (a) producing customised letters
   (b) producing short occasional letters
   (c) producing long legal documents with many identical clauses
   (d) producing complex medical documents containing many pharmaceutical terms
4. A triple-underline symbol on a corrected document means that we must:
   (a) start a new paragraph
   (b) use a capital letter
   (c) use a lower-case letter
   (d) correct the spelling of a word
5. Which of the following keys, when pressed, will move the cursor a number of spaces horizontally?
   (a) Alt
   (b) Esc
   (c) F8
   (d) Tab

6. The 'find and replace' facility:
   (a) finds all occurrences of words longer than eight characters and offers a list of alternatives from the thesaurus
   (b) finds a block of text you may have marked for moving and allows you to replace the markers with 'move' symbols
   (c) searches for all words at the beginning of sentences and checks that they start with a capital letter
   (d) finds one or all occurrences of the given text and changes it to the given replacement
7. The term 'text' means:
   (a) letters, numbers and symbols (excluding pictures and diagrams) that make up a document
   (b) documents that consist of letters only
   (c) all documents (excluding business letters)
   (d) a document that does not contain any typing errors
8. A font is the same as:
   (a) the pitch
   (b) the typeface
   (c) the size of the characters
   (d) none of the above

Short-answer questions

1. Briefly describe the main text editing facilities of a word processor.
2. Suggest three advantages and two disadvantages of word processor use.
3. Briefly describe the main features you would look for in buying a word processor program.
4. Describe the following styles of text alignment and give examples of where each one might be used: justified, flush left, flush right and centred.
5. Illustrate, by means of an example, the 'stored paragraphs' facility of a word processor.
6. What is merge printing? Give an example of an application where it might be used.
7. Distinguish between the spelling check and thesaurus facilities of a word processor.

▦ Glossary of word processing terms

alignment: the way in which the text of a document is adjusted relative to the left and right margins, whether flush left, flush right, justified or centred.

bold type: a typeface design matching the one in normal use but made up of thicker lines to give emphasis.

carriage return: the keystroke or command that ends the current line of text and sends the cursor to the first character position on the next line, invoked in word processing by pressing the 'enter' key.

centred: the style of alignment in which the text is placed halfway between the left and right margins of the document.

data file: a computer file on disk that contains text or other data that the user has created and stored, as distinct from program files, which contain the computer code that runs the program.

editing: making corrections and other changes to a text, including substitutions, deletions, and insertions.

'find and replace': a facility that automatically replaces a selected word or phrase with an alternative word or phrase, at selected occurrences or at every occurrence in the document.

flush left: the style of alignment in which lines are of different length and the text has a straight left margin and uneven right margin, exactly as it was typed into the word processor.

flush right: the style of alignment in which lines are of different length and the text has a straight right margin and uneven left margin.

font: a special type of program file that contains instructions for creating a particular typeface on the printer, usually with a separate font for each size.

justification: the style of alignment in which all the lines are forced out to equal length by increasing the space between words, with straight left and right margins.

line spacing: the adjustable vertical distance between lines of text.

menu: a list of the options available at any stage in the execution of a program.

merge printing: a facility that allows the user to customise standard documents by automatically reading in variable data.

page break: a code in a word processor file that causes the printer to start printing on a new page: it may be a 'forced page break' entered by the user or one that occurs automatically when the amount of text entered would fill the defined page size.

spelling check: a facility of most word processors that checks the spelling of words in a document by comparing them against a list of words in one of the program files.

stored paragraph: a paragraph stored in a separate file on disk that can be combined with other paragraphs to make up a composite document.

tab key: a key that causes the cursor to jump a number of spaces horizontally to user-defined positions on the typing line in order to set the width of columns and the space between them.

thesaurus: a facility that allows the user to choose alternative words from lists of words with a related meaning.

typeface: a distinctive style of type with its own name.

underlining: the printing of a continuous line under a selected group of words to emphasise them.

word processor: a computer program used in the creating, editing and printing of text.

word wraparound: a feature of a word processor that causes the cursor to move automatically to the beginning of the next line in the display when the end of a line is reached.

work area: the area of the display excluding the status line, menu and ruler line, where text is typed and edited.

Chapter 8
Practical Word Processing Assignments

These assignments are graded, and we advise that you work through them in the order in which they are given. Unless otherwise stated, set up the document for A4 page size with one inch left and right borders for all assignments. Justification should be off unless otherwise stated. **Note: The text for assignments 3, 4, 6, 7, 8, 9, 10, 16 and 20 are available in ASCII format and Word format from the Gill & Macmillan website at www.gillmacmillan.ie.**

◣Functions and commands required
As you progress through these assignments, you will need to check on the functions and commands specific to your word processor program. You will also be practising commands and functions learned in earlier assignments. (Note: If you do not have access to a printer, you can display the results of that task instead.)

The functions and commands required for each assignment are as follows.

ASSIGNMENT 1
- Text entry in a document file
- Cursor movement
- Saving a document to disk

ASSIGNMENT 2
- Deleting and inserting text
- Retrieving a file

ASSIGNMENT 3
- Consolidation assignment

ASSIGNMENT 4
- Moving a block of text

ASSIGNMENT 5
- Dividing and joining paragraphs
- Letter format

ASSIGNMENT 6
- Consolidation assignment
- Find and replace

ASSIGNMENT 7
- Centring
- Fonts

ASSIGNMENT 8
- Underlining and bold
- Bullets
- Case changes
- Hanging indent

ASSIGNMENT 9
- Setting margins
- Block format

ASSIGNMENT 10
- Consolidation assignment
- Indent paragraphs
- Line spacing

ASSIGNMENT 11
- Setting tabs

ASSIGNMENT 12
- Setting tabs

ASSIGNMENT 13
- Tables

ASSIGNMENT 14
- Tabs and tables, layout

ASSIGNMENT 15
- Clip art
- Font sizes

ASSIGNMENT 16
- Clip art
- Columns
- Frames
- Header and footer

ASSIGNMENT 17
- Stored paragraphs

ASSIGNMENT 18
- Merge printing

ASSIGNMENT 19
• Merge printing

ASSIGNMENT 20
• FETAC sample exam

Assignment 1

1. Key in the following text.
2. Proofread carefully.
3. Use the backspace key or delete key to delete any errors, and retype.
4. Save on disk using the filename LOCHHUNT.

Nessie lies low

A prize of €5,000 in the Loch Ness monster hunt was won yesterday by Oceanscan, an American survey company. The prize, however, fell far short of the €500,000 on offer for conclusive proof of Nessie's existence.

Oceanscan made sonar contact on Saturday with a large unidentified object measuring up to 8 m long. The sonar contact was made near the loch's northern shore, where most sightings of Nessie have been reported.

Andy James (42), the team leader, said yesterday: 'We are thrilled to win the prize for the best search method. The object, which showed up on Saturday, registered as two blips on the sonar screen, but it moved out of range quickly.'

The organising committee of the hunt have decided to hold the event again next year. It will be held over a ten-day period in July, and the prize money for conclusive proof of Nessie's existence will be increased to €750,000. Many teams, including those from Canada and the United States, have agreed to participate again.

Assignment 2

1. Key in the following text.
2. Proofread carefully.
3. Save on disk using the filename OILFIND1.

New oil reserves

Saudi Arabia has discovered extensive new crude oil reserves in previously unexplored areas, according to a report from Reuters news agency today.

One Saudi government source said that the new find was bigger than the total known reserves of some other OPEC member-states. The Saudi state company has reportedly been drilling in areas well away from its existing oil pipeline network.

The agency quotes unnamed Saudi officials as saying that the find could boost the country's oil reserves by as much as 20 per cent. The discovery could have a significant impact on oil markets in lowering the price of crude oil from its recent record price of around $80 per barrel.

This is good news for the consumer, who has recently been experiencing steadily increasing prices on all oil products. Increased oil prices automatically lead to increased inflation and invariably to increases in unemployment.

4. Retrieve the file OILFIELD1.
5. Edit the file by making the alterations shown below and proofread carefully.

New oil reserves

Saudi Arabia has discovered extensive new crude oil reserves in previously unexplored areas, according to a report from Reuters news agency ~~today.~~ *yesterday*

One Saudi government source said that the new find was bigger than the total known reserves of some other OPEC member-states. The Saudi state *oil* company has reportedly been drilling in areas well away from its existing oil pipeline network.

discovery
The agency quotes unnamed Saudi officials as saying that the ~~find~~ could boost the country's oil reserves by as much as 20 per cent. The discovery could have a significant
world
impact on oil markets in lowering the price of crude oil from its recent record price of around $80 per barrel.

This is good news for the consumer, who has recently been experiencing steadily increasing prices on all oil products. Increased oil prices ~~automatically~~ lead to increased inflation and invariably to increases in unemployment.

6. Save this edited version of the file onto your diak, using OILFIELD2 as the filename.

Assignment 3

◤Carry out the following tasks:

1. Retrieve the file DUNBEG1 from the Gill & Macmillan website (www.gillmacmillan.ie).

2. Edit the document by making the alterations shown below and proofread carefully.

Dunbeg development proposals

There is an ~~immediate~~ _urgent_ need for a children's playground in the area. The association considers Knockmore Meadow ~~as~~ _to be_ a suitable site for a playground, as it is close to Dunbeg swimming pool and gymnasium. The association is prepared to organise and supervise sports events and barbecues _at the playground_ during the summer holidays.

There is an immediate need for a pedestrian crossing on Castledean Road near the shopping ~~arcade~~ _centre_ . Residents of Beechwood Road and Fitzgerald Avenue have great difficulty crossing Castledean Road during working hours.

The association urges the county council to honour its 2005 commitment to install street lighting on Bishopstown Road and Gasfinn Road. These roads are close to the railway station, and the lack of adequate street lighting, especially during winter months, is a problem for those who commute _by rail_ to Castledean every day

3. Save the edited version of the file to disk, using DUNBEG2 as the filename.

Assignment 4

■ **Carry out the following tasks:**

1. Retrieve the file NEWS from the Gill & Macmillan website (www.gillmacmillan.ie).

2. Edit the document by making the alterations shown below and proofread carefully.

Mason & Co.

COMPANY NEWSLETTER   *position here*

INTERCOMPANY FOOTBALL. The annual intercompany football tournament took place at Murrenstown ~~football~~ sports grounds. Many local firms entered a team. The tournament was eventually won by Slaney Meats PLC. Our team reached the semi-final but was beaten by Marymount Electrical Ltd. *in a penalty shootout*

FISHING TRIP. Twenty-five people have enlisted for the fishing trip to the ~~Slaney~~ Boyne valley on Saturday next. A coach will leave from the town hall at 10 a.m. A limited number of places is still available; if you are interested, please forward your name *and address and telephone number* to John Martin or Susan Conway.

NEW ARRIVAL. Best wishes to Andrew and Niamh Boylan on the birth of their first child, a baby girl. She is to be called Ciara.

DRAMA SECTION. Mary McEvoy would like to hear from anyone who would be willing to participate in this year's drama production of John B. Keane's 'Many Young Men of Twenty'. Performances would be in ~~late March~~ early April of next year.

SECURE PARKING. In the light of last month's vandalism of two cars in the company car park, a new gate has been installed at the entrance to the car park. This gate will be locked from 10 a.m. to 1 p.m. and from 2.15 to 4.45 p.m. each day. *position where shown by asterisk**

3. Save the edited version of the file to your disk, using NEWS1 as the filename.

4. Produce a print-out of NEWS1.

Assignment 5

1. Create the following letter.
2. Proofread.
3. Save the letter using CARSALE1 as the filename.

Cox Motors Ltd
Gort Road
Ballymore
Co. Tipperary

Mr Ruairi O'Connell
25 Golden Vale Road
Ballymore
Co. Tipperary

11 May 2007

Dear Mr O'Connell,

Thank you for your enquiry about the Astra car range. As requested, we are sending you a brochure giving full details of all six cars in the range.

You will notice that the fuel consumption is excellent and all new Astra cars have a three-year warranty on all parts. A leaflet is also enclosed outlining the retail prices of our new cars, together with a comprehensive list of quality used Astra cars in stock.

Please feel free to drop into the garage at any time for a test drive.

Yours sincerely,

Robert Cox
Sales Department

---

4. Make the following edits to the letter. You may practise using the editing symbols for this exercise:
(a) replace the date given with today's date
(b) in paragraph 2, replace 'cars' with 'models' throughout the paragraph
(c) delete the word 'also' in paragraph 2
(d) insert the word 'now' before 'in stock' at the end of paragraph 2
(e) replace 'drop' with 'call' in paragraph 3
(f) join the first two paragraphs together
(g) make the sentence that begins 'A leaflet is…' the start of a new paragraph.
Save this version of the letter to your disk, using CARSALE2 as the filename.

Assignment 6

1. Retrieve the file AGM1 from the Gill & Macmillan website (www.gillmacmillan.ie) and make the following edits.
2. Save the changed file as AGM2.

Minutes of the annual general meeting of members of Corrugated ~~Steel Products~~ **Iron Process** Ltd, held at 34 Riverside Road, Navan, on Tuesday 30 October 2004[7].

Mr Aidan Dooley, Chair ~~of the Board~~, presided.

The Secretary read the notice convening the meeting, and the auditors' report.

The Chair addressed the meeting, and proposed: That the directors' report and the accounts for the year ending 30 September 2004[7] produced at the meeting **in Navan** be hereby received and adopted, and that a dividend of ~~15~~[18] per cent less income tax be declared, to be payable to members on ~~20~~[27] November 2004[7].

The Chair proposed that Mr Patrick Matthews, the director retiring by rotation, be re-elected as a director of the company, Mr Declan Murphy seconded the motion, which was put to the meeting and carried by nine votes to three.

Ms Niamh Sheridan, a shareholder, proposed that Jackson, Brady and Company, having agreed to continue in office as auditors for a further year, receive a fixed fee of €17,000. This was seconded by Mr Seán Moran, another shareholder, put to the meeting, and carried unanimously.

There was no other business.

Operator: change all occurrences of chair to chairperson throughout

Chair

7 November 2004[7]

228

Assignment 7

◨ Carry out the following tasks:

1. Retrieve the file MENU from the Gill & Macmillan website (www.gillmacmillan.ie).
2. The menu is to be displayed outside the hotel, but the manager is not pleased with the format. He has asked you to centre all the text, including the hotel name and address and to use fonts to enhance the appearance of the menu.
3. Save the centred menu to disk, using MENUC as the filename.

Assignment 8

1. Retrieve the file REPORT from the Gill & Macmillan website (www.gillmacmillan.ie) and make the following edits.
2. Save the edited file as REPORTA.

REPORT OF THE SUBCOMMITTEE ← (Point size 18, bold, Centre and underscore)

This is the report of the subcommittee appointed according to the terms of the Board resolution of 5 July 2007 'that a subcommittee be appointed to investigate and report on the decline of paper sales in the southern region for the period ending 30 November 2006, and to make recommendations.'

Subcommittee members   **Bold Headings**

Indent 2.5 cm

Frank Brady (chairman)
Valerie Byrne
Ian Caprani
Ciarán Dunne
Madeleine Dunne
Dermot Moyne
Mary Purcell

(Operator: Change all company names in the report to bold print)

Summary
The full report is in the hands of the marketing manager. Some of the more important findings are:

(a) Competition has increased considerably, especially with the entry into the market of Reprotext Ltd.

clients

(b) Two of our reliable ~~customers~~ have ceased trading in the last twelve months: Southprint Ltd and Speedprint Ltd.

(c) There is a cheaper imported paper on the market, which is affecting sales from department C.

(d) Because of the high rate of absenteeism in the dispatch department some orders were cancelled.
and more expensive
(e) The haulier for the southern region is less reliable /than those of any of the other regions.

Recommendations
1. Find a new haulier for the southern region.
2. Obtain more information on possible cheaper sources of paper.
3. Assign two more sales representatives to the region.
4. Establish the reason for the absenteeism in the Dispatch Department.
5. Make a closer examination of the activities of Reprotext Ltd.

change numbering to bullet format

Data
Details of data relevant to this report are attached.

Signed: ....
1 December 2007

Assignment 9

1. Retrieve the file OUTDOOR from the Gill & Macmillan website (www.gillmacmillan.ie) and make the following edits.

---

91 St Peter's Drive
Dublin 24

5 July 2007

Dear Sir,/**Madam**,

I am writing to describe a recent experience that ~~might~~ **will** be of interest to your readers.

I decided to do something different for my holidays this year. I booked an adventure holiday at the Slievemore Mountain Lodge adventure centre in Co. Wicklow **Ireland**. From the very minute I arrived at the centre I began to unwind. The scenery was beautiful, with peaceful lakes, rolling heather-covered hills, and sparkling streams. *run on*

The centre has a choice of daily activities, including hill walking, canoeing, sailing, orienteering, and rock climbing, to mention only a few. I tried ~~nearly~~ all of the~~se~~ activities
N.P. during the week. //The walks covered an area where we saw no signs of human habitation, which made a pleasant contrast with the 'concrete jungle' I am used to most of the year! The accommodation was very comfortable: it was a real pleasure to return from a day's activity to a roaring log fire and a hot meal.

We hear so much about disappointed holidaymakers nowadays. This was **one of** the best holiday of my life, and I would wholeheartedly recommend such a holiday ~~to anyone who wants a real break from it all~~.

Yours sincerely,

Pádraig Whelan ———— *leave 4 lines for the signature*

Carry out the following tasks:

2. To make it more acceptable to the editor of the paper, the letter should be put into two narrow columns of equal width.
3. Change the alignment to block format.
4. Save the edited file as OUTDOOR1.

Assignment 10

1. Retrieve the file SURVEY from the Gill & Macmillan website (www.gillmacmillan.ie) and make the following edits.

HEART DISEASE SURVEY ← (Bold, centre, point size 20)

More than half of a group of patients screened for heart disease risk factors were found to be overweight, and nearly a quarter had high blood pressure, it emerged today. ⌐ run on
third (inserted above "quarter")

examined
The researchers looked at forty patients in the Dún Laoghaire area. GPs screened the patients for such things as excess weight, high blood pressure, and high cholesterol levels.

already
Now researchers are planning a second screening project, to study a larger number of patients, following the disturbing results of the pilot study carried out by the Department of Preventive Medicine in University College, Dublin.

Nearly 60 per cent of the people examined were overweight, according to the 'Irish Medical Times'. A quarter had high cholesterol levels, while 20 to 30 per cent had high blood pressure. (*italics*)

Now, GPs in the wider area of south-east Co. Dublin are to become involved in a second trial to screen a larger number of patients.

◼ Carry out the following tasks:

2. Alter the left margin to 4 cm.
3. Produce a 1.5 cm hanging indent on each paragraph.
4. Change the entire documnet to double line spacing.
5. Save the edited file to disk.
6. Name the file SURVEY2.

Instructions for Assignments 11 and 12

The tab settings for each task are given in centimetres.

L = Left, R = Right, C = Centre and D = Decimal.

For example, L6 means set a left tab at 6 cm while D13 means set a decimal tab at 13 cm.

Assignment 11

◣Task 1

1. Create a new document and enter the following text using the tab settings provided.

	FIRST YEAR BUSINESS STUDIES LECTURES			
Subject	Lecturer	Room	Day	Time
Accountancy	Mr R Lee	34A	Mon	18:30
Economics	Ms P Walsh	42C	Wed	20:00
Law	Mr J Smyth	38B	Mon	20:00
Statistics	Mrs A. O'Reilly	36B	Wed	18:30

Tab settings: Heading and table – L4, L8, L11 and L13

2. Save the document as **Tabs1** to your disk and close the file.

◣Task 2

1. Create a new document.
2. As two sets of tabs are required, this task should be tackled as follows:
   - Set the tabs for the headings
   - Enter the details, e.g. Quarter, Blocks, Cement and Sand
   - Press the enter key to move to a new line
   - Clear the existing tabs
   - Set the new tabs for the table data, e.g. Qtr 1, 18000, 6700, 12000
   - Enter the data in the table
   - The tab settings are given beneath the following table.

QUINN BUILDING SUPPLIES - QUARTERLY TURNOVER			
Quarter	Blocks	Cement	Sand
Qtr 1	18000	6700	12500
Qtr 2	7900	13400	8600
Qtr 3	12300	4800	9100
Qtr 4	9600	11500	17600

Tab: Headings – C5, C9, and C13, i.e. Quarter, Blocks, Cement and Sand
Settings: Table – R5.5, R9.5 and R13.5, i.e. Qtr 1, 18000, 6700, 12500

3. Save the document as **Tabs2** to your disk and close the file.

Assignment 12

◣Task 1

1. Create a new document and enter the following text using the tab settings provided.

BESTMATCH PERSONNEL RECRUITMENT			
Name	Age	Position	Experience
R Allen	22	Clerk	3
L Byrne	42	Secretary	22
Y Murphy	31	Engineer	10
S Ryan	52	Teacher	31

Tab settings: Headings – C4, L7, and C12 **and** table – C4, L7, and R12.5

2. Save the document as **Tabs3** to your disk and close the file.

◣Task 2

1. Create a new document and enter the following text using the tab settings provided.

McCANN'S SUPERMARKET - WEEKLY NEWSPAPER SALES			
Newspaper	Number Sold	Cost	Number Returned
Irish Independent	134	€1.60	12
Irish Times	91	€1.60	4
The Star	202	€1.30	23
The Daily Mirror	107	€1.00	9

Tab settings: Headings – C5, C9, and C13 **and** table – R5.5, D9 and R13.5

2. Save the document as **Tabs4** to your disk and close the file.

◼Task 3

1. Create a new document and enter the following text using the tab settings provided.

SLIEVE RUSSELL HOTEL - WEDDING BANQUETS			
Couple	Main Course	Cost/Head	Guests
Allen/Nolan.......	Turkey/Ham	€39.00.......	230
Conway/Keogh......	Fillet of Beef	€48.00.......	165
Dolan/Brennan.....	Salmon	€45.50.......	79
Moran/McHugh......	Pork	€36.50.......	270
O' Reilly/Lee......	Turkey/Ham	€39.00.......	91

Tab settings: Headings – L4, L8 and L12 **and** table – L4, D9 and R13

2. Use leader dots for each tab setting.
3. Save the document as **Tabs5** to your disk and close the file.

Assignment 13
◼Task 1

1. Create a table with three columns and five rows.
2. Enter the information given below into this new table.

Country	Capital	Continent
Canada	Ottawa	North America
Ireland	Dublin	Europe
Japan	Tokyo	Asia
Nigeria	Lagos	Africa

3. Save this table as **Country** to your disk and close the file.

◥ Task 2

1. Create a table with five columns and six rows.
2. Enter the information given below into this new table.

Course	Tutor	Hours	Exam	Students
Access	L Browne	40	City & Guilds	19
Excel	K Kennedy	35	FETAC	23
PowerPoint	F Mason	25	MOUS	15
Publisher	D O' Brien	32	FETAC	20
Word	F Wilson	35	City & Guilds	11

3. Centre the information in the table.
4. Format the headings to bold type.
5. Save this table as **Classes** to your disk.
6. Insert a row between the *Publisher* and *Word* rows and enter the following into this new row.

Visual Basic	S O' Neill	120	MCSD	30

7. Resave the table as **Classes2** to your disk and close the file.

◥ Task 3

1. Create a table with six columns and eight rows.
2. Merge the cells on row 1.
3. Enter the information given below into the new table.

SUMMER FISHING COMPETITIONS					
Trout	58	€4000	€2500	€1200	7 May
Salmon	65	€5000	€3000	€1800	1 January
Pike	28	€1500	€750	€400	14 April
Bream	55	€2000	€1000	€500	28 June

4. Format the main heading to bold type and to point size 14.
5. Italicise the column headings.
6. Centre the information in the table.
7. Ensure that the columns are wide enough to accommodate the information.
8. Sort the table in alphabetical order of fish.
9. Save this table as **Competition** to your disk.
10. Delete the row containing the details on the pike competition.
11. Resave the file as **Competition2** to your disk and close the file.

◥Task 4

1. Create a table with six columns and seven rows.
2. Merge the cells on row 1.
3. Enter the information given below into the new table.

GOOD FURNITURE LTD – CUSTOMER ORDER FORM					
Table	3	€400	€1200	€50	€1250
Armchair	10	€220	€2200	€30	€2230
Wardrobe	8	€165	€1320	€65	€1385

4 Format the main heading and column headings to bold type.
5. Italicise the column headings.
6. Centre the information in the table.
7. Change the background colour of the heading to black and the text to white.
8. Add a 1.5 point border to the table.
9. Save this table as **Furniture** to your disk and close the file.

Assignment 14

1. Create the following document using a combination of tabs and tables.
2. Save on disk using the file name QUEST.

QUESTIONNAIRE

A. Personal Profile

Q1. Sex   Male [ ]   Female [ ]

Q2. Number of years teaching [ ]   Number of years teaching with computers [ ]

Q3. Number of years as computer/IT co-ordinator [ ]

Q4. Qualifications [   ]

Q5. Age   20–30 [ ]   31–40 [ ]   41–50 [ ]   50+ [ ]

Q6. Computer owner   No [ ]   Yes [ ]

B. School Profile

Q7.

1	Location of school (e.g. Dublin 12)	
2	School type (e.g. vocational)	
3	Is your school co-educational? (Y/N)	
4	Number of students in the school	

C. Hardware Facilities

Q8. Please indicate the number of each of the following computers in your school.

	No.	Networked (Y/N)
IBMs or compatibles		
Apples		
Nimbus		
BBCs		
Commodores		

Thank you for your co-operation!

Assignment 15

1. Create the poster using clip art, font sizes and borders.
2. Save the file as POSTER.

Congratulations!

to
all the students of City Community College

on your Graduation

You are invited to the graduation ceremony at The College Hall

**On 25th November 2007
At 8.00pm sharp**

Assignment 16

1. Retrieve the file IDEAL from the Gill & Macmillan website (www.gillmacmillan.ie).
2. Change the documnet to appear as given below using columns, bullet points, frames and clip art.

The Ideal of Integration The Way Forward

Computers were introduced into the education systems of some countries in the late 1960s and early 1970s. However, the development of the microcomputer in the 1980s has produced the most significant developments in computer use in education systems worldwide.

The global effect of the use of computers on the curriculum as outlined by Wellington has been threefold.

- Firstly, the emergence of a new subject called *Computer Science*. This has been incorporated in to the vocational and upper secondary level curriculums worldwide.
- Secondly, the development of computers and information technology as an integral part of culture and society, which all students should experience. The subjects **Computer Awareness** and *Computer Literacy* seem to fulfil this role.
- Thirdly, the development of computers and information technology as teaching and learning resources where computers are integrated across the curriculum.

Some countries opted initially to concentrate on the first option only. Such countries include Greece, Japan, Denmark, Ireland, Austria and Belgium. Other countries such as France, UK and Canada developed comprehensive policies where all

three options have been followed. However, more recently the general trend in all countries is towards a comprehensive approach where all three options are being introduced as outlined in a recent report by the OECD.

With respect to the detailed curriculum many claims have been put forward about the possible impact of using computers in the school curriculum. Educational goals may change by having more emphasis on productive rather than reproductive tasks (as there is often quicker learning of practice and drill activities) such as problem solving, information handling and inquiry skills.

It is claimed that greater opportunities will be more available to work on more real life problems. The benefit to special needs students is particularly evident where multimedia (combination of video and text images) computer systems are used. This will mean that the curriculum can be expanded for special needs students. It is possible for students to do things never possible before, such as severely handicapped students learning and communicating via the computer. The assessment of students' achievement may change to more responsive and quicker methods. The role of the teacher may change to that of a facilitator and hence the operational curriculum may also change.

3. Insert 'ICT in Education' as a header.

4. Insert your own name as a footer.

Assignment 17

You have just been appointed to the complaints department of Hewson Electrical Ltd. Your duties include responding to letters of complaint from dissatisfied customers.

1. Create the following paragraphs in separate files on your disk. The files should be named PT1, PT2, PT3, PT4 and PT5, respectively.

[File 1]
We have received your letter concerning the item that you bought at our store. We are sorry to hear that it is causing problems.

[File 2]
As the goods are still under guarantee, please call our maintenance department to arrange a suitable time for our repair technician to call to you.

[File 3]
As the goods are no longer under guarantee, repair work cannot be carried out free of charge. Our repair technician, however, can call to you to give a quotation for the cost of repairs.

[File 4]
As this is an old model, parts are extremely difficult to obtain. We have an excellent range of new models in our showrooms, and we would be happy to offer you a reasonable trade-in discount off the cost of a new model.

[File 5]
Your faithfully,

Desmond Joyce
Repair Control Department

---

2. Use the correct combination of stored paragraphs and today's date to compose letters of reply to the following customers. Your are also given suitable names for your letter files.

LETTER	PERSON	STORED PARAGRAPHS
LTR1	Ms Joyce Noonan 55 Kilmore Road Castlebawn, Co. Donegal	Files: PT1, PT2, PT5
LTR2	Mr Seán Ryan 73 Ormond Road Invermore, Co. Limerick	Files: PT1, PT3, PT5
LTR3	Ms Róisín Nestor 6 Mount Nugent Road Dunfinn, Co. Cavan	Files: PT1, PT4, PT5

Assignments 18 and 19 require the use of the merge printing facility of your word processor. Here the <> symbol is used to enclose the variables: different indicators may be required on your word processor.

Assignment 18

Produce four personalised letters to members of the Irish Anglers' Association based on the following form letter and accompanying data file.

Form letter: save as ANGLER

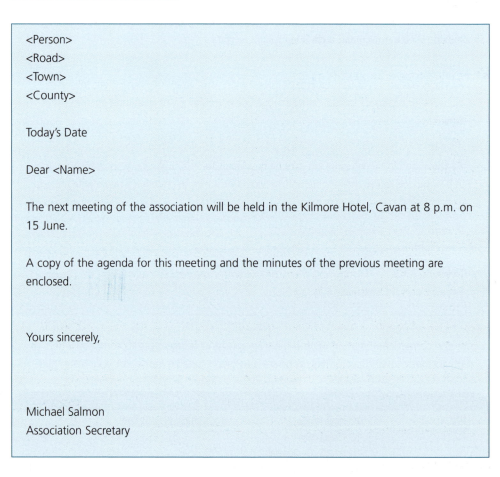

<Person>
<Road>
<Town>
<County>

Today's Date

Dear <Name>

The next meeting of the association will be held in the Kilmore Hotel, Cavan at 8 p.m. on 15 June.

A copy of the agenda for this meeting and the minutes of the previous meeting are enclosed.

Yours sincerely,

Michael Salmon
Association Secretary

PERSON	ROAD	TOWN	COUNTY	NAME
Mr J Richards	14 Main St	Tullamore	Co. Offaly	Mr Richards
Mr S O'Reilly	12 Farnham Rd	Cavan	Co. Cavan	Mr O'Reilly
Mrs T Quinn	2 Fenagh Way	Ballinamore	Co. Leitrim	Mrs Quinn
Ms U Dolan	30 Brooke St	Sligo	Co. Sligo	Ms Dolan

Assignment 19

Produce four personalised letters and accompanying mailing labels based on the following form letter and accompanying data file:

◤Form letter: save as INTERVIEW

<Person>
<Road>
<Town>
<County>

Today's Date

Dear <Name>

I have received your enquiry about any opportunity that may be available at this club for you to act in the capacity of <Job>.

I am pleased to tell you that there is, in fact, such a vacancy at the moment and would like you to visit the club to discuss the matter with me as soon as possible.

The next club night is Monday, 16 August and I would be grateful if you could call in then, preferably at <Time>.

Can you let me know if you can come at that time?

Yours sincerely,

John Martin
Secretary

PERSON	ROAD	TOWN	COUNTY	NAME	JOB	TIME
Mr T Ward	32 Dargle View	Rathfarnham	Dublin 16	Mr Ward	Stagehand	6.15 p.m.
Ms E O'Reilly	4 Market Square	Clones	Co.Monaghan	Ms O'Reilly	Prompter	6.30 p.m.
Ms R Nolan	2 Ferndale Grove	Drogheda	Co. Louth	Ms Nolan	Usher	6.45 p.m.
Mr S Ryan	3 Tuam Road	Ballinasloe	Co. Galway	Mr Ryan	Set Designer	7.00 p.m.

The mailing labels will be produced from the first four fields in the JOBSEEKER file.

Assignment 20

FETAC sample exam
Practical Assignment 1

1. Retrieve the file TASK4 from the Gill & Macmillan website (www.gillmacmillan.ie).

2. Proofread and correct where necessary, and make the amendments as indicated.

3. Ragged or justified line endings are accepted (unless otherwise instructed within the document).

4. Take great care with pagination.

5. Save your document as **HEALTH** for printing as instructed by your Specialist Teacher.

- All abbreviations should be typed in full where appropriate.
- Block or centre style is acceptable once used consistently throughout an assignment.
- Dictionaries are not allowed.

Assignment 1.

HEALTH & SAFETY AT WORK ← *(Bold, Centre + U.S)*

OPERATOR: Change Font size to 12 litel throughout document

In order to ensure health and safety at work the employer must first prepare a safety statement. The safety statement identifies the risks or hazards to which the workers are exposed. When these risks or hazards have been established action must be taken. Good Codes of Practice as well as staff training and information, form an *del* essential part of the strategies involved in promoting a healthier and safer working environment.

1.   REPETITIVE STRAIN INJURY (RSI) *Bold Headings*

Repetitive Strain Injury (RSI) is the result of awkward or constrained working postures, repetitive movements or tasks. The strain usually affects the neck and upper limbs. The cost of hours lost to the workforce is enormous, not to mention costs involved due to early retirement and medical attention required; or reduced quality and quantity of work produced.

The factors that lead to RSI are still not quite known, but some of the risk factors can be outlined as follows:

INDENT ½"
- awkward posture
- repetitive work
- poor social relations
- heavy manual handling
- lack of influence in the organisation

} double line spacing

Justify R.H. Margin throughout document

INSERT TEXT HERE

2.   FIRE AND ELECTRICITY

use side Heading Fire. Most substances burn quickly and the fumes produced can be deadly. It is smoke and fumes that kill people, not flames.

It is imperative that the Fire Escapes are adequate and clearly marked.

Electricity. Common sense prevails in this instance. Every year many people are killed or badly injured at work due to electric shock.

Cable joints that are frayed or damaged should be replaced. Make sure all plugs are connected properly. Light bulbs or items which could be easily broken should have a protective guard.//Appliances should be unplugged before making adjustments or cleaning. *N.P.*

It is the responsibility of the Employees to ensure that they know and understand the Company Safety Statement.

With due care and consideration given to the factors outlined above better productivity will ensue and there will *del* be reduced insurance costs as well as less disruptions to work which are caused by accidents or ill health. *TR?*

3.   SURVEY ← *(Block Caps + Bold Heading)*

L.c.   Finally, a Recent survey indicates :

- over 16,000 accidents occurred at work
- approx. 80 people died
- some 4,000 suffered occupational diseases
- 750,000 working days lost through absences

} double line spacing

Assignment 1.

Insert at "*"

The on-set of RSI is usually slow + involves a series of steps. At first the person feels tired or fatigued with slight discomfort. This later develops into more severe pain + usually constrains daily activities. If allowed to continue it can lead to chronic disability for the individual. Rehabilitation at this chronic stage is more difficult than if

STET.   measures ~~had been~~ were in place to prevent RSI. <u>Prevention</u> is better than <u>cure</u>.   (Bold + Italics)

~~Psychological~~ factors such as stress, monotonous work, (which requires an amount of attention or precision + fixed posture) along with lack of work satisfaction contribute to RSI.

(PSYCHOSOCIAL)

OPERATOR: Replace the phrase "at work" with "in the workplace" throughout the document.

Note:
Print out the document with Page numbers included.

Practical Assignment 2

1. Key in and display the information attractively.

2. Information should be on a single page.

3. Save your document as **AGENDA** for printing as instructed by your Specialist Teacher.

- All abbreviations should be typed in full where appropriate.
- Block or centre style is acceptable once used consistently throughout an assignment.
- Dictionaries are not allowed.

Assignment 2.

"H+S" - Health and Safety in full

H+S Seminar   caps, centre & bold

17-19 June 2007   centre

Day 1. General Office Safety + Stress Management   Block Caps + Bold

9.00 - 9.30 Registration

9.30 - 11.00 Ergonomics in the Office

11.00 - 11.30 Coffee Break

11.30 - 12.30 Stress Management

12.30 - 1.30 Q. + A. Session

"Q + A" - Question and Answer in full

Day 2. Safety Assessment + Controls in the Lab. → in full

9.00 - 9.30 Registration

9.30 - 11.00 Fundamentals of Industrial Measurement + Process Controls

11.00 - 11.30 Coffee Break

11.30 - 12.30 Respiratory Exposure to Volatile Solvent Vapours

12.30 - 1.30 Q + A Session

Day 3. Safety skills with mechanical Equipment

9.00 - 9.30 Registration

9.30 - 11.00 Rotating Equipment Preventative Maintenance

11.00 - 11.30 Coffee Break

11.30 - 12.30 Dust Suppression in Suction - type machinery

12.30 - 1.30 Q + A. Session

Reservation Form here

Assignment 2.

(H + S) Seminar Reservation Form (Bold Text)
in full

NAME (Block Caps) ....

DEPT. .... Position ....

Seminar Title ....

Date of seminar .... Time of seminar ....

(words) → 1st Choice ....

→ 2nd Choice ....

double line spacing

Lunch Required   Yes [ ]   no [ ]

Signature .... Date ....

Note: Please return to your Dept manager. Reservations cannot (only) be confirmed when this form is received.

Bold text

Operator : Please ensure that both the Agenda for the seminar and the Reservation Form are on the one page.
All Abbreviations in full

Practical Assignment 3

1. Key in the following draft letter, being careful to insert the symbols for the variables exactly as shown.

2. Save your document as **DRAFT** for printing later as instructed by your Specialist Teacher.

3. Create **three** separate letters with the variables given: save each one for printing later.

Please save first letter as **MOONEY**
Please save second letter as **SEARCHER**
Please save third letter as **FIXET**

Assignment 3.

[1]

[2]

Dear [3]   *("H+S" - Health and Safety in full throughout document)*

H + S Seminar – June 2007   *(Caps, Bold + U.S. Heading)*

This company has a very positive approach to H + S
del. in all its aspects. *activities* To ensure implementation
of its policies, it is proposed to hold seminars
on different aspects of H + S at work.
I shall be grateful if you will deliver a one-
day seminar to our employees in relation to [4].
NP [The date for this seminar is [5].
I enclose a programme indicating details of each
days proceedings. The location of your seminar
is [6].
Please confirm with me at your earliest convenience
if you can give the seminar on that date.
Looking forward to a favourable response.

yours sincerely   *(WINNING WIDGET COMPANY)*

Block Caps. + Bold

_____
A M O'Neill
General manager

Enc

Assignment 3
Variables

Letter 1

[1] Today's Date

[2] Mr C.D. Mooney
     Director
     Human Resources
     A.D. Communications Company
     63 Central Mall
     DONEGAL

[3] Mr Mooney

[4] General Office Safety and Stress Management

[5] Tuesday, 17 June 2007, from 9.00 a.m. – 2.00 p.m.

[6] First Floor, Boardroom, Head Office, Dublin

Letter 2

[1] Today's Date

[2] Dr E.F. Searcher
     Chief Analyst
     Laboratory Division
     R.O. Chemicals Ltd
     37 Alder Industrial Estate
     CORK

[3] Dr Searcher

[4] Safety Assessment and Controls in the Laboratory

[5] Wednesday, 18 June 2007, from 9.00 a.m. – 2.00 p.m.

[6] Block B of Annex at Manufacturing Site, Dundalk

Letter 3

[1] Today's Date

[2] Mr G.H. Fixet
     Mechanical Services Section
     Melting Engineering Company
     4 New Quays
     DUBLIN

[3] Mr Fixet

[4] Safety Skills with Mechanical Equipment

[5] Thursday, 19 June 2007, from 9.00 a.m. – 2.00 p.m.

[6] Room 22, Assembly Building at Manufacturing Site, Dundalk

Chapter 9
The Internet and the World Wide Web

▦ History and structure of the Internet

What is the Internet?

The Internet is a global computer network. The computers on this network can be divided into two types – *clients* and *servers*. The clients are the computers that are similar to yours and mine: they can request information from the network. The servers, sometimes called *hosts*, are the computers that store and provide the information.

How does the Internet work?

The essential elements of the Internet are the *server* computers that are linked by a *permanent communications link*. This link is like a special-purpose telephone line that is always open and talking to the server computers, which are always on. The computers communicate over the network using the same 'language', called *TCP/IP (Transmission Control Protocol/Internet Protocol)*. Each server computer has a unique address that tells the other computers on the Internet how to find it. A client computer can connect to the Internet by linking to a server computer that is permanently connected to the Internet.

When you send or receive information through the Internet, it is broken down into smaller pieces called *packets*. Each packet is 'passed' from server computer to server computer on the Internet until it reaches its destination. On arrival, the packets are re-assembled into the original information. The packets travel independently through the Internet and may take different routes to their destination. Special computers, called *routers*, regulate the traffic on the Internet. A router, like a good travel agent, picks the most efficient route based on the volume of traffic and number of stopovers.

Information transfer on the Internet

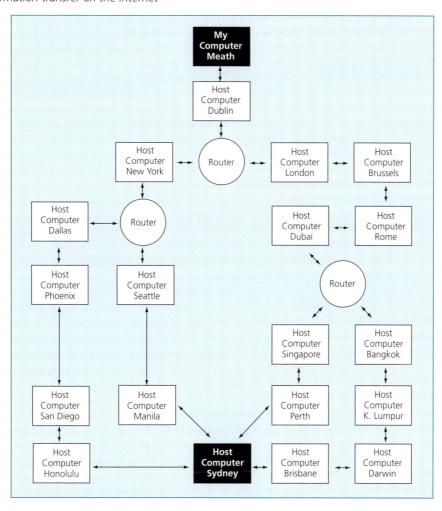

Referring to the diagram above, I may request information on Sydney's Opera House. Let us assume that this information is held on a server computer in Sydney, Australia. The packets that go to make up the requested information may travel between the server computer in Sydney and my computer in Meath via a number of different routes:

- Sydney ➔ Manila ➔ Seattle ➔ New York ➔ Dublin ➔ Meath

- Sydney ➔ Honolulu ➔ San Diego ➔ Phoenix ➔ Dallas ➔ New York ➔ Dublin ➔ Meath

- Sydney ➔ Brisbane ➔ Darwin ➔ Kuala Lumpar ➔ Bangkok ➔ Dubai ➔ Rome ➔ Brussels ➔ London ➔ Dublin ➔ Meath

- Sydney ➔ Perth ➔ Singapore ➔ Dubai ➔ Rome ➔ Brussels ➔ London ➔ Dublin ➔ Meath

What is the World Wide Web?

The World Wide Web (WWW), sometimes called the 'Web', consists of millions of pages of information stored on thousands of server computers all over the world. A collection of related web pages is called a website.

The terms 'Internet' and 'Web' are often confused with one another. The Internet is the physical structure of the network, including server computers, routers and the communications lines that connect everything. The Web refers to the collection of websites and the information that can be accessed when one is using the Internet.

How did the Internet develop?

During the Cold War, the American Department of Defence embarked on a project to link military and research computer systems in a fail-safe network. The principal problem to be solved was how to design a network of computer systems, situated in different geographical locations, that would not be entirely disabled in the event of a nuclear attack.

In 1964, Paul Baran wrote a proposal for such a computer network. Every computer (node) of the network could equally send or receive information. Most importantly, if one node was 'down', the rest of the nodes could still communicate. Though not the most efficient way to transmit information, the network would be reliable and not dependent on any particular computer. In 1969, the Pentagon's Advanced Research Projects Agency (ARPA) used these principles to install the first such network in the United States. It was called the ARPANET and it connected Stanford Research Institute, University College Los Angeles (UCLA), University College Santa Barbara and the University of Utah.

The ARPANET offered two main services:

- *Electronic mail (e-mail):* This meant that people could compose documents on their computers and post them 'electronically' to each other.
- *Electronic publishing:* This meant that people could make information from their computers available to everyone else using the service.

By 1971, the ARPANET was connecting twenty-three agencies, including universities and government research centres, in the United States. In 1973, the ARPANET became international with initial connections to the University College of London and the Royal Radar Establishment in Norway. By the end of the decade, the ARPANET had moved from its military/research roots and was being used for commercial purposes and as a discussion platform for various groups. Computers attached directly to the network became known as servers.

In the early 1980s, a team led by Bob Kahn and Vint Cerf developed a set of rules, or protocols, for transferring data between different types of computer networks. These protocols tell computers how to locate and exchange data with one another. This standard set of protocols, as we have already seen, became known as *Transmission Control Protocol/Internet Protocol (TCP/IP).*

In 1984, the American National Science Foundation (NSF) built a network to connect its six supercomputer centres. The new network soon connected many of NSF's regional centres and became known as NSFNET. The ARPANENT and NSFNET were then connected and the growth of this 'network of networks', or Internet, became exponential.

In other countries, educational and research computer networks were being constructed. For example, the Higher Education Authority Network (HEANET) and the Joint Academic Research Network (JANET) were developed in Ireland and Britain, respectively. By the late 1980s, it became clear that all of these national networks would be more useful if they were connected together. Since the Internet in the United States was the largest and best tested system, the other national networks adopted their technologies and connected to it. By 1987, the number of Internet servers exceeded 10,000; two years later the number had exceeded 100,000.

The concept for the World Wide Web was developed in 1990, when Tim Berners-Lee and Robert Cailliau wrote a proposal for using a simple interface and 'HyperText' to access and 'browse' data and information. The software was developed for CERN (the European Institute for Particle Physics) in Switzerland; the original 'Web' was meant to be only for the physics community. In 1991, Berners-Lee and Cailliau put their 'Web' software on the Internet for free. Soon afterward, Marc Andreessen incorporated graphical capabilities into a new browser, and the Mosaic browser was released from the American National Center for Supercomputing Applications (NCSA) to the public in January 1993.

By 1996, a number of new browsers had emerged, with *Microsoft Internet Explorer* and *Netscape Navigator* leading the way. The year 1996 also saw the launch of *Macromedia's Flash* program, which allowed website designers to add interactive animations to web pages. In 1998, *Google*, the search engine of choice used by most people nowadays, was launched.

The early years of the new century saw an exponential growth in the number of Internet users. At the time of writing, it is estimated that 1.5 billion people access the World Wide Web on a regular basis. Its range of uses also continues to expand. The web is now used for:

- research
- communication, e.g. e-mail
- publishing
- e-business
- downloading music and films, e.g. iTunes
- playing games
- membership of online communities.

With the continuing roll-out of broadband (or 'always-on' high-speed Internet access), it is anticipated that Internet usage will continue to grow.

Who owns and pays for the Internet?

No single person, group, company or government owns or controls the Internet. The owners of an individual server computer are responsible for maintaining it and its connection to the Internet.

The server computers on the Internet are permanently connected by thousands of miles of telephone lines and fibre optic cables that require routers to co-ordinate the flow of information. The cost of maintaining these links must be met. Some users, particularly those on government or university networks, do not pay for access to the Internet because their employers or superiors pay for the costs. The vast majority of users, however, pay a subscription fee and/or a telephone charge for access to the Internet.

Internet connection requirements

In order to connect to the Internet, you need:

- a computer
- telephone line and modem – dial-up access
- telephone line and/or devices supplied by the Internet service provider (ISP) – broadband
- appropriate Internet software
- an account with an Internet service provider (ISP).

◪ Connecting to the Internet

Before examining the different methods of connecting to the Internet, we must first look at **bandwidth**. This can be defined as the rate of data transmission and is measured in bits per second. The faster your transmission (or the greater the bandwidth of your connection), the less time you will spend waiting for text, images, sounds and video clips to upload or download from computer to computer.

Bandwidth is often compared to road width, e.g. many cars will travel more quickly on a four-lane highway than on a single-lane road.

◪ Connection methods

The two most common methods of connecting to the Internet are **dial-up** and **broadband**.

◪ Dial-up access

A person connecting his/her computer to a standard phone line using a device called a modem is permitted to dial into an Internet service provider's (ISP) server computer to establish a connection to the Internet. Dial-up access is temporary because either the user or the ISP terminates the connection.

A standard dial-up connection offers access speeds of up to 56 kilobits per second (kbps). Despite being the way people have connected to the Internet for years, it is being steadily replaced by broadband.

◪ Broadband

Broadband comes from the words 'broad' and 'bandwidth'. It is an always-on Internet connection that gives you high-speed access and downloads for a flat-rate monthly charge.

Advantages of broadband:

- web pages download in a fraction of the time it takes when compared to traditional dial-up access
- e-mail messages download instantly
- flat-rate fee makes the costs predictable
- able to talk on the telephone at the same time as surfing on the Internet
- file transfers are very fast, e.g. music downloads take seconds, not minutes, when compared to traditional dial-up access
- receive Internet radio and other real-time services without interruption
- allows businesses to conduct net-meetings or videoconferencing, thus minimising travel costs for in-person meetings.

Disadvantages of broadband:

- always-on nature of the service makes the computer more susceptible to viruses and other forms of attack
- you may be tempted to spend more time on the Internet than you currently do
- may not be available in your area.

ISPs normally offer broadband Internet access in one or more of the following ways:

1. **Asymmetric digital subscriber line (ADSL)** connections operate over a conventional telephone line using digital technologies and allow you make and receive telephone calls while simultaneously using the Internet. Voice and data are carried on the line by using different frequency ranges. Voice is transferred on lower frequency bands and data on higher ones.
2. **Cable** uses a special type of modem that connects to a cable TV line to provide a continuous connection to the Internet. A cable modem uses the cable TV feed to your home and so is restricted to those areas that have a cable TV provider.
3. **Fixed wireless** connects your computer to the Internet using radio signals. A small aerial is erected on the outside to the building and this sends and receives signals to and from a connection point on the inside, which in turn is connected to your computer.
4. **Satellite** is a specialised form of wireless communication, using a satellite dish erected on the building to connect your computer to the Internet. Its main disadvantage is that there is a delay on the signal, making it unsuitable for voice and video communications.

Broadband access speeds vary depending on the type of broadband and the ISP. The following table gives a summary of access speeds.

Internet connection speed	Time to download a typical web page (assuming 100 kilobytes of data)	Time to download a typical 5-minute song (assuming a 5 megabyte MP3 file)	Streaming video quality
56 K dial-up modem	14 sec	12 min 30 sec	
256 K broadband	3 sec	3 min	Low quality
512 K broadband	1.6 sec	1 min 30 sec	
1 Mb broadband	0.8 sec	41 sec	
2 Mb broadband	0.4 sec	20 sec	Medium quality
4 Mb broadband	0.1 sec	5 sec	
6 Mb broadband	Instantaneous	Instantaneous	
8 Mb broadband	Instantaneous	Instantaneous	TV quality
Note: All figures are approximate and represent best-case download speeds. Actual speeds will generally be lower.			

Courtesy of www.broadband.co.uk.

Note that Internet connection speeds are usually expressed in kilobits per second (kbps) or megabits per second (mbps) – these are not the same as kilobytes (KB) or megabytes (MB), which we use when talking about computer memory and storage media capacities. The rule is lower case b for bits and a capital B for bytes. Remember, one byte equals eight bits.

Hardware required

The World Wide Web is expanding at a phenomenal rate. Better websites, with a high multimedia content, are appearing all the time. These websites may contain sound, graphics and video clips as well as text. Modern computers running up-to-date software are now required to view these sites successfully. As of going to print, we would recommend the following personal computer hardware specification for connection to the Internet using a standard telephone line:

HARDWARE	RECOMMENDED SPECIFICATION
CPU	Intel Pentium 4 3.0 Ghz processor
RAM	1 GB
Hard Disk	250 GB
Graphics	AGP 4/8X graphics card
Modem or network interface card (NIC)	56 kbps or integrated 10/100 LAN card
DVD	16x DVD+/-RW drive
Sound support	Yes
Operating system	Windows XP or Vista

We also recommend that you buy a standard webcam that will allow you to record and share video over the Internet.

Improvements in PC technology mean that faster and better components are being included in new personal computers. For the latest hardware specifications, you should visit the websites of leading PC manufacturers like Dell or Packard Bell.

Software required

The software required in order to access and use the Internet can be categorised into three types:

- *Communications software* – this should typically come with your modem or other communication device. It enables your computer to make contact with your ISP's server computer.
- *Protocol software* – this enables your computer to communicate with computers used by other Internet users.
- *Applications software* – these enable you to actually do things on the Internet, such as send e-mail, read news and transfer files. Two examples of applications software are your web browser and e-mail program.

The protocol and applications software is usually available on one CD, from an Internet service provider, as a 'start-up kit' and can be installed quite easily on your computer.

Internet service provider

An Internet service provider (ISP) is a company that provides access to the Internet. Most ISPs offer a number of Internet access options. In making a decision about an ISP, the following areas are important:

- cost
- performance
- help and installation
- security.

◤Evaluating an ISP

The quality and cost of service can vary significantly from one ISP to another. In evaluating an ISP, you should ask the following questions:

1. Do you offer dial-up access?
2. Which broadband access methods do you offer – ADSL, cable, wireless or satellite?
3. Is ADSL available in my area?
4. Other than my computer, what additional equipment and software do I need?
5. What connection packages do you offer?
6. What are the typical data transfer rates for each connection package – download and upload?
7. What is the contention ratio for each package? (Contention ratio applies to the number of people connected to an ISP who share a set amount of bandwidth.)

8. What is the cost of each connection package?

9. Are there any usage limits placed on download and upload before additional charges are incurred?

10. Which connection package do you suggest based on my anticipated usage?

11. What other costs do I need to incur to get your Internet service?

12. If I change my ISP, are there any exit fees?

13. Will you send an engineer to my home or business to set the Internet up for me?

14. What type of technical support do you provide? Is there a telephone helpline?

15. What is the maximum size of an e-mail I can send or receive?

16. What are the factors that contribute to my usage allowance?

17. What is your policy on unsolicited e-mail ('spam')?

18. Where do I find out about downloading music and video?

19. Do you have any software to protect my computer when I am on the Internet?

20. What can I do to protect children from inappropriate content on the internet?

A number of the leading ISPs in Ireland are listed below.

COMPANY	WEBSITE
BT Ireland	www.btireland.ie
Chorus	www.chorus.ie
DigiWeb	www.digiweb.ie
Eircom	www.eircom.net
Gaelic Telecom	www.gaelictelecom.ie
Irish Broadband	www.irishbroadband.ie
NTL	www.ntl.ie
UTV	www.utvinternet.ie

IP addresses and domain names

Server computers on the Internet are able to communicate with one another because each one has a unique code number called an *IP (Internet protocol) address*. Each IP address is made up of a series of numbers separated by periods. A typical example would be: 128.92.32.187.

Human beings have difficulty remembering long strings of numbers. This is where domain names come in. A *domain name* is a unique word that acts like a nickname for the IP address. A typical example would be: www.rte.ie.

The domain names are significantly easier for us to remember but computers prefer to communicate with each other using the numerical IP address. In order that we can use addresses that we can remember and understand, the IP address and its corresponding domain name must be linked or cross-referenced.

The *Domain Name System (DNS)* takes care of this cross-referencing for us. DNS is a large database that holds all the IP addresses and corresponding domain names of all servers connected to the Internet. When you specify the address of a server using its domain name, a process called *domain name resolution* takes place to find the server computer.

Domain name resolution takes place on the Internet on special computers known as domain name servers. The other servers on the Internet access the *domain name servers* many times per second. If one domain name server does not know how to translate a domain name into its IP address, the task will be sent to the next closed domain name server, all within milliseconds.

Intranet

An intranet can be defined as an 'internal Internet' designed for use within the confines of a company or organisation. Technologies and software originally developed for the Internet are used to establish the internal network. What distinguishes an intranet from the Internet is that the former is private. Outside users can be prohibited access, ensuring high security. It is ideal for companies who want to avail of all the benefits of the Internet, but in an internal environment. Intranets can be used to:

- distribute information throughout a company or to specified recipients, especially in multimedia format
- facilitate effective and highly secure communication between employees.

The World Wide Web and other Internet facilities

The Basics

We have already established that the World Wide Web (WWW or Web) comprises millions of pages of information stored on thousands of server computers all over the world. We know that in order to view pages on the Web we need special software known as a web browser. Three examples are *Microsoft Internet Explorer, Mozilla Firefox* and *Netscape.*

Uniform resource locator (URL)

Each web page has its own unique address, known as a *uniform resource locator (URL).* An imaginary URL is shown below:

http://www.gaa.ie/leitrim/results.htm

This URL consists of four distinct parts:

- *http://* – this is the protocol that the browser uses to read the web page.
- *www.gaa.ie* – the domain name of the server where the web page is located.
- *leitrim* – the folder on that server where the web page is stored.
- *results.htm* – the file or web page name.

This imaginary page might contain club results for Leitrim GAA matches.

◤Hyperlinks

It is easy to move within the same page or between pages on the Web using *hyperlinks*. A hyperlink can be text, graphics or pictures. When you click with your mouse on a hyperlink, the browser takes you to another place within the same page or to another web page containing related information. A text hyperlink is frequently known as *hypertext*, it is frequently underlined and normally appears in a colour different from the normal text colour on the web page.

◤The browser

When you load your browser software and connect to the Internet, you will most likely be brought to the home page of your ISP. You will observe that your browser window is divided into two main areas:

- a top panel – containing an address line, a menu and a tool bar
- a bottom area – where the web page is displayed.

If you know the URL of a web page, you can type it directly into the *address line* in the browser window. The page will be then be downloaded from the server into the browser window. The following screen shot shows the Irish government's home page displayed in *Microsoft Internet Explorer:*

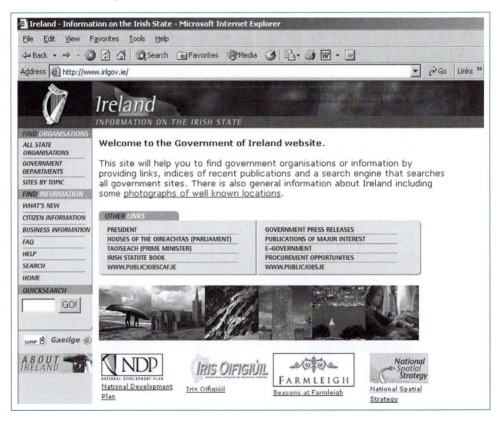

The *menu* presents you with a range of options and sub-options. The *print* and *save* options are particularly useful as they allow you to print a web page or save it to disk. Other menu options that are frequently used include *select* and *copy*. These latter options facilitate you in copying text from a web page into a word processor document.

The *tool bar* contains a number of useful buttons to aid your browsing:

- *Back* – allows you to revisit the page immediately before the one you are currently looking at.
- *Forward* – will move you forward again to the next page.
- *Home* – takes you back to your browser's default page. In many cases, this will be the home page of your ISP.
- *Stop* – halts the downloading of a page.
- *Refresh/Reload* – requests the server to send the same page again.
- *History* – displays a list of all the pages you have viewed since the last time you started your web browser.
- *Favorites/bookmarks* – is a list of your favourite web pages. You can return to any of the pages listed by simply clicking on its name in the *favorites* or *bookmarks* list. (Notice the American spelling of 'favorites'.)

Web browsers offer the facility to switch off graphics. This means that only the text on a web page will be downloaded and allows the Internet user to 'surf' the Web more quickly.

Plug-ins

A *plug-in* is a program that works with your web browser to give it an extra capability. For example, some popular plug-ins include the following.

- *Adobe Acrobat Reader* allows you to read files created in portable document format (pdf) (www.adobe.com).
- *Flash Player* enables you to see animation produced using Adobe (formerly Macromedia) Flash as well as streaming audio and video (www.adobe.com).
- *Quicktime* allows you to view video clips on web pages (www.apple.com).
- *RealPlayer* plays audio and video transmissions (www.realnetworks.com).
- *Shockwave Player* enables you to see animation on a web page and is useful for playing online games (www.adobe.com).

On the Internet, sound and video can be sent from a server to a client computer in either of two ways:

- *Complete download* – all of the data must be downloaded from the server before you can hear sound or see video images.
- *Streaming* – this is similar to listening to the radio or watching television. You hear the sound and/or see the images as your computer receives the data from the server. You do *not* have to wait for complete files to be downloaded before you hear sound or see video images.

Conducting a search

In searching for specific information on the Web, you should be:
- familiar with search tools and their different searching methods
- comfortable in using the range of search techniques necessary to refine a query.

◪Search tools

A *search tool* is a computer program that helps us to find information on the Web. There are many search tools available and each one has access to its own large database of information on web pages. These databases are continually being updated with new website or web page references. Search tools may be categorised into two main types:
- directories
- search engines

◪Directories

A *directory* search tool looks for information by subject matter. An example of a directory search tool is *Yahoo!*. Using a directory search tool, you can conduct a search in a hierarchical manner starting with a general subject heading and following with a succession of increasingly more specific subheadings. The search method is known as a *subject search*.

An example of a subject search in Yahoo! (http://dir.yahoo.com) for information on *Star Wars* films was conducted as follows:

Entertainment ➜ Movies & Film ➜ Genres ➜ Science Fiction & Fantasy ➜ Series ➜ Star Wars

The database of websites for directory search tools are usually compiled and categorised by human beings. A website owner would normally register a new website with the directory for inclusion in its database. Directory search tools are useful when you want to find entire websites on a particular topic. Other examples of directory search tools are *Magellan* and *Onekey*.

When Yahoo! was launched in 1995, it was classified as a directory search tool rather than a search engine because indexing specialists and not software decided which category a web page would fit into. Today, Yahoo! also uses special software called *spiders* to automatically index the web pages because the web has grown too large to index manually. Yahoo! now offers the options of either searching the web using keywords or by subject matter.

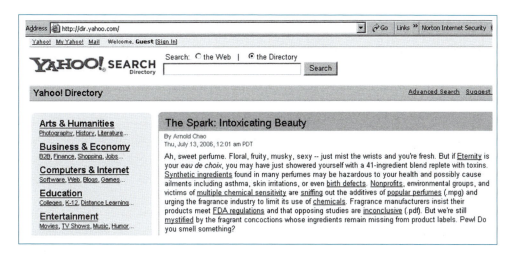

Search engines

A *search engine* searches database(s) by using keywords. It responds to a query with a list of references or *hits*. This search method, known as a *keyword search*, differs from the *subject* method of searching used by the directory search tools.

Search engines rely on special software called *spiders* to maintain and update their databases of web information. The most popular search engine is Google (www.google.ie).

◼Multi-engine search tools

A *multi-engine search tool*, also called a *meta-search tool*, uses a number of search engines simultaneously. The search is conducted using keywords; it then lists the hits either by search engine or by integrating the results into a single listing. One of the most popular multi-engine search tools is Dogpile (www.dogpile.com).

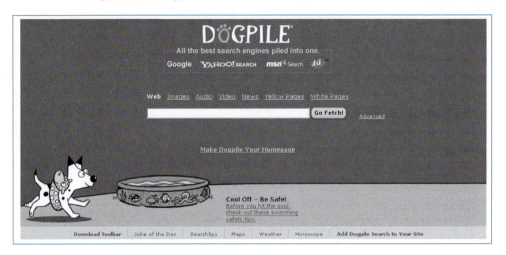

These are the addresses of some of the most popular directories and search engines:

All-In-One – www.allonesearch.com

AltaVista – www.altavista.com

Ask Jeeves – www.ask.com

Excite – www.excite.com

HotBot – www.hotbot.com

Go – http://go.com

Google – www.google.ie

Dogpile – www.dogpile.com

MSN – www.msn.com

Onekey – www.onekey.com

Yahoo! – www.yahoo.ie

◼Portal sites

Portal, or gateway, sites are large websites considered as entry points to other websites. A search engine may be incorporated into the website. The information on the website is vetted by human beings to ensure that it is relevant and up to date. An example is Library.ie, the portal site to Ireland's libraries (www.library.ie).

◤Advice on how to search the World Wide Web

The best advice to give regarding how to search the Web is *to read the directions*. Every search tool has its own website giving detailed information on how best to use its services. There are, however, a number of search tips that can be applied when using most search tools.

1. Be specific

Let us assume that you are using a search engine to find information on fish. If you enter 'fish' as a keyword, a long list of references to web pages that contain the word 'fish' will result from the search. It may take hours to go through each one to find the exact information that you require. The search criterion entered was not specific enough. You must decide what information you require about fish, e.g. a search for 'freshwater trout' would yield a shorter list of references, as it is more focused.

2. Use quotation marks for associated words

Words enclosed within double quote marks denote an exact phrase. It is treated like a single term. An example would be: "tennis for beginners".

Exact phrases will help find information more quickly. For example, if you know a line from a poem and you wish to look for the entire poem, enclose the line in quotes in the search window before clicking the search button.

3. Plus and minus

Let us assume that you wish to search for a restaurant in Galway. You should enter the keywords as follows:

Galway + restaurant

The plus ensures that the search engine will look for references that contain both keywords: *Galway* and *restaurant*.

Let us say that you require a restaurant in Galway that does *not* specialise in seafood. You should enter the keywords as follows:

Galway + restaurant - seafood

The minus sign here will ensure that references containing the word *seafood* will not be shown. Note there is no space between the minus sign and the word following it. The plus and minus signs are invaluable tools when you wish to refine a search.

4. Stemming

This refers to the ability of a search tool to include the stem or the main part of a word. For example, sing is the stem for sings, singer, singing and singalong. Stemming may require use of a *wild card*, symbolised by an asterisk (*). In our example, the search would be conducted using 'sing*' as the reserved word.

5. Connection operators

You can choose from a number of operators to help construct search criteria:

- AND (similar to '+') requires that both words are present somewhere within the document being sought, e.g. *football* AND *Gaelic.*
- NEAR is used when you expect to find certain words occurring near each other, *or* do not know the order in which words will occur in relation to each other, e.g. searching for *Shakespeare'* NEAR *comedies'* will find *"The wonderful comedies of Shakespeare are ..."* as well as *"Shakespeare's greatest comedies number only three."*
- OR requires that at least one word is present, e.g. *classical* OR *opera.*
- NOT (similar to '-') excludes a word from a query, e.g. *football* NOT *soccer.*
  When using these operators, remember to capitalise them as shown above.

6. Case sensitive

If you capitalise letters in your search, then you narrow the search to only occurrences of that word with the exact same capitalisation. If your entry is in all lower case, then the search engine will search for all occurrences of the word, regardless of capitalisation.

- Adjacent capitalised words are treated as a single proper name, e.g. Michael Collins
- Commas separate proper names from each other, e.g. Damien Duff, Derval O'Rourke.

7. American English

As many websites are American, the text on these sites will be in 'American' English. Words such as *colour* and *metre* will be spelled as *color* and *meter.* Americans use words like *automobile* and *gas* for *car* and *petrol,* respectively. A search for "American automobiles" may be more fruitful than one for "American cars".

Other Internet facilities

◪ File transfer protocol

File transfer protocol (FTP) is the name for a set of rules for transferring files from one computer to another via the Internet. The files are stored on server computers all over the world called *FTP sites.* The URLs of FTP sites have the prefix *ftp://. FTP* is a separate Internet facility from the World Wide Web. A web page, however, can have a hyperlink to a file stored on an FTP site.

Each FTP site limits the number of people who can use it simultaneously. If the site is busy, you will get an error message when you try to connect. Many FTP sites have alternative sites that provide identical information. The latter, known as *mirror sites,* help reduce the traffic on popular FTP sites.

Downloading software

You may wish to download software from an FTP site to your computer, e.g. a new version of your browser software. Programs stored at FTP sites usually consist of a large group of files. To avoid downloading each program file individually, these are normally grouped or *archived* into one file. This file may then be *compressed* or *zipped* to reduce its size. Compressed files save storage space on the FTP site and transfer more quickly on the Internet. After downloading the software file to your own computer, you will then have to decompress it before you proceed with the its installation. Popular compression/decompression programs include:

- *WinZip* – for personal computers
- *Stuffit* – for Apple Macintosh computers.

Voice over IP

Voice over IP (VoIP), or Internet telephony, is a technology that allows you to make telephone calls over the Internet. A major benefit of VoIP is that these telephone calls do not incur a call charge beyond the fee to the ISP for Internet access. To use VoIP, you must have broadband access to the Internet.

There are three different methods of using VoIP to make telephone calls:

- **ATA:** Use a device called an analogue telephone adaptor (ATA). The ATA allows you to connect a standard phone to your computer or your Internet connection.
- **IP phone:** Use a specialised phone, which resembles a normal phone that connects directly to your router or broadband modem.
- **Computer-to-computer:** Use a computer equipped with a microphone, speakers, sound card and broadband Internet access as well as the necessary software. The latter is provided for free by most Internet telephony companies.

Most VoIP companies provide the same features as standard telephone companies, e.g. caller ID, call waiting, call transfer and three-way calling. Many also permit the use of webcams to make video calls. Security is not a problem, as Internet telephony companies encrypt every conversation, thus ensuring confidentiality. One of the leading Internet telephony companies is Skype (www.skype.com). Skype's software can be downloaded for free from their website.

Internet relay chat

Internet relay chat (IRC) enables you to communicate with many different people simultaneously, regardless of where they are in the world, by simply typing back and forth. When you type text, it immediately appears on the screen of each person involved in the conversation. Every person in the group chooses a nickname. This lets the others know who is speaking and preserves the identity of that person.

A chat group, also known as a channel, focuses on particular topics for discussion. There are thousands of chat channels on topics as diverse as politics, hostess catering, English Premiership soccer and yoga.

The IRC channels are controlled by special computers on the Internet called IRC servers. To join an IRC, you will need an IRC client program (e.g. mIRC) installed on your computer. This program can be downloaded from a website, e.g. www.download.com.

Instant messaging

Instant messaging allows you to have a private conversation with a person over the Internet. Each message you send will appear on the other person's screen and vice versa. Instant messaging permits you to compile a **contact list** of people that you wish to interact with. Once you connect to the Internet, the instant messaging program will automatically alert you if any member of the contact list is also on-line, as you may wish to have a 'conversation'.

Most of the leading instant messaging programs possess a range of features:

- **Instant messages:** Send notes back and forth with a person who is on-line.
- **Images:** Look at an image stored on a contact's computer.
- **Sounds:** Play sounds for other people.
- **Files:** Share files with others.
- **Talk:** Use the Internet to talk with family or friends.

To engage in instant messaging, you must have an instant messaging program installed on your computer. Any one of the most popular programs can be downloaded from the websites given:

- AOL Instant Messenger: www.aim.com
- ICQ: www.download.com
- MSN Messenger: http://messenger.msn.com
- Yahoo! Messenger: http://messenger.yahoo.com.

Blogs

A blog (short for web log) is an online diary or e-zine (electronic magazine) made available on the web. It has facilities for readers' comments. Most blogs are created by individuals, but group blogs also exist.

Creating and maintaining a blog or adding an article to an existing blog is called **blogging**. Individual articles on a blog are called posts.

A blog entry typically consists of the following:

- **Title:** The blog's title.
- **Date:** The date of the most recent post.
- **Post title:** The title of the most recent post.
- **Text:** The actual text of the most recent post.
- **Posting information:** Information telling who wrote the post.
- **Comments:** An area for readers of the blog to add their comments.
- **Previous posts:** A list of the most recent posts.
- **Archives:** A link to view the archive section containing older posts.

There is a range of blog hosting services on the web, which help you create and store your blog. Two popular websites are:

- Blogger: www.blogger.com
- Weblogs Compendium: www.lights.com/weblogs/.

A popular website to help search for blogs is:

- Blog Search Engine: www.blogsearchengine.com.

You can also use Google and Yahoo! to search for blogs.

Multimedia conferencing

A range of software products is available that allows the Internet to be used to hold on-line conferences. The people 'attending' the conference can be located anywhere in the world. The services that these products provide include some or all of the following:

- a broadband service over the Internet
- video capabilities
- shared whiteboard – this allows the participants to show drawings, plans or sketches to each other. A whiteboard is visible in a window of each participant's screen. An item inserted on the whiteboard, by one participant, is visible to the others.

Popular multimedia conferencing products include:

- Click to Meet
- Microsoft NetMeeting
- Netscape Conference.

Radio and television on the Web

Thousands of radio stations and hundreds of TV channels are now webcasting their programmes on the Internet. The word '**webcast**' is derived from 'web' and 'broadcast'. It can be defined as the live or delayed transmission of audio or video content over the Internet. A webcast uses streaming audio or video to deliver programmes to its listeners or viewers. RTÉ and the BBC currently webcast many of their services.

To listen to or view a webcast, you need a computer equipped with good graphics and sound cards, a multimedia playing software package, e.g. RealPlayer, and a fast, reliable Internet connection. Companies like *WorldTVRadio* (http://worldtvradio.com) offer tuner software to access a huge range of worldwide radio stations and TV channels over the Internet.

Podcasts

A podcast is a web-based audio broadcast. You are permitted to save programmes to your PC or digital music player, i.e. MP3 player, so you can listen to them at your leisure.

To access podcasts, you need to:

- obtain podcasting software – leading programs include *iPodder* (or *Juice*), *jPodder*, *Doppler* and *Nimiq*

- subscribe to a podcast – this is achieved by copying the address of the podcast into the podcasting software
- download the latest version of the podcast.

RTÉ and the BBC have many radio programmes now available for download as podcasts from their respective websites. A useful portal website to a wide range of podcasts is available at Podcast.net (www.podcast.net).

On-line games

There are many sites on the Internet providing games that you can download and install on your computer. You can also play on-line games with other games enthusiasts anywhere in the world. For example, you can have an on-line game of chess with a person in Los Angeles or Singapore. Games known as multi-user dungeons (MUDs) are very popular; these take place in imaginary kingdoms. Many MUDs are text-based but some do include pictures.

Massively multi-player online games (MMOG) have become very popular with the advent of broadband Internet access. These games allow thousands of players to play together. Some examples of the different styles of these games are:
- MMORPG (on-line role-playing)
- MMORTS (real-time strategy)
- MMOFPS (first-person shooter).

To play an on-line game, you will need to download and install a client program. This software will allow you to communicate with the server on the Internet on which a particular game is taking place.

Electronic business (e-business)

Electronic business (e-business) is the conducting of business on the web. Many companies and shops have websites where products or services are described and where purchases can be made on-line. A diverse range of products or services is available, e.g. airline tickets, books, clothing, computers, flower delivery and food.

A growing number of shopping malls are a feature of the Internet. Each mall has a set of hyperlinks to all the different shopping pages. You can browse through products or services and make a purchase on-line.

The method of ordering a product or service can vary. You may be required to either:
- complete an on-line order form
- simply tick the product or service on a data entry form
- select an 'Add to the shopping basket' button.

Tesco is an example of a company selling a comprehensive range of household goods and foodstuffs on the web. You can do your weekly shopping on-line and have it delivered to your home.

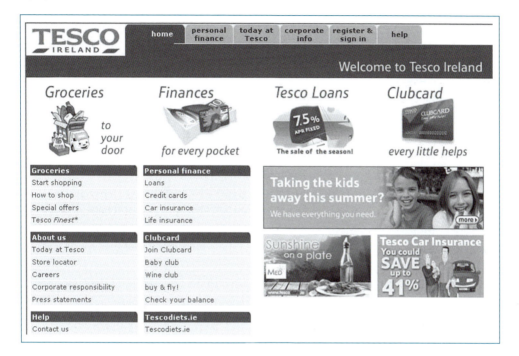

There are two methods of paying for your on-line purchases:

- *Credit card* – this is the most widely used method. You are asked to enter your credit card details using an on-line form before completing the purchase. Most reputable companies that are conducting business on the Internet have security measures in place to prevent unauthorised access to credit card details.
- *Digital cash* – before you make a purchase on-line, you withdraw money from your bank in digital form using special software. The digital cash is stored on your hard disk. When you wish to complete a purchase, you send the digital money over the Internet to the seller of the product or service.

Security and confidentiality

Security and confidentiality on the Internet are issues that are important for both the individual user and organisations. We will now examine some of the main security and confidentiality matters concerning the Internet and the World Wide Web.

Virus protection

In connecting to the Internet, your computer may become infected by computer viruses in either of two ways:

- An infected file downloaded from the Internet to your computer.
- An infected file sent as an e-mail attachment to you.

Some common symptoms that could indicate your computer has been infected are:

- Unusual messages or displays on your monitor.
- Unusual sounds or music played at random times.
- Your system has less available memory than it should.
- A disk or volume name has been changed.
- Programs or files are suddenly missing.
- Unknown programs or files have been created.
- Some of your files become corrupted or suddenly don't work properly.

There are several programs (called virus protection software, anti-virus software, or virus checks) that will check your system for known viruses, scan incoming files and warn you before any infected files are let in. An important fact about these programs is that they are only as good as their database of known viruses.

Since new and different viruses are being introduced all the time, anti-virus databases need to be updated often. When you buy anti-virus software, monthly or quarterly updates of the software are sent to you for a period of time (usually one year). The fee for these updates is usually included in the initial price. Two of the most popular anti-virus software products available are *McAfee Anti-Virus* (www.mcafee.com) and *Norton Anti-Virus* (www.symantec.com). Anti-virus software is also available as shareware on the World Wide Web. The quality of these shareware products can vary greatly.

If you have a computer that is not currently running virus protection software, the first thing you should do is install one of these programs and have it scan your hard drive. It will identify any files that have been infected by any virus it recognises and offer you the option to repair the file if it can. In most cases infected files can be 'cleaned' by your virus protection software; in some, however, the files may have to be discarded. Once you have determined that all the files in your system are virus-free, this would be a good time to do a complete back-up of your system. If your computer gets infected in the future, you will really appreciate having clean copies of your files.

Filtering software

The World Wide Web is a wonderful source of information. There are, however, sites on the World Wide Web that contain material unsuitable for children and vulnerable groups of people. For example, websites dedicated to gambling, pornography or subversive activities can be accessed quite easily using any of the popular search tools. Programs which prevent access to objectionable information on the Internet are available. These programs, known as *filtering software* products, monitor and search for keywords. The software can prevent the user from downloading or sending information containing certain words, address details, credit card details as well as audio, picture or video files. These programs can also prevent users from accessing specific sites by maintaining a list of forbidden URLs, newsgroups and addresses.

Popular filtering software products include:

- Cyber Patrol (www.cyberpatrol.com)
- Net Nanny (www.netnanny.com)
- 8e6 Technologies (www.8e6.com)

Firewalls

A *firewall* is a combination hardware and software buffer that many companies or organisations have in place between their internal networks and any outside network, including the Internet. A firewall allows only specific kinds of messages from the Internet to flow in and out of the internal network. This protects the internal network from intruders or hackers who might try to use the Internet to gain access to those systems.

In general, firewalls are configured to protect against unapproved interactive log-ins from the 'outside' world. Some firewalls permit only e-mail traffic through them, thereby protecting the network against any attacks other than attacks against the e-mail service. Other firewalls provide less strict protections, and only block services that are known to be problems. Some elaborate firewalls block all traffic from the outside to the inside, but permit users on the inside to communicate freely with the outside.

◪Encryption

Encryption is a way of coding the information in a file or e-mail message. If a third party intercepts the encrypted file or message as it travels over a network, it cannot be read. Only the person or persons who have the appropriate decoding software can decode or unscramble the message.

Some of the encryption methods available are:

- *PGP* – Pretty Good Privacy (PGP) is used to make e-mail messages private.
- *ROT13* – Rotate 13 (ROT13) is used to make newsgroup messages private.
- *SHTTP* – Secure HyperText Protocol (SHTTP) is used for security on the World Wide Web.
- *SSL* – Secure Sockets Layer (SSL) is used for security on the Internet and the World Wide Web.

◪Digital signatures

A digital signature is a code that can be attached to an electronically transmitted message that uniquely identifies the sender. Like a written signature, the purpose of a digital signature is to guarantee that the individual sending the message really is who he or she claims to be. Digital signatures are especially important for electronic commerce and are a key component of most authentication schemes. Encryption techniques are used to guarantee the security of digital signatures.

When you use digital signature software, you create a matched pair of keys. One is the private key, which is typically installed on your computer. The *private* key is used only by you and is required during the signing process.

The second key is the public key. The *public* key is available for use by anyone wishing to authenticate documents you sign. The public key will 'read' the digital signature created by the private key and verify the authenticity of documents created with it. It would be similar to the process of accessing a safety deposit box. Your key must work with the bank's key before the box opens.

◪Cookies

A *cookie* is a message sent by a web *server* to a web *browser*. The browser software usually saves the cookie, as a text file, to the hard disk of the user's computer. The cookie can be sent back to the server whenever the browser makes additional requests. The main purpose of cookies is to identify visitors to a website and possibly prepare customised web pages for them, e.g. personalised greetings.

Other reasons for using cookies include:

- Helping with on-line sales/services, e.g. *Amazon Books* or *Microsoft*.
- Tracking popular links or demographics, e.g. *DoubleClick*.

As a cookie is a simple text file, it *cannot* be used to:

- Transmit viruses to your computer.
- Access your hard drive.
- Ascertain your e-mail address.

Cookies are very small files. Both Netscape and Microsoft, however, have measures in place that limit the number of cookies that will be saved on your hard disk at one time. These measures make it impossible for cookies to fill the hard disk of your computer. Netscape limits your total cookie count to 300. If you exceed this, the browser will discard your least-used cookies to make room for the new ones. Microsoft saves cookies into the *Temporary Internet Files* folder. The default size of this system folder is set to 2 per cent of your hard disk capacity.

A negative aspect of the use of cookies is that they can be used in conjunction with Web servers as a 'tracking device' to build a profile of an individual's surfing and buying habits. Many people consider this as an invasion of privacy.

Spyware

Spyware is any software that secretly gathers information on your use of a computer and reports back to another computer on the Internet without your permission.

Two main types of spyware are:

- **Advertising spyware:** Keeps a record of websites you visit in order to build a profile of your interests. This information can be used by advertising companies to send you advertisements on products or services related to your interests.
- **Malicious spyware:** Can record every keystroke and mouse click, making it possible to obtain personal information, even bank details and credit card numbers, while a person is conducting business on-line, e.g. making an on-line purchase.

To determine if your computers has contracted spyware, you should look out for the following symptoms:

- Do pop-up ads frequently appear even when you are not accessing the Internet?
- Was your homepage reset?
- Are there any changes to your browser toolbar?
- Do you recognise a slowdown in your computer's performance?

Spyware can be restricted by:

- installing anti-spyware protection software
- updating this software regularly
- using a firewall
- adjusting security settings on your browser to a high level
- downloading files only from trustworthy websites.

Phishing

Phishing is a dishonest scheme conducted on the Internet to lure people into revealing important information, e.g. bank account or credit card numbers, which can then be used to make unauthorised bank account withdrawals or to pay for purchases.

A typical phish is carried out as follows: an official-looking e-mail is sent to a potential victim pretending to be from his/her bank. The e-mail states that due to internal accounting errors or some other pretext, certain information must be updated to continue the service. A link in the message directs the user to a fraudulent website that asks for personal financial information. Many of these websites look genuine, with a professional appearance complete with company logos.

Phishing fraud can be avoiding by:

- phoning your bank and speaking with an official regarding the e-mail
- never providing your personal information in response to an unsolicited e-mail, fax, pop-up advertisement or unexpected website address
- reviewing bank and credit card statements for problems or inconsistencies.

Chapter 10
Electronic Mail and Web Publishing

▦ Electronic mail

Electronic mail, or e-mail, is the most widely used feature of the Internet. E-mail is similar to conventional mail except that the letters are delivered over the Internet. A number of e-mail messages can by typed off-line. When you are ready to send your e-mail, a connection to your ISP can be established and all of the messages can be sent together.

E-mail has a number of advantages over standard mail:

- Speed – a message can travel around the world in seconds.
- Cost – there is no charge for sending or receiving e-mail other than the cost of the connection to your ISP's server.
- Content – full working computer files can be attached to the e-mail message, e.g. spreadsheets and databases.
- Multiple copies – any number of copies of the same message can be sent to different destinations at the same time.

E-mail also has a number of disadvantages when compared with standard mail:

- Security – e-mail messages can be intercepted. However, with the increasing use of encryption, it is likely that this problem will disappear in the future.
- Reading files – when you receive a file as an e-mail attachment, it is necessary to have the appropriate software to access it, e.g. if you receive a *Microsoft Excel* spreadsheet as an attachment, it is necessary to have *Microsoft Excel* installed on your computer to work with the spreadsheet.
- E-mail documents are not legally binding (as of going to print).

How does e-mail work?

You send your message using an e-mail program; it travels via your ISP over the Internet to a destination server computer. It is stored on that computer in a special folder called a *mailbox*. Most people have a mailbox provided to them by their ISP. If you send an e-mail message to somebody, it will go to his or her mailbox, which is located on his or her ISP's mail server computer. It will stay there until they access the mailbox to collect their messages. In order to send the e-mail message, however, you must have the *e-mail address* of the would-be recipient.

What is an e-mail address?

An e-mail address defines the location of an individual's mailbox on the Internet. Examples of typical e-mail addresses would be:

jdoe@eircom.net

or

glineker@bbc.co.uk

The address consists of two parts separated by the '@' symbol. The part before the '@' symbol is called *the user name*, which can be a real name or an alias. The part after the '@' symbol is called the *domain name* and gives the location of that person's account. In the first example the user name is 'jdoe' while the domain name tells us that John Doe's mailbox is located on a server belonging to the Eircom company, which is based in Ireland (.ie).

An e-mail address cannot contain spaces. The last few characters in an individual's e-mail address usually indicate the type of organisation and/or country the person belongs to. For example:

ORGANISATION	COUNTRY
.com – commercial	.ie – Ireland
.gov – American government	.uk – United Kingdom
.org – non-profit organisation	.au – Australia
.net – network	.ca – Canada
.mil – American military	.it – Italy

Characteristics of an e-mail program

An e-mail program lets you send, receive and manage your e-mail messages. Currently, the most popular e-mail programs are Microsoft's Outlook Express and Qualcomm's Eudora.

All e-mail programs have similar characteristics:

- *Compose* – you can compose a message; this is similar to writing a letter using a word processor.
- *Reply* – you can reply to a message that you have received.
- *Forward* – you can send a copy of a message you have received to another person with an e-mail address.
- *Store* – you can store important messages so you can review them later. E-mail programs let you create folders to organise all of your stored messages.
- *Delete* – you can delete messages you no longer need.
- *Print* – you can produce a hard copy of a message.
- *Attachments* – the sender of an e-mail message can attach files created by other programs. You can open an attached file provided that you have the program in which the file was created installed on your computer.

Component parts of an e-mail message

The e-mail message below was created using *Outlook Express*. However, the component parts of any e-mail message are very similar regardless of the e-mail program used to create it.

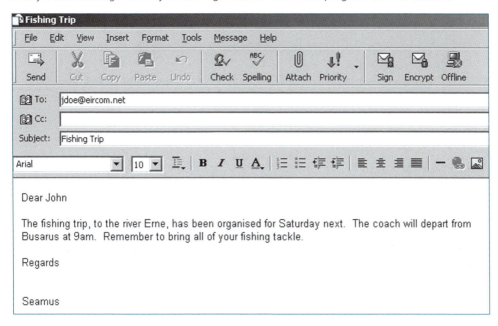

- *To*: This line holds the e-mail address of the person who will receive the message. In this case, it is jdoe@eircom.net.
- *Cc*: This stands for carbon copy. If you wish to send the e-mail to more than one person, you can enter a number of other e-mail addresses on this line (separated by commas or semi-colons). In our example, this line is blank, meaning that we are only sending the message to John Doe.
- *Bcc*: This stands for blind carbon copy. This is similar to carbon copy except that each recipient of the message does not know that others have received the message. Again, in our example, this line is left blank.
- *Subject*: This identifies the content of the message. It is important to enter a short title or reference for your message, indicating what it is about. Appropriate subject titles makes it easier for the recipient to organise incoming mail. In our example, we have entered 'Fishing Trip' in our subject line.
- *Body of the message*: This area holds the text of the message. In our case, it is notification of a forthcoming fishing trip to the river Erne. Most e-mail programs have an in-built spellchecker facility. We recommend that you use it before sending the message.

Managing mailboxes

The e-mail program uses a number of mailboxes or folders to help you manage the mail on your computer. These mailboxes must not be confused with the mailbox that the ISP provides for you on their server.

The five mailboxes common to most e-mail programs are:

- *Inbox*: When you download a new e-mail message from your mailbox on the server, it is stored in the inbox on your computer.
- *Outbox*: A message that you have composed, but not yet sent, is stored in an outbox.
- *Sent items box*: Copies of e-mail messages that have been mailed are automatically placed in the sent items box.
- *Drafts box*: Copies of unfinished e-mail messages are usually held in the drafts box.
- *Deleted items box*: E-mail messages that you have deleted from the other boxes are moved to the delete box. You can retrieve messages from the delete box and restore them to the inbox or outbox. However, once you empty the delete box, any e-mail messages that were previously held in it cannot be retrieved.

The e-mail program allows you to create your own mailboxes or folders. This is useful in that you can move e-mail messages from your inbox or sent items box to appropriately named folders, e.g. business, personal, family.

Emoticons and acronyms

It is often hard to convey emotions in written communication. The task of conveying emotion is even more difficult if we are corresponding with people whom we have never met, who have different cultural values to our own or whose native language may not be English.

Fortunately, a useful set of symbols has evolved to help us in conveying emotions in our e-mail messages. This set of symbols is continually growing. These symbols are called emoticons ('emotional icons') or 'smilies'. Some common examples and their meanings are shown below:

EMOTION	MEANING
Smile	:-)
Frown	:-(
Laugh	:-D
Cry	:'-(
Surprise	:-O
Wink	;-)

Try looking at the symbols in the table with your head tilted to the left.

Acronyms are frequently used in e-mail messages to save time typing and to convey emotion. Again, the number of e-mail acronyms is growing all the time.

Some of the more commonly used acronyms are shown below:

ACRONYM	MEANING
BTW	By the way
FAQ	Frequently asked question
FOAF	Friend of a friend
IMHO	In my humble opinion
FYI	For your information
L8R	Later
LOL	Laughing out loud
ROTFL	Rolling on the floor laughing
SO	Significant other
WRT	With respect to

You may be sending an e-mail message to your cousin in Chicago informing her of your forthcoming visit there. You could include the following sentence, which includes an acronym and an emoticon, in the e-mail message:

'BTW, we have just booked our flight tickets and we are really looking forward to the holiday in Chicago :-)'

Good e-mail etiquette

E-mail has evolved a much less formal style than traditional business writing. We advise, however, that you take a little care in composing e-mail messages. It is always a good idea to read through the message again before clicking the 'send' button. The message may contain spelling mistakes and poorly constructed sentences. This will convey an unfavourable impression of you to the recipient of the e-mail.

We recommend that you follow the guidelines set out below when using e-mail:

• E-mail messages should be relatively short and unambiguous.
• Check for incorrect spellings and poor grammar.
• Take care to enter the correct e-mail address of the would-be recipient.
• Never include anything in the e-mail message that you may later regret.
• Always enter a title for the message on the subject line.
• A message should not be written entirely in capital letters; this is known as *shouting*.
• Do not overuse acronyms and emoticons.
• Do not send large attachments without prior approval.
• Do not engage in *flaming*. A flame is an angry or insulting message directed at one person.
• Reply to e-mail promptly.
• Do not engage in *spamming*. This is the unsolicited mass distribution of e-mail messages.

Web-based e-mail accounts

Some companies with websites on the World Wide Web offer a free web-based e-mail service. The most widely used service of this type is *Hotmail*. To register for a free web-based e-mail account, you simply call up Hotmail's website and fill the on-line form. Hotmail's site can be found at www.hotmail.com. To access or send mail, all a person has to do is:

- connect to the Internet through any server
- call up Hotmail's website
- enter his/her user name and password
- download any new messages from their mailbox at Hotmail
- compose and send new messages if he/she wishes.

This facility is of tremendous benefit to people who are travelling. No matter where they are, once they can connect to the Internet they can download their e-mail messages from their mailbox at Hotmail.

Mailing lists

A *mailing list* is a discussion group that uses e-mail to communicate. There are thousands of mailing lists on the Internet. They cover a very wide range of interests, from Andrew Lloyd Webber to zoo animals. When you send a message to a mailing list, a copy of the message is sent to the mailbox of each person on the list. You must subscribe to the mailing list to join the discussion group. You can unsubscribe from a mailing list at any time.

Each mailing list has two e-mail addresses. One address receives messages for the entire group while the other address is for administration. When you subscribe initially to a mailing list, make sure that you send your request to the administration address. If you are on one or more mailing lists, make sure that you check your e-mail frequently, as e-mail messages can mount up in a very short time.

Some mailing lists are *moderated*. This means that one member of the group reads each message. If the message is suitable, it is sent to the other members on the list. A moderated mailing list keeps discussion on-topic by screening out irrelevant messages. In an unmoderated mailing list, all messages are sent to everyone in the group. If you receive many messages from a mailing list, check if the list is available as a *digest*. A digest is a set of messages that have been grouped together and sent as one message.

Mailing lists can be *manually maintained* or *automated*. An administrator manages a manually maintained mailing list while a *mailing list manager* is software residing on a server computer that automates the process of maintaining a mailing list. The *mailing list manager* accepts messages e-mailed by subscribers and sends copies of the messages, which may be first screened by a moderator, to all of the subscribers. The most commonly used mailing list managers are *Listserv* and *Majordomo*.

Usenet newsgroups

Let us digress for a moment to examine how a public notice board, say in a shopping centre, works. Anybody can pin notices to the notice board. The notices can be read by anyone who looks at the board. A person might place a notice advertising a computer for sale. An interested party could pin a reply notice with an offer or a request that the advertiser make contact with him or her. A shopping centre employee may take charge of organising the notice board. The different notices could be arranged under different category headings:

- Items for sale
- Accommodation offered
- Childminders
- Work available
- Miscellaneous.

Newsgroups (sometimes called message boards) work in a similar way. They allow people with common interests to communicate with one another. Usenet consists of thousands of newsgroups (like our categories on the notice board). A newsgroup can be defined as an electronic discussion group consisting of collections of related postings (also called articles) on a particular topic. Making a posting to a newsgroup is similar to placing a notice on the notice board.

Usenet was the original worldwide newsgroup or message board system made available on the Internet. It now contains more than 14,000 newsgroups, covering a wide range of interest groups.

There are newsgroups on a diverse range of topics. For example, there are newsgroups on African music, artificial intelligence, comics, equestrian sports, Japanese culture, pharmacy and wines. The name of a newsgroup describes the type of information it discusses. A name consists of two or more words separated by periods:

rec.sport.soccer

The first word describes the main topic area (rec for recreation). Each of the following words narrows the topic area.

Some of the main newsgroup topic areas are:

NAME	TOPIC AREA
Alt	Alternative newsgroups covering a variety of topics
Biz	Business-oriented newsgroups
Comp	Computer-related newsgroups
Misc	Miscellaneous newsgroups
News	Newsgroups covering Usenet itself
Rec	Recreational and hobby newsgroups
Sci	Science-oriented newsgroups
Soc	Newsgroups for discussion of social issues
Talk	Newsgroups for discussing often controversial issues

You *subscribe* to newsgroups that you want to read on a regular basis. This is similar to subscribing to a magazine but in this case there is no charge. You can reply to an article or supply additional information. A program called a *newsreader* allows you to read and send articles to newsgroups. Both *Internet Explorer* and *Netscape Navigator* have built-in newsreader programs.

Newsgroup articles are stored on *news server* computers around the world. An ISP will operate at least one news server computer. It is very unlikely that the ISP will carry all of the newsgroups. For each newsgroup that it supports, the ISP will hold all the postings to that newsgroup for a period of time. The length of time will vary from newsgroup to newsgroup and range from as little as one day to several months. When a message has been on a server for longer than the specified time, the server deletes it. When you post an article to a newsgroup on a certain server, it is automatically passed on to all the other news servers around the world that carry the same newsgroup.

Google and *Yahoo!* operate mailing list and newsgroup facilities through their *Google Groups* and *Yahoo! Groups* websites, respectively:

- Google groups: http://groups.google.com
- Yahoo! groups: http://groups.yahoo.com

◤Spam

Spam is an unsolicited e-mail message, usually sent to many recipients at the same time, or a news article posted to many newsgroups. It is the Internet equivalent of junk mail.

While it is difficult to avoid spam completely, there are steps that you can take to greatly reduce it:

- avoid giving your e-mail address to unknown or unfamiliar persons
- obtain two e-mail addresses – one for personal messages and one for newsgroups and chat rooms
- use your e-mail program's message filtering features
- check if your ISP has e-mail filtering software available, e.g. Eircom's *Email Protector*
- look for a privacy statement before you fill out an on-line form
- when completing on-line forms, always look for and tick any data protection opt-out boxes if you do not wish to receive advertisements
- never reply to spam
- report spammers to your ISP.

▦Web publishing
Website evaluation

In evaluating any website, we advise that you examine a number of different aspects.

1. Appearance and layout

- *Consistency*: The web pages that go to make up the website should look as if they belong together. They should have common:
  - text colours and fonts
  - backgrounds
  - illustrations (if applicable).

The website should have a consistent and easy-to-use navigation system, i.e. anyone should be able to move around the website with ease using the hyperlinks. A navigation bar is often used for this purpose. This is a bar of icons or buttons with hyperlinks to other pages on the website.

- *Readability*: As it is more difficult to read on-screen as opposed to printed text, short paragraphs are better for web pages (no longer than five sentences).
- *Placement:* Text and graphic elements must not appear as if they were thrown onto the page. They should have a common alignment; it is not a good idea to centre, left-align and right-align different elements on the same page. A common alignment does not mean that all of the elements must be placed along the same invisible vertical line in the margin of the page. Indenting of elements, using the same alignment, may suit a particular web page.
- *Closeness*: Headings, subheadings, body text or graphic elements that belong to each other should be placed close together. A subheading separated by blank lines from the text to which it belongs does not look right.
- *Contrast*: Most students know the importance of colour contrast on websites. A bright colour on a dark background (or vice versa) is much easier to read. Contrasting elements also show priorities. Text that is in a different colour, point size or font can indicate that it is a heading or subheading.
- *Page size*: The entire website home page should fit in the browser window. Wherever possible, horizontal scrolling should be eliminated on every web page in the site.
- *Site map*: On larger websites, one web page should include a site map or index. A site map shows how the various pages in the site are linked.

2. Appropriate use of graphics

- *Overuse of graphics*: Some websites can have too many images or animations, which can detract greatly from the message of the website.
- *Large images*: Some websites contain graphics that do not fit on the screen. They have not been scaled to suit the particular pages.
- *File size*: A large graphics file can take a considerable length of time to download. Thumbnails, smaller versions of the same file, are recommended. If the user wishes to see a larger version of the image, he or she may click on the thumbnail that should have a hyperlink to a file containing a larger version of the image.
- *Alt labels*: Graphic images without alt labels are not advisable. An alt label is a text alternative for an image. If an individual has disabled the graphics mode in his or her browser, he or she will be at a loss if there is no alt label displayed instead of the image.

3. Technical considerations

- *Working links*: It is of the utmost importance that all of the hyperlinks in the website work properly. Sometimes when you click on a hyperlink, you can get the message: 'URL not known'. This is evidence of a 'broken' link or a missing web page.

- *Browser compatibility*: A website should be tested using at least two different browsers. For example, a site may appear fine when viewed using Internet Explorer but may not look right in Netscape or vice versa. Versions of web browsers should also be given consideration; some websites may not appear as they should when viewed using an older version of a browser.
- *Necessity of plug-ins*: Some websites require the use of at least one plug-in program in order to be viewed successfully. For example, in order to view a video clip, you will probably need to install a plug-in called *QuickTime*.
- *Meta tags*: These are used to document web pages and/or provide information that can be used by search engines to classify or index the page. There are several meta tags, but the most important for search engine indexing are the description and keywords tags. The description tag summarises the contents of a web page. The keywords tag provides a selection of words that the search engine can associate with the web page.
- *Frames*: The browser window can be divided into a number of panes known as frames. Different web pages in the site can appear in each of the frames. Too many frames in the browser window make it look cluttered and can convey an unfavourable impression.
- *Image map*: Image maps are used for navigation purposes on a website. An image map is a graphic with a number of hyperlinks on it. For example, a photograph of a group of people could have a hyperlink from each person's face to a web page for that individual.
- *Interactivity*: Some sites are interactive. The user can enter details onto a web page and these are then processed. For example, you can order a book from Amazon's website by simply completing an on-line form; the order will then be processed and the book dispatched to you. The interactivity of a website normally depends on programs written in programming languages such as *Java, JavaScript* or *Perl*.

4. Linguistic considerations
- *Spellings and grammar:* Poor grammar and spelling can convey an unfavourable impression of the person who created the website. Great care should be taken to eliminate grammatical and spelling errors.
- *Vocabulary range*: The range of words used in the website should be appropriate to the target audience. A website for children should contain words appropriate to their level of development.
- *Humour/sarcasm*: A person from a different cultural or ethnic background may access a website and not understand attempts at humour or sarcasm.
- *Colloquialisms or slang*: These have no place on a website.

Creating a web page
There are two main ways of creating a web page.
1. Use a web editor program. This is also known as a web authoring program.
2. Enter the page details and relevant HTML tags using a text editor program. HyperText Mark up Language (HTML) instructs the browser how to display a page.

Web editor program

A web editor program has many features that are similar to those of a word processor. For example, the user is allowed to enter text, apply text formatting and insert graphics. The web editor facilitates the establishment of hyperlinks between pages. When you create a web page using a web editor program, the HTML tags are applied automatically. Popular web editor programs include *Microsoft FrontPage, Adobe Go-Live, Netscape Composer* and *Adobe (formerly Macromedia) Dreamweaver.*

Text editor and HyperText Mark-up Language (HTML)

Any program that allows the user to enter and save text as a text-only document can be used as a text editor, e.g. *Microsoft Word, WordPad* or *NotePad*. To specify that the document is a web page, the file extension '.htm' must be added to the file name.

Each HTML tag is surrounded by angle brackets. For example: <B>Irish Tourism</B> gives the instruction – 'Make the text Irish Tourism appear in bold type' – to the Web browser. It is a good idea to capitalise the HTML tags so they stand out from the document text.

Many HTML tags work in pairs – *opening* and *closing* tags – that affect the text between them. The following table shows twenty frequently used HTML tags.

OPENING TAG	CLOSING TAG	PURPOSE
<A HREF>	</A>	Specifying the URL of the page where the link goes
<B>	</B>	Displaying text in bold face
<BODY>	</BODY>	Enclosing the main section of a web page
<BGSOUND>		Inserting background sound for a web page
 		Creating a line break
<CENTER>	</CENTER>	Centring text, images or other elements
<FONT>	</FONT>	Changing the font face, size and colour of text
<HEAD>	</HEAD>	Creating the head section of a web page
<Hn>		Creating headings of different sizes
<HR>		Inserting a horizontal rule
<HTML>	</HTML>	Identifying a text document as a web page
<I>	</I>	Displaying text in italics
<IMG>		Inserting images on a web page
<LI>		Creating a list item
<OL>	</OL>	Creating an ordered list
<P>		Creating a new paragraph
<PRE>	</PRE>	Displaying text exactly as it appears in the editor
<TITLE>	</TITLE>	Creating a caption in the title bar area
<U>	</U>	Underlining text
<UL>	</UL>	Creating an unordered list

Sample travel agent website

We will now examine how to construct a very basic website, consisting of only two web pages, using a text editor and HTML. The pages below appear as they would in the browser window:

Page 1

Going Places

Going Places, a travel agency founded by Mary O'Connor in 1996, is going from strength to strength. It has offices in Dublin, Cork and Galway. The company offers a variety of holiday types:

- <u>European city breaks</u>
- Sun holidays
- Skiing packages
- Long haul tours
- Customised holidays

The company's policy is to provide quality low-cost holiday packages to its customers. On examining the phenomenal growth in its turnover over the years, it would appear that *Going Places* is living up to its name.

Page 2

European City Breaks

Going Places offers wonderful short holiday packages to a host of European destinations:

1. London
2. Paris
3. Brussels
4. Munich
5. Florence

The 'two-night special' is popular with customers. This holiday break includes flights, two nights bed & breakfast with dinner on one evening in one of the cities listed above. The package also includes insurance, tax and transfer costs.

There is a hypertext link from <u>European city breaks</u> on page 1 which, when clicked, calls up page 2.

The following shows the two pages, complete with text and the appropriate HTML tags, as each would appear in the text editor window.

Page 1

```
<HTML>
<HEAD>
<TITLE>Going Places</TITLE>
</HEAD>
<BODY BGCOLOR = WHITE TEXT = BLACK>
<H1>Going Places</H1>
<P>
<I>Going Places</I>, a travel agency founded by Mary O'Connor in 1996, is going from
strength to strength. It has offices in Dublin, Cork and Galway. The company offers a
variety of holiday types:
<UL>
<LI><A HREF = "holiday2.htm">European city breaks</A>
<LI>Sun holidays
<LI>Skiing packages
<LI>Long-haul tours
<LI>Customised holidays
</UL>
<P>The company's policy is to provide quality low-cost holiday packages to its customers.
On examining the phenomenal growth in its turnover over the years, it would appear
that <I>Going Places</I> is living up to its name.
</BODY>
</HTML>
```

This file is saved as *holiday1.htm*.

```
<HTML>
<HEAD>
<TITLE>Going Places</TITLE>
</HEAD>
<BODY BGCOLOR = White TEXT = Black>
<H1>European City Breaks</H1>
<I>Going Places</I> offers wonderful short holiday packages to a host of European
destinations:
<OL>
<LI>London
<LI>Paris
<LI>Brussels
<LI>Munich
<LI>Florence
</OL>
The 'two-night special' is popular with customers. This holiday break includes flights, two
nights bed & breakfast with dinner on one evening in one of the cities listed above. The
package also includes insurance, tax and transfer costs.
</BODY>
</HTML>
```

This file is saved as *holiday2.htm*.

How the HTML tags work

1. Each web page starts and finishes with the opening and closing 'HTML' tags – <HTML> and </HTML>. These tags tell the browser that whatever appears between them should be treated as a web page.
2. The <HEAD> and </HEAD> tags create a head section for the page.
3. The text between the <TITLE> and </TITLE> tags gives a brief title or description of the page. This text is displayed in the title bar of the browser program.
4. The contents of the web page appear between the <BODY> and </BODY> tags. This tag is used, in our website, with attributes; we have specified in the <BODY> tag the background and text colour attributes for each page. Notice the American spellings.
5. The header tags, <H1> and </H1>, specify that enclosed text will appear as a major heading on a text page.
6. The <P> tag indicates the start of a new paragraph.
7. The italics tags, <I> and </I>, specify that enclosed text will be shown in italics.

8. The unordered list tags, <UL> and </UL>, specify that enclosed text will be shown in a bulleted list.
9. The ordered list tags, <OL> and </OL>, specify that enclosed text will be shown in a numbered list.
10. The <LI> tag specifies items that should be bulleted or numbered.
11. The line, <A HREF = "holiday2.htm">European city breaks</A>, specifies a hypertext link from 'European city breaks' to the file saved as 'holiday2.htm'.

Inserting a graphic

A graphic image may be placed on a web page using the IMG tag. For example, let us replace the line: *<H1>Going Places</H1>* with the line *<IMG SRC = "logo.gif">* in the 'holiday1.htm' file. The newly updated 'holiday1.htm' appears in the browser window as follows:

Going Places, a travel agency founded by Mary O'Connor in 1996 is going from strength to strength. It has offices in Dublin, Cork and Galway. The company offers a variety of holiday types:

- European city breaks
- Sun holidays
- Skiing packages
- Long-haul tours
- Customised Holidays

The company's policy is to provide quality low-cost holiday packages to its customers. On examining the phenomenal growth in its turnover over the years, it would appear that *Going Places* is living up to its name.

The IMG tag has an SRC (source) attribute that inserts the file containing the logo graphic, *logo.gif*, onto the web page. IMG has another attribute that can be used to align the graphic on the web page. For example, the instruction *<IMG SRC = "logo.gif" ALIGN = RIGHT>* would insert the logo onto the web page but align it along the right margin of the browser window. We advise that you save all files making up a website in the same folder.

Changing colours

Our web pages have black text on a white background. If we replace the tag *<BODY BGCOLOR = White TEXT = Black>* with *<BODY BGCOLOR = Green TEXT = Yellow>*, we will get yellow text on a green background. We can use choose combinations from the following sixteen predefined colours:

THE SIXTEEN PREDEFINED COLOURS			
Silver	Maroon	Navy	Olive
Grey	Red	Blue	Yellow
White	Green	Purple	Teal
Black	Lime	Magenta	Cyan

You can choose from a greater range of colours by using the hexadecimal code for the colour. A discussion on hexadecimal colour codes is beyond the scope of this book. However, we can use the codes to give our web pages a greater burst of colour. For example, if we substitute *<BODY BGCOLOR = white TEXT = black>* with *<BODY BGCOLOR = "#C6EFF7" TEXT = "#AD0000">*, we get bright blue text on a burgundy background. When using a hexadecimal colour code, you should always place the # symbol before the code and enclose it in quotation marks. A selection of colours and their hexadecimal equivalents can be found on the next page.

Using backgrounds
A graphic can be used as a background instead of a specific colour. The *background* attribute is used instead of *bgcolor* for the body tag. Let us assume that we have a photograph of a partially clouded sky stored in a file called 'sky.gif'. We could get black text on a sky background by using the following:
<BODY BACKGROUND = "sky.gif" TEXT = black>

File formats
The most common file formats on the World Wide Web are shown below:

FILE TYPE	FILE EXTENSION	MEANING
Web Page	HTM	HyperText Mark-up Language
Graphics	GIF	Graphics Interchange Format
Graphics	JPG	Joint Photographics Expert Group
Sound	AU	Audio Player
Sound	RA, RM, RAM	Real Audio
Sound	WAV	Wave
Sound	MID	Midi
Animation and Video	DCR	Shockwave
Animation and Video	SWF	Flash
Sound	MP3	MPEG Audio Layer 3
Other	PDF	Portable Document Format
Animation and Video	AVI	Audio Video Interleaved
Animation and Video	MPG	Motion Picture Experts Group
Animation and Video	MOV	QuickTime

Hexadecimal Colour Codes

Alice Blue F0F8FF   Antique White FAEBD7   Aqua 00FFFF
Aqua Marine 7FFFD4   Azure F0FFFF   Beige F5F5DC
Bisque FFE4C4   Blanched Almond FFEBCD   Blue 0000EE
Blue Secondary 0000FF   Blue Violet 8A2BE2   Brown A52A2A
Burly Wood DEB887   Cadet Blue 5F9EA0   Chartreuse 7FFF00
Chocolate D2691E   Coral FF7F50   Cornflower Blue 6495ED
Corn Silk FFF8DC   Crimson DC143C   Cyan 00FFFF
Dark Blue 00008B   Dark Cyan 008B8B   Dark Golden Rod B8860B
Dark Grey A9A9A9   Dark Green 006400   Dark Khaki BDB76B
Dark Magenta 8B008B   Dark Olive Green 556B2F   Dark Orange FF8C00
Dark Orchid 9932CC   Dark Red 8B0000   Dark Salmon E9967A
Dark Sea Green 8FBC8F   Dark Slate Blue 483D8B   Dark Slate Grey 2F4F4F
Dark Turquoise 00CED1   Dark Violet 9400D3   Deep Pink FF1493
Deep Sky Blue 00BFFF   Dim Grey 696969   Dodger Blue 1E90FF
Fire Brick B22222   Floral White FFFAF0   Forest Green 228B22
Fuchsia FF00FF   Gainsboro DCDCDC   Ghost White F8F8FF
Gold FFD700   Golden Rod DAA520   Grey 808080
Green 008000   Green Yellow ADFF2F   Honey Dew F0FFF0
Hot Pink FF69B4   Indian Red CD5C5C   Indigo 4B0082
Ivory FFFFF0   Khaki F0E68C   Lavender E6E6FA
Lavender Blush FFF0F5   Lawn Green 7CFC00   Lemon Chiffon FFFACD
Light Blue ADD8E6   Light Coral F08080   Light Cyan E0FFFF
Light Golden Yellow FAFAD2 Light Green 90EE90   Light Grey D3D3D3
Light Pink FFB6C1   Light Salmon FFA07A   Light Sea Green 20B2AA
Light Sky Blue 87CEFA   Light Slate Grey 778899   Light Steel Blue B0C4DE
Light Yellow FFFFE0   Lime 00FF00   Lime Green 32CD32
Linen FAF0E6   Magenta FF00FF   Maroon 800000
Medium Aquamarine 66CDAA   Medium Blue 0000CD   Medium Orchid BA55D3
Medium Purple 9370D8   Medium Sea Green 3CB371   Medium Slate Blue 7B68EE
Medium Spring Green 00FA9A Medium Turquoise 48D1CC   Medium Violet Red C71585
Midnight Blue 191970   Mint Cream F5FFFA   Misty Rose FFE4E1
Moccasin FFE4B5   Navajo White FFDEAD   Navy 000080
Old Lace FDF5E6   Olive 808000   Olive Drab 688E23
Orange FFA500   Orange Red FF4500   Orchid DA70D6
Pale Golden Rod EEE8AA   Pale Green 98FB98   Pale Turquoise AFEEEE
Pale Violet Red D87093   Papaya Whip FFEFD5   Peach Puff FFDAB9
Peru CD853F   Pink FFC0CB   Plum DDA0DD
Powder Blue B0E0E6   Purple 800080   Red FF0000
Rosy Brown BC8F8F   Royal Blue 4169E1   Saddle Brown 8B4513
Salmon FA8072   Sandy Brown F4A460   Sea Green 2E8B57
Seashell FFF5EE   Sienna A0522D   Silver C0C0C0
Sky Blue 87CEEB   Slate Blue 6A5ACD   Slate Grey 708090
Snow FFFAFA   Spring Green 00FF7F   Steel Blue 4682B4
Tan D2B48C   Teal 008080   Thistle D8BFD8
Tomato FF6347   Turquoise 40E0D0   Violet EE82EE
Wheat F5DEB3   White FFFFFF   White Smoke F5F5F5
Yellow FFFF00   Yellow Green 9ACD32

Note: Use the '#' symbol before the colour code.

Questions

1. Distinguish between the terms *Internet* and *World Wide Web*.
2. Who owns and pays for the Internet?
3. How would you evaluate an *Internet service provider*?
4. List the basic hardware and software necessary in order to use the Internet.
5. Define the term '*broadband*'. Describe the four main ways of accessing broadband in Ireland.
6. Distinguish between *IP addresses* and *domain names*.
7. What are *plug-ins*? Give examples of how they are used.
8. Examine briefly the different software tools available for searching the Web.
9. What is *voice over IP*? What are the different ways of using *VoIP*?
10. What is a *blog*? What are its main components?
11. How does *multimedia conferencing* work?
12. Distinguish between a *podcast* and a *webcast*.
13. Outline the chief methods of paying for goods or services over the Internet.
14. Describe how viruses may spread from the Internet to your computer. How can this be prevented?
15. What is *filtering software* and how does it work?
16. Define the term *firewall*. What is its purpose?
17. In the context of the Internet, what are *cookies*? Outline their positive and negative aspects.
18. What is *spyware?* How can it be limited?
19. What are the advantages of *e-mail* over standard or *snail* mail?
20. Describe the components of an *e-mail address*.
21. Outline the chief characteristics of an e-mail program.
22. Outline the various parts of an e-mail message.
23. List some elements of what you consider as good e-mail etiquette.
24. Describe how a web-based e-mail account works.
25. Distinguish between *mailing lists* and *newsgroups*.
26. Define the term 'spam'. Outline ways of reducing it.
27. What elements do you look out for when evaluating a website?
28. What are the two main ways of creating a web page?
29. Choose any five HTML tags and explain the purpose of each one.
30. List the most common graphic, sound and video file formats on the Web.

Glossary of Internet terms

Advance Research Projects Network (ARPANET): an early US network that forms the basis of the Internet.

bandwidth: the rate of data transmission measured in bits per second.

blog: an online diary or e-zine made available on the web.

broadband: always-on high-speed Internet access.

browser: a program to help users view and search for information on the WWW.

cookie: a piece of information sent by a web server to a web browser that the browser software is expected to save and to send back to the server whenever the browser makes additional requests from the server.

digital signature: a code that can be attached to an electronically transmitted message that uniquely identifies the sender.

domain name: a unique word that acts like a nickname for the IP address of a server computer.

Domain Name System (DNS): regulates the naming of computers on the Internet.

download: the act of copying a file from a server computer on the Internet to your own computer.

electronic business (e-business): the administration of conducting business over the Internet.

electronic mail (e-mail): messages sent from one computer to another on a network.

e-mail address: defines the location of an individual's mailbox on the Internet.

emoticon: symbol composed of punctuation marks designed to express some form of emotion.

encryption: a way of coding information in a file or e-mail message so only the intended recipient can read it.

File Transfer Protocol (FTP): a set of rules for transferring files from one computer to another via the Internet.

filtering software: programs that prevent access to objectionable information on the World Wide Web.

firewall: a combination hardware and software buffer that many companies or organisations have in place between their internal networks and any outside network, including the Internet, to prevent unauthorised access.

flame: an angry or insulting e-mail message.

hyperlink: a link from one web page to another or within the same web page. Clicking on the link with a mouse activates it.

hypertext: a word or group of words that are hyperlinks.

HyperText Mark-up Language (HTML): the coding language used to create web pages.

instant messaging: allows you to have a private conversation over the Internet.

Internet: global computer network connecting millions of computers.

Internet protocol (IP) address: a unique code number assigned to each computer on the Internet.

Internet relay chat (IRC): a service that allows users connected to the Internet to chat with each other over many channels.

Internet service provider (ISP): a company that provides access to the Internet, usually for a fee.

intranet: the use of technologies and software developed for the Internet on an organisation's internal network.

mailbox: special folder on a computer for holding e-mail messages.

mailing list: a discussion group that uses e-mail to communicate.

netiquette: behaviour guidelines evolved by users of the Internet.

newsgroup: a discussion group on the Internet.

off-line: not connected to the Internet.

on-line: connected to the Internet.

phishing: a dishonest scheme conducted on the Internet to lure people into revealing important information.

plug-in: a program that works with your web browser to give it an extra capability.

podcast: a Web-based audio broadcast.

portal: large website with hyperlinks to a wide range of topics and issues.

router: special computer that regulates traffic on the Internet.

search engine: remotely accessible program to help users find information on the Internet.

search tool: a computer program that helps us to find information on the Web.

site map: shows how the various pages in a website are linked.

spamming: the unsolicited mass distribution of e-mail messages or postings to multiple Internet newsgroups.

spider: a program that combs the Internet for new documents such as web pages and FTP files. All the references found are supplied to a database that can be used by a search engine.

spyware: any software that secretly gathers information on your use of a computer and reports back to another computer on the Internet without your permission.

streaming: sending data, for example radio broadcasts or video frames, in a steady flow over the Internet.

uniform resource locator (URL): the unique address of each web page on the World Wide Web.

Usenet: a global collection of newsgroups with comments passed among hundreds of thousands of computers.

voice over IP (VoIP): a technology that allows you to make telephone calls over the Internet.

webcast: the live or delayed transmission of audio or video content over the Internet.

website: a collection of related web pages.

World Wide Web (WWW or Web): consists of millions of pages of information stored on thousands of server computers all over the world.

Chapter 11
Practical Internet
Assignments

▦ E-mail assignments

◤ E-mail

The class tutor is advised to create a Web-based e-mail account. The students can then direct e-mail messages, given in the following assignments, to the address of this account.

Assignment 1

1. Find a free Web-based e-mail service on the Web.
2. Use this service to create your own Web-based e-mail account.

Assignment 2

Use your new e-mail account to send the following e-mail message to the e-mail address provided to you by your tutor:

> Subject: Fishing Trip
>
> Dear Conor,
> The fishing trip to the river Boyne will take place on Saturday next. The coach to Trim will leave from the Ambassador cinema at 10 a.m. Don't forget your fishing tackle :-)
>
> Regards,
>
> Sarah

Assignment 3

1. Enter the following text in a new word processing document:

Agenda
1. Chairperson's address
2. Minutes of the last meeting
3. Secretary's Report
4. Treasurer's Report
5. Competitions for the forthcoming year
6. Election of club officials
7. Any other business

2. Save the file as *Agenda* to your disk.
3. Use the e-mail program to compose the following e-mail message:

Subject: Annual General Meeting

The Annual General Meeting of Carrigallen GAA club will take place in the Community Centre on Sunday next at 3 p.m. Please find the agenda for the meeting attached to this e-mail.

Yours faithfully,

Sean Cooke
Club Secretary

4. Attach the *Agenda* file to the e-mail message.
5. Send the e-mail message and attachment to the e-mail address provided for you by your tutor.

Assignment 4

1. Use your e-mail program to create a new mailbox or folder called *Hobbies*. Copies of the two messages composed and sent in the previous two tasks are now stored in the Sent Items mailbox.
2. Move both messages from the Sent Items mailbox to your new *Hobbies* mailbox.

Assignment 5

Tutor Instruction

The **tutor** is advised to e-mail the following message to the Web-based e-mail accounts of all students in the class:

> Subject: Printing
>
> Dear Class Member,
> Remember to check for misspellings before printing your document. It is also a good idea to use the print preview option if this is available. This latter option allows you to see the layout of your page before you decide to print.
>
> Orla O'Brien
> Class Tutor

Student Instruction

Check for any new mail. The message above should be downloaded to your *Inbox* folder.

▦ Searching the World Wide Web

Use a search engine of your choice to complete the following assignments:

Assignment 6

1. Find a recipe for apple pie.
2. Save the page as *pie* to your disk.

Assignment 7

1. Find a web page that contains the poem 'The Road Not Taken' by Robert Frost.
2. Save the web page as *road* to your disk.

Assignment 8

1. Find a web page containing the lyrics of the song 'The Sound of Silence' by Simon and Garfunkel.
2. Copy the lyrics of the song to a word-processing document.
3. Save the document as *silence* to your disk.

Assignment 9

I wish to buy a book on the software product *Adobe Photoshop* from an on-line bookstore. Find three different books on *Adobe Photoshop*, together with their respective prices. You must:

a. Enter the details found into a word processing document.

b. Include the addresses (URLs) of the pages where you found the relevant information.

c. Save the file as *adobe* to your disk.

Assignment 10

Assume that you are a qualified web master or web designer. Find suitable positions in this field that are currently available in Ireland.

1. Copy the specifications of three positions found to a word processing document.

2. Save this document as *Webjobs* to your disk.

Assignment 11

Assume that you wish to buy a house in either counties Cavan or Leitrim. You do not wish to spend more than €350,000.

1. Find five houses on the market that meet these criteria.

2. Use your browser software to save the details on each house as *house1* to *house5*, respectively.

Assignment 12

A close family relative is travelling to the west coast of America and has asked you to use the WWW to find:

1. The cost of a return flight from Dublin to San Francisco.

2. The name of a good hotel in San Francisco.

3. The nightly rate at this hotel.

   • You can quote prices in the local currency, i.e. USD (US dollars).

   • You must enter the details found as follows into a word processor file:

      → Flight cost = €XXX or $XXX

      → Airline(s) = AAAA

      → Hotel name = HHHH

      → Nightly hotel cost = €NNNN or $NNNN.

   • You must also include the addresses (URLs) of the pages where you found the relevant information.

   • Save the file as *travel* to your disk.

Assignment 13

1. Find a website that has free web page backgrounds available.

2. Download the background of your choice, saving it as *backgrnd* to your disk.

Assignment 14

1. Find a web page that has a picture of a Claddagh ring.
2. Save the picture only, under the file name *Claddagh*, to your disk.

Assignment 15

1. Find a midi sound file of the Irish national anthem.
2. Save this file as *anthem* to your disk.

▦ Web publishing

Assignment 16

1. Using a text editor, enter the *holiday1* and *holiday2* files as shown in the web publishing section. Save both files in htm format to your disk.
2. Load your browser program and view both files.
3. Using the text editor and appropriate HTML tags, create the following web page on the Italian city of Florence.

> **Florence – the capital of Tuscany**
>
> Florence, set in the heart of the Italian province of Tuscany, is a wonderful old city. The sights and smells of this city will live long in the memory of the traveller.
>
> A browse in the antique shops on the Ponte Vecchio, a visit to the Sante Croche church and a pasta meal in one of the old trattorias is a beautiful way to spend a day.

4. Save the web page as *holiday3*, in htm format, to your disk.
5. Create a hyperlink from the word 'Florence' in the holiday2 file to the holiday3 file. Re-save the holiday2.htm file.
6. View the three-page website – holiday1, holiday2 and holiday3 – and ensure that hyperlinks are working properly.

In the following tasks, you may use a web editor program or a text editor and appropriate HTML tags.

Assignment 17

1. Produce the following web page:

Billie Holiday (1915–59)

Billie Holiday, one of the greatest jazz-blues singers of all time, was born in Baltimore, USA on 7 April 1915. She had an impoverished childhood before moving to New York City in the late 1920s, where she began singing in Harlem clubs.

A recording session in 1935 brought Billie to public attention. Thereafter, she was vocalist with various orchestras, including those of Count Basie and Artie Shaw. Billie made many recordings with the saxophonist Lester Young and with the pianist Teddy Wilson.

Throughout the 1940s and 1950s, Billie appeared in clubs throughout the United States with great success, although her voice increasingly showed the effects of her long-term drug addiction. She died in the Metropolitan Hospital, New York City on 17 July 1959.

Billie rarely sang traditional blues, but her reputation rests on her ability to transform popular songs into emotionally profound pieces. Her autobiography, *Lady Sings the Blues*, was published in 1956.

2. Download a suitable background from the Internet.
3. Use the background for this web page.
4. Choose an appropriate text colour to contrast with the background.
5. Save the web page as *billie.htm* to your disk.
6. Use your web browser to view the page.

Assignment 18

1. Produce the following web page:

The Titanic

One of the worst maritime disasters in history was the sinking of the *Titanic*. The British liner, on its maiden voyage from Southampton to New York City, struck an iceberg about 100 miles south of Newfoundland just before midnight on 14 April 1912. The mighty ship sank in less than three hours. Of the 2200 people aboard, over 1500 lost their lives.

Subsequent investigations found that:
• The ship had been steaming too fast in icy waters.
• Lifeboat space had been provided for less than half of the passengers and crew.
• The *Californian*, a ship close to the scene, had not come to the rescue because its radio operator was off duty and asleep.

In 1985, the wreck of the *Titanic* was located by a joint French-American expedition. They found that the ship had broken into two parts; these are lying over a half a mile apart on the ocean floor. A year later, an American research team explored the *Titanic* and took photographs of the wreck site.

---

2. Use appropriate background and text colours for the page.
3. Use a search engine to find a picture of the *Titanic* on the Web.
4. Save this picture to your disk.
5. Insert the picture beneath the final paragraph on the web page.
6. Use a search engine to find a midi sound file of the theme music 'My Heart Will Go On' from the 1998 film *Titanic* on the Web.
7. Download the midi file to your disk.
8. Insert the midi file as background sound on your web page.
9. Save the file as *titanic.htm*.
10. Use your web browser to view the page.

Assignment 19

Produce your own personal web page. You may include information on some or all of the following:
- family and friends
- interests and hobbies
- achievements in the past
- hopes and plans for the future.

Include a photograph of yourself on the web page.

Assignment 20

Produce a web page for a business or organisation in your local area. Include a logo, if one is available, on the web page.